METROPOLIS NOW

PLANNING AND THE URBAN IN CONTEMPORARY AUSTRALIA

**Edited by
Katherine Gibson
& Sophie Watson**

PLUTO PRESS
AUSTRALIA

First published in November 1994 by
Pluto Press Australia Limited,
PO Box 199, Leichhardt, NSW 2040

Cover design: Trevor Hood

Index: Neale Towart

Typeset, printed and bound by
Southwood Press, 80 Chapel Street, Marrickville, NSW 2204

Australian Cataloguing in Publication Data

Metropolis now.

Bibliography.
Includes index.
ISBN 1 86403 014 3.

1. Suburbs — Australia. 2. City planning — Australia.
3. Suburban life — Australia. 4. Sociology, Urban — Australia.
I. Gibson, Katherine, 1953-   . II. Watson, Sophie.

307.740994

Contents

PART 2: RETHINKING URBAN PLANNING AND POLICY IN THE NINETIES

Tables and Figures

TABLES

FIGURES

Acknowledgements

Putting together an edited collection can be a lot of work and angst. Yet putting together this book has been a great pleasure to us both. Apart from the fun of working with a diverse and lively set of contributors, we were very fortunate in having the excellent assistance of Qingsheng Zhou and Jenny Cameron. In the final stages of the project their meticulous help with putting together the manuscript was invaluable. We would also like to thank Robin Connell for her support for the project and Rosemary Pringle for the title.

Part 1

Suburban Discourses

Introduction

Katherine Gibson and Sophie Watson

What is it about the Australian suburb that is so disturbing? Why is there a sense of embarrassment about the very urban context in which almost all Australians live? Is it the embarrassment of facing up in the stark light of day to what is revealed in a dream — in this case the 'great Australian dream'? Or is it the disturbingly polarised nature of academic debate about 'the suburbs'—variously judged as good/bad, wasteful/efficient, ugly/satisfying, oppressive/liberating?

Currently Australians in many different contexts are taking on the suburbs and coming to terms with the often contradictory emotions and thoughts that they inspire. For example, many recent Australian films have had suburban rather than the classic rural settings (here *The Big Steal*, *Spottiswood*, even *Strictly Ballroom* come to mind), as though it were now alright to anchor fantasy, crime and romance in those places usually associated with reality, safety, the mundane and everyday. What this cultural turn signifies is, perhaps, a willingness to let down the opposed moral, aesthetic and political guards which have surrounded 'the suburban' for so long and to allow suburban discourses to proliferate.[1]

In *Metropolis Now* we take a look at Australian suburbia through a variety of lenses, all of which highlight the positioning of 'the suburban' with respect to 'its other' or 'an other'. *Metropolis* was the title of Fritz Lang's famous 1926 film fantasy of modernist city life made in interwar Germany. Against such images of a 'real' metropolis, the suburban sprawl we call cities in Australia have appeared as faint, thinned out, de-eroticised reflections. It seems a paradox that in one of the most highly urbanised societies in the world, 'real city life' has been equated with the metropolis of the core — London, New York, Berlin — and not with the red roofs of Sydney or the tree-lined streets of Melbourne. This has changed. Now we see Los Angeles portrayed as the quintessential postmodern city, its sprawling streetscape inspiring filmmakers and academics alike in a new form of urban celebration.[2] And now it may be easier to see Australian cities as metropolises as well.

Our book *Metropolis Now* incorporates a rethinking of what constitutes urban life and how we might challenge the restrictive hierarchies that have often influenced our approaches to living in Australian cities. In Part 2 these issues are taken up in a number of practical contexts where authors engage with important contemporary policy questions concerning city life. The collection of essays in Part 1 challenge many of the ways in which contemporary urban discourse places the suburbs (distinctive parts of Australian cities), women, non-English speaking residents and Aboriginal histories in positions of subordination, positions of 'otherness'.

Based upon recent social research, the following chapters present distinctive insights into various discourses of the suburban. Jean Duruz and Susan Thompson each take up the positioning of women with respect to suburbia. Variously portrayed in popular and academic representations as oppressed by, or guardians of the suburbs, women are rarely allowed to speak for themselves. The pieces by Duruz and Thompson are both based upon extensive in-depth interviewing with women about the meaning of home and place — the former with a middle-class woman living in a leafy north shore Sydney suburb, the latter with migrant women from non-English speaking backgrounds living in Sydney's inner western suburbs. We see how women's views can be seen as both participating in and challenging established representations which (usually negatively) map the suburbs onto the feminine, the materialistic and the domestic.

Louise Johnson in her chapter draws a parallel between the white/British colonisation of black/indigenous Australia and the suburban colonisation of rural-urban fringes of the city. In both processes of 'colonisation' Johnson draws attention to the violence by which 'places' are 'made' (via the eradication of difference) and hegemonic identities (whether nation or community) are constructed. Kathleen Mee takes up some of these points in the context of the place-making advertising strategies adopted by local government authorities in western Sydney. Mee shows how local councils, in attempting to overcome the process by which western Sydney has been rendered subordinate to Sydney proper, vie with each other to claim aspects of Sydney's essential character for themselves.

George Morgan traces one of the historical bases for the establishment of suburbs in modern cities — the quest for an open and spacious living environment in which the disorders of disease, crime and revolution could not take root. He provides interesting insight into the way in which discourses of the suburban as healthy/good/pure are built upon the moral panics of yesteryear. He also points to the ironic contrast between fears of 'a dense and public sociability' then, and fears now of 'a lack of sociability in street spaces that are not occupied or controlled'. Jean Hillier and Phil McManus take up the issue of space and its defence as they turn our attention to the extreme way in which policing of the suburban environment takes place in new estate developments in Perth. Property protection and social segregation are developed to a new height in these walled and semi-walled enclaves of wealth and conspicuous consumption. In an attempt to overcome the discourse of suburban monotony and mediocrity, the developers and residents of these new (or renamed) Perth localities have erected both discursive and material barriers to create and then protect an elite identity. In the process another discourse, that of suburban egalitarianism is actively being undermined with full support from the planning authorities.

The construction of suburbia as new, raw, and undistinguished is challenged by the concept of 'heritage' and the practice of conservation. As Helen Armstrong argues, the heritage industry highlights historical continuity, creating a place-based history where one had never been before. No longer are suburbs and urban neighbourhoods seen as part of an undifferentiated urban sprawl. Countless heritage studies have contributed to the identification of place markers in the physical and built environments of suburbia that attest to permanence and culture. Armstrong points to the ethnic and monumental bias of heritage practice in contemporary Australian cities. She argues that cultural discontinuity is a more useful representation of our urban heritage and explores what the elements of a multicultural heritage practice might be which emphasises remembered lived experiences in place as well as monuments to past cultural practices.

Finally in Part 1, Peter Murphy and Robert Freestone draw our attention to the ways in which we might conceive of our cities as multiply centred upon a diverse set of activity nodes, rather than focused upon a single and dominant centre. They explore the relevance of the 'edge city debate' to Australian urban areas, particularly Sydney.

Their chapter highlights the changes which have taken place in the spatial organisation of urban functions within the city. Suburbs are no longer necessarily positioned at a great distance from centres of business, industrial and cultural activity. It would seem that the spatial, economic and cultural isolations upon which many of our images of suburbia rest have in many areas been overcome by the reorganisation of urban space.

Perhaps, as Murphy and Freestone suggest, we now live in post-suburban cities. If this is the case then there is all the more reason to take a long hard look at the images, representations and discourses of the suburban which have to date contained and influenced urban and suburban social/spatial practices. The following essays go a considerable way towards identifying the gender, ethnic and class specific assumptions, exclusions and resonances of the suburban discourses we have currently available.

NOTES

1.   See, for example the recently published book edited by Ferber, S; Healy, C. and McAuliffe, C. (1994) *Beasts of Suburbia: Reinterpreting Cultures in Australian Suburbs*, Melbourne: Melbourne University Press.

2.   Los Angeles has most recently been immortalised as a paradigmatic post-modern place by writers such as Soja, E. (1989) *Postmodern Geographies*, Verso, London; and Davis, M. (1990) *City of Quartz: Excavating the Future in Los Angeles*, Verso, London.

1

Romancing the suburbs?

Jean Duruz

In her recent book *The Sphinx in the City*, Elizabeth Wilson, a city dweller and unashamed, uses the sphinx as metaphor of female sexuality—dangerous, uncontrolled, engulfing—that lurks at the labyrinthine heart of city spaces. Fear of the sphinx, Wilson says, results in continual policing of women within urban environments, and—at least for cities in Britain and America—in women's historic banishment to the suburbs.[1] Obviously, this is not a pretty tale. With women marginalised in urban environments or literally excluded from these, and with a 'corrosive anti-urbanism' issuing from both the left and the right, Wilson concludes:

> The result is that today in many cities we have the worst of all worlds: danger without pleasure, safety without stimulation, consumerism without choice, monumentality without diversity. At the same time, larger and larger numbers of people inhabit zones that are no longer really either town or countryside.[2]

Tracing 19th century movements of population in England to these nether-zones, Wilson evokes the romance that accompanied and supposedly softened women's exile. This, she says, is a romance of rest, peace and comfort, of country houses and their gardens, of secluded spaces set apart and protected from the physically dangerous, alienating, fragmented ones of the emerging industrialised city. At the centre of this rural idyll was not the sphinx, but its guardian angel—woman.[3]

17

Furthermore, this is a romance the outlines of which, if not the details, persist with some tenacity. Leonore Davidoff, Jean L'Eperance and Howard Newby, discussing 20th century British suburbs as feminised landscapes, remark wryly: 'In their suburban homes, wives are still expected to . . . wait, albeit with less resignation as well as less hope, for the hand upon the latch'.[4]

Meanwhile, in Australia, the great suburban romance has had a chequered history. While we could claim to be one of the first sub-urbanised nations (in the sense of suburbanisation preceding industri-alisation)[5] and the reality is that most Australians live in suburbs, meanings of the 'suburbs' and 'suburban' are subject to constant debate. These range from Robin Boyd's attack on the 'suburb' as a kind of demi-monde of the 1960s — that 'half world between city and country in which most Australians live'[6] — and Patrick White's 1961 creation of Sarsaparilla as an outer-suburban cultural desert —'a geographic hell ruled by female demons'[7] — to Steve Bedwell's recent enthusiastic celebration of remembered suburban bliss and its imagery — Bob and Dolly Dyer on *Pick-a-Box*, the Kingswood in the drive, the kids jumping through the sprinkler or swinging from the Hills Hoist.[8] Is this the great suburban romance reinvented for the 1990s, a retrospective viewing of that 'world we have lost'?[9] Is this a utopian world of home ownership, of bungalows with their own gardens in leafy suburbs, and above all of the constant presence of women in proper aprons, deftly wielding electrical appliances?

Here I do not intend discussing in detail the history of 'public' discourses and debates in regard to meanings of 'suburbs', for this history is well documented.[10] There is also a substantial body of feminist work that examines the contradictory positioning of women in suburban landscapes, and counts the costs for women of the 'suburban dream' of home ownership and pursuit.[11] Building on work such as this but taking a different direction, my interest centres on women's own negotiations with the 'dream' and its imagery. To dismiss Australian suburbs as 'geographic hell' or to cast these spaces unproblematically in a golden glow of nostalgia is to miss the fine textures of women's continuing engagement with romance, with myth, with memory in everyday life. On the other hand, by tracing these engagements we may gain a sense of 'the making and remaking of individual and collective consciousness, in which both fact and fantasy, past and present, each has its part'.[12]

Specifically I want to select, as a reference point, suburban develop-ment in Australia in the late 1950s and early 1960s — a period of rapid expansion and an historic moment of high levels of home ownership.[13]

The critical questions I want to ask are: how do women — traditional guardians of suburban living — now redraw those suburbs of the 1950s and 1960s in memory and imagination? What meanings are encoded in women's memories and dreams for rethinking the 'private' domain and constructing suburbs of the future? My approach is through textual readings of interview material, and in particular of those fragmentary images of 'suburbs' occurring in one woman's story.[14] Though this approach is a necessarily limited and partial one (in both senses of the word), it does allow an 'inside' look at connections of place, identity and gendered relations of power, and hints at possibilities for challenging romance, for narrating 'other' stories.

IMAGINED HOUSES, SUBURBS—WORKING SKETCHES

> Women are practised on the peripheries . . . We live in houses that weren't built for our dreams, in suburbs connected by transport systems we can't control. We fit our stories to the worlds we inherit. Or do we?[15]

In the story that forms the basis of this chapter, drawn from interviews with Sue McInnes, memory and imagination intertwine to produce varying accounts of the suburbs and, I shall argue, differing — sometimes competing — identities within femininity. To develop this argument I need to introduce two brief working sketches of landscapes. These provide us with points of entry to Sue McInnes' story, and to analyses that follow.

In the early 1960s, Sue and Tom McInnes were renting a 'pretty little cottage' in one of Sydney's northern suburbs. In remembering both courtship and early married life, Sue describes the stuff of dreams in relation to plans for the McInnes' future home:

> Sue: I didn't have a dream house . . . I hadn't thought ahead at all in my life . . . I hadn't really calculated on being married and having a home and what sort of home it would be. It wasn't really until we started going together that we started thinking what kind of lifestyle we'd like . . . we were thinking of living somewhere with a very large garden and having dogs and lots of children . . . I suppose . . . rather like what we were used to . . . just a nice home and a nice garden . . .[16]

. . .

> Sue: . . . we certainly had no dreams of brick veneer, triple
> frontreds and [so on] . . . our ideal would have been a boatshed
> somewhere, or . . . a chalet [in the mountains] . . . just some-
> thing a bit different. But . . . we were never tempted to go
> through project homes . . .
> Jean: I wondered whether [you did] in those early days.
> Sue: I think we would have gone and visited some . . . [to see]
> some of the . . . newer ideas, but we weren't at all attracted to
> them. We liked older houses — preloved. [17]

While Sue denies pursuing the 'dream home', it is clear from these
fragments of her story that she envisages 'the house' and neighbourhood as significant settings for her marriage and for family life.
Although she constructs herself as a 'dreamer' in the sense of not a
'planner', once the decision to marry is taken there is an inevitability
about the house, garden and children to follow, at least in dreams.
The linking of the home as site for the labour of child-rearing is well
established in the literature, and is reflected too in the interviews I
conducted for this project. [18] Just as there is a proper time to marry, so
too must the home be a proper place for children and family life.

For Sue McInnes, what constitutes a 'proper place'? It may appear
that her wishes in relation to the future home and neighbourhood seem
vague and modestly expressed. She wanted 'just a nice home and a nice
garden' and 'just something a bit different', while at the same time
stresses that she and Tom had 'no dreams of brick veneer', 'were never
tempted' by builders' display homes, and 'weren't at all attracted' to
these. It seems that, to some extent, the dream that is not wanted is
expressed more clearly and more forcefully than the one that is. It is
worth tracing threads in Sue's rejections in order to build sharper
outlines of preferred settings — settings glimpsed fleetingly here as
'what we were used to' or 'something a bit different'. By focusing on
rejected landscapes of dreaming and desire, we may gain a sense of
'inner' landscapes of femininity and of possible ways in which its paths
and boundaries are negotiated.

TALES OF ESCAPE: THE FLIGHT FROM THE TRIPLE FRONTEDS

Despite Sue's initial claim to want 'just a nice home and a nice garden',
later in the same interview imagination ranges more freely. It is here
that wanting 'something a bit different' becomes significant. While
Sue's remembered dreams persistently include gum trees and perhaps
'a bigger acreage', [19] she is scornful of the uniformity that the 'suburbs'

and 'suburban' had come to signify. The mass production of dreams, the valuing of 'new' over 'old', the race for status through 'triple fronteds' and 'brick veneer'—these are to be avoided. Instead of blind following of fashion or rampant consumerism, she seeks in memory a dream house which though modest, probably, in its appointments, has 'character' (it is 'preloved') and individuality, and is distinguished by its setting: 'a pretty garden' . . . 'somewhere with gum trees' . . . 'a hills area' . . . 'the mountains'.[20] For Sue, this is the kind of 'nest' to which Game and Pringle refer, 'the place where you could express your 'real self'', the place where you chose to spend your time'.[21]

By the late 1950s and early 1960s, criticisms of the development of Australian suburbs and suburban housing was not new. Karskens documents, for example, comments of architects such as Annear and Wilkinson in the period before the mid-1920s and says these and 'a host of others' all condemned suburbia.[22] Houses were criticised as poorly planned, cheaply built, and repetitive in style, with the overall effect of meanness, monotony and conformity. Later, Robin Boyd, in a similar vein, was to declare: 'Australia is the small house . . . This is a story of material triumph and an aesthetic calamity'.[23] Furthermore, it is not simply suburban houses that stand condemned, but their owners and occupiers as well. Spearritt says: 'By the 1960s . . . those red-tiled expanses had . . . been peopled with equally sterile stock characters. Suburban people, to many "refined" and "educated" commentators, were figures of fun, suburban life something they loved to hate.'[24]

Does wanting 'something a bit different' then represent a refusal of the 'other'—the mythic 'otherness' and 'ugliness' of 'suburban' land-scapes and their inhabitants? Furthermore, if the 'other' in its 'public' representations is to be rejected, what possibilities lie ahead for building dreams of the 'home' and the life within it? In developing this tale of escape, I want to unravel further Sue's replacement of the 'pretty little cottage' of early married life — the material basis for dreams — with her broader vision of the house with gum trees, the boatshed, the chalet, the hobby farm.[25] In doing this, I am arguing that a number of 'public' linkages could be suggested for this imagined imagery.

The first of these 'public' links relates to discourses of the 'rural' and of the 'garden suburb'. While specific forms of suburban houses and suburban planning have had both critics and defenders,[26] the 'suburban dream' itself has ideological roots in that rural idyll of 19th century Britain. More recently, echoes of it are found in Australia in the garden suburb movement of the first 30 years of this century. This movement was based in the belief that social reform could be engendered through the provision of clean, orderly and aesthetically pleasing environments for detached owner-occupied dwellings.[27]

While the garden suburb movement could be regarded as a failed experiment in that its reformist goals were unrealised, Freestone points to its continuing influence in residential planning after World War II, and to the adoption of 'garden suburb' in popular imagination as a place of trees, flowers and room to move. So, space, beauty and the 'natural' combine here to form a class-based vision of the 'suburban dream': it is a dream originally born of middle-class notions of the relationship of 'nature', aesthetics and morality, and of middle-class resources for its realisation.[28] In desiring space and 'natural' beauty, does Sue McInnes, in her dreaming, confirm 'the suburbs' after all, or rather particular class constructions of 'garden suburb' that stand outside the 'other' of 'suburban', as popularly constituted?

As well as the appeal of the garden suburb movement, we could speculate on other 'public' meanings sketched in Sue's imagined house, garden, neighbourhood. In creating an image of a house with gum trees, it is possible that Sue acknowledges criticism of suburban housing, such as Boyd's, and popular ideologies of the 'suburban'— suburban landscapes as 'ugly', suburban dwellers as materialistic, and suburban life as intellectually sterile.[29] Persistent themes in Boyd's work emerge in his attack on Featurism — fashions in the built environment for highlighting design features at the expense of the whole, and the use of excessive ornamentation, veneer or disguise.[30] In Boyd's mocking description of the modern home and its interiors he mounts a scathing attack on feature windows, fireplaces 'faced with autumnal stone veneer' and tinted venetian blinds with every slat bearing 'a printed pattern, perhaps of tiny animals done in aboriginal style'.[31] Here beauty and ugliness are read in specific ways, with a privileging of 'wholeness' in design and 'the natural'. Perhaps Sue McInnes' rejection of 'triple fronteds' and 'brick veneer' could be interpreted as a similar rejection of particular construction and style features as well as a more general rejection of snobbery and excessive concern for fashion.[32]

Constructions of beauty, space and 'the natural' converge in Boyd's second major criticism of suburban housing development. In company with the artifice of Featurism in house design and furnishings goes the denuding of the Australian landscape — the 'shorn look'. Describing an imaginary hillside on which stands a farmhouse and a small orchard, Boyd says: 'Look at it two or three years later when a subdivider's bulldozers lurch in. A grid of streets is laid across it. All the trees, native and fruit are cut down.'[33] Inevitably, rows of ever-marching electricity poles and wires, and houses surrounded by 'tidy beds of English annuals' are to follow.

To avoid landscapes like these, says Boyd, it is necessary to retain as many trees as possible, build roads following natural contours, and design houses with an eye to creating an aesthetic wholeness of landscape.[34] In a similar fashion, I want to argue that perhaps, for Sue McInnes, gum trees are invested with iconic qualities. Not only does their absence define the 'city' as unsuitable;[35] this absence might also allow 'shorn' suburbs to be dismissed. Furthermore, presence of gum trees in wooded suburbs or in picturesque rural settings (the hills, the mountains) is seen as a guarantee of space and beauty — a respect for the 'natural' and a commitment to art, not artifice. These are the 'beautiful things' that will rise above consumer items intended as fashion statements — the 'beautiful things' that provide resources of spiritual nourishment.[36]

So, it seems that 'good taste' and greenery are to offer protection from the threat of the 'other'. However, who or what precisely is the 'other'? I want to suggest that lurking behind Boyd's criticisms is the spectre of class — the 'other' of working-class families who supposedly have more money than taste, and of the 'North Shore Executive Zone'[37] where capital abounds, but high culture is thin on the ground. Furthermore, spectres of gender intersect with these class identities. The excessive ornamentation of Boyd's Featurism could be regarded not only as forms of working-class culture to be dismissed, but also as a reflection on all women as the keepers of home decor.[38] Likewise, Boyd's rejection of the 'shorn look' could be constructed as a class attack on tidiness at the expense of beauty — in fact, tidiness as 'ugliness', and as a gendered attack — an abhorrence of 'masculine' assaults upon the 'natural' environment.[39] Following this line of argument we could conclude that Sue McInnes, in opting for space, beauty and the 'natural', affirms her class position as preserver of 'good taste' and of high culture, while at the same time her femininity as nurturer, not destroyer, of the 'natural' environment.

However, for Sue, space and visually attractive settings are not valued only for their aesthetic qualities. These can also provide a defined landscape in which productive labour and leisure as a family become possible. The image of the productive back yard or hobby farm as a context for family life occurs and re-occurs during interview discussion of preferred neighbourhoods:

> Sue: I think I've always had a . . . bit of an earth mother strain in me and I was . . . interested in just having babies and dogs and gardens and . . . vegetables. . . .[40]

> Sue: . . . we both used to talk about houses in a hills area or just somewhere with gum trees and a pretty garden, and we'd have animals and ducks and things like that.[41]

What is the significance of these preferences? Are Sue's desires for 'gardens', 'vegetables', 'ducks and things like that' a reflection of a long tradition of Australian back yards, or a conscious critique of industrialisation and consumerism? It is worth tracing briefly both of these historical developments.

Writers documenting 20th century suburban development in Australia comment on the strongly established tradition of the productive plot. While the front garden of ornamental trees, shrubs, flowers and lawns presents its respectable face to the street, it is the back yard that is the proper site for family activity— for its work and leisure. Here children and dogs are contained, washing hung out, vegetables and fruit trees tended, and chooks kept.[42] Marion Halligan, for example, in her memories of a Newcastle childhood of the 1950s, provides a glimpse into an economy based in the products of the back yard and its surrounding neighbourhood — an economy based in home-grown fruit and vegetables, judicious marketing at local orchards, picking wild fruit, jam-making and preserving.[43]

This is an economy where labour, thrift and gratuitous exchange of products predominate. However, here I want to note that it is women's labour that is crucial to its functioning. With the separation of home and work (for men), it is probably women who have the daily responsibility of food-growing, tending animals, and transforming products into meals for family consumption. Furthermore, it could be argued that the tradition of the back yard plot locates women within a vestigial rural economy, an economy in which both men and women would have originally participated, though in different ways. Meanwhile, their husbands as wage labourers are positioned differently. In entering the market economy, men acquire a defined income, defined conditions of work, and through constructions of what constitutes 'work', privileged positions in domestic relations of power.[44]

The challenge to this productive, and it could be argued predominately female, economy occurred in Australia primarily during the 1960s when images of the car and the supermarket began to replace those of vacant allotments covered in blackberries and the back yard of chooks and rampant choko vines.[45] However, it is possible that in remembering dreams associated with the first years of married life, Sue McInnes is drawing on experience of this productive economy, both as a child during the 1950s and as a young wife in the early 1960s. The plum tree that Sue mentions as the 'pride of the garden' in her rented cottage not only provides forms of aesthetic pleasure;[46] the fruit of the tree offers opportunities for thrift, labour and sustenance — opportunities to practise housewifely arts, and to confirm specific images of femininity.

So, I am arguing that Sue McInnes' memories could be linked with a long tradition of productive back yard culture (despite challenges and changes to this). Alternatively, these memories could be a reading back into experiences of the early 1960s responses to a later movement in protest against mass-production and mass-commodification.[47] Michael Symons charts the history of the 'back to the land' movement of the 1970s, with its antecedents in forms of youth movements of the late 1960s. These forms were based in counter-cultural practices and 'alternative' lifestyles. Symons, however, is cynical of the degree of self-sufficiency attained in Australia during the 1960s and 1970s, and is gloomy in regard to future prospects under capitalism.[48]

Protest, nevertheless, can take milder forms. Larger gardens and hobby farms can suggest the culture of self-sufficiency or provide nostalgic references to rural life, without threatening capitalism's base of waged labour. To this end, the farm or garden takes on qualities of class: it is a postmodern playing with the 'rural' that rests on the satisfactions to be gained from productive activities, and not on the land as livelihood. Accordingly, in 1978 the *National Times* was to announce the emergence of a new class: this was one of 'middle-class peasants'.[49] Is this the identity positioning suggested by Sue's narrative? At this point, some comment by way of summary is necessary.

Garden suburbs, gum-studded hillsides, chooks in the back yard, hobby farms — what do these versions of escape narratives suggest for meanings of the 'feminine' and for feminine identity? I want to suggest that the imagery of Sue's dreams could be shaded in tones of class and gender. It is from middle-class positionings that one can afford to reject cramped city housing or the suburban sprawl on the cheap land of treeless plains. Likewise, middle-class positions provide a location for developing critiques of one's own class, and for seeking housing alternatives.

Conspicuous consumption in the suburbs can be shunned, and the rural idyll favoured, without the loss of class or culture. At least, this may seem the case to Sue, though as a married woman and unpaid worker, her class position is an ambiguous one.[50] Nevertheless, it appears that it is the possession of material and cultural resources that enables the choice of space, beauty and the 'natural' as this escape narrative's significant themes.

However, this supposed power to choose raises further questions. Is the desire to escape from the 'suburbs', as popularly constituted, yet another example of middle-class hegemony? Is this an example of those with financial resources rejecting established structures of social life and moving on, leaving working-class people securely embedded in these?[51] Alternatively, does this class location allow space for post-modern nostalgia — a flirtation between the otherwise contradictory categories of 'middle classes' and 'peasants'? A different interpretation would adopt a less conservative position, unpacking the intersections of class and gender more thoroughly, and allowing scope for resistance. The following section presents only brief hints of possibilities.

TALES OF ROMANCE AND 'OTHER' STORIES

In developing alternative analyses, two running threads from interview texts are useful for our purposes. The first of these concerns the McInnes' refusal to 'buy big', and Sue's denial of 'wanting' in relation to new commodities.[52] A feminist interpretation of Sue's dreams might focus on the gendered dimensions of 'not wanting', together with the contradictory aspects of Sue's class positioning. It could be suggested that 'not wanting' represents a realistic tailoring of dreams to the income resources of the marriage, or a refusal of capitalism's soft sell, and a class vision of beauty and 'good taste'. This, however, is to assume the shared class positioning of Sue and her husband. On the other hand, if Sue is constructed as a dependant — as an unpaid worker, who exchanges her labour for 'maintenance'— the picture that emerges is a different one. As a dependant, Sue is reliant on the extent of her husband's income, and on his good will in its distribution. In the case of dreams of 'the house' and 'the suburb', Sue is tied also to Tom's choice of employment and its location. An irony of Tom's career change during the early 1960s (a change that, although negotiated, was his choice and not Sue's), was that the McInnes' were to move from the 'pretty little cottage' first to the 'other' of Sydney's outer western suburbs, and then to the 'other' of the inner city.[53]

'Wanting' and 'not wanting' take on different meanings within gendered relations of power, despite the illusion of a shared class position between husband and wife, and that of a similar access to shared resources. Perhaps one of the lessons of femininity is to learn not to want, or to curtail one's dreams to 'just a nice home' and no more. Here I am arguing a tension between capitalist and patriarchal relations of power. In this example of dreams for 'the house', capitalist and patriarchal relations appear to be at odds: whilst capitalism urges that the way to femininity is through class-based consumption, patriarchy demands restraint. Possible conflict is resolved, however, as dreams still require purchase of private property, with 'natural' beauty of setting and the charm of 'the old' offering compensation for modesty of aspirations. Furthermore, the balancing act of desire and restraint promises the reward of escaping the 'other'.

The second thread — the valuing of labour, freely given on behalf of others — could also be considered from feminist perspectives. A feminist interpretation might claim Sue's yearning to return to a 'productive' culture as nostalgia for constructions of housewife as 'homemaker', as 'home producer', in contrast to those of housewife as 'chauffeur/shopper'. Although housework as a whole is devalued, within the range of tasks that constitute housework it is possible that some, like growing vegetables or preserving, offer more scope for demonstration of skill and expression of self than others that focus more on household maintenance and servicing.[54] Sue's dreams then go beyond a fanciful play with the 'rural'. Instead, they may be concerned with reasserting a space, however limited, for valuing women's work as producers.[55]

Nevertheless, the extent to which such dreams constitute 'resistance' should not be exaggerated. First, we might argue that such choices are reactionary ones, reaffirming 'feminine' arts and housewifely skills within a traditional division of labour and income. Second, such choices could be designated resistant only in the sense of attempts to make life habitable within existing structures, though without radical challenge to these. A space is opened up certainly to assert feminine identities that offer possibilities for pleasure, but its boundaries are circumscribed.

So, in Sue's opting for 'just a nice home and a nice garden' and 'just something a bit different', particular social relations and structures remain intact. The goal of ownership of a detached dwelling in a semi-rural or rural setting is an unquestioned one. Likewise, the sexual division of labour, and gendered separation of home and paid work receive no challenge.[56] In Sue's memories, the broad outlines of the great suburban romance survive, though, as discussion has indicated, negotiations with its details are complex and contradictory. Whilst dreams may reject various spectres of 'otherness' (images of 'sterile' environments of working-class life, or of the rapacity of the middle classes, for example), they endorse relations of power which construct both women and suburbs as 'other', locating the 'other' of women within the 'suburban other'.

TOWARDS THE SUBURBAN HAPPILY EVER AFTER

Women's stories of suburbs as places for families, homes, work and pleasure provide a fruitful ground for exploring negotiations with romance narratives in everyday life. Through women's remembering, complex meanings are produced that suggest possibilities for 'other' stories to dominant 'public' romances—'other' stories that are neither idealisation on one hand, nor demonisation on the other. Negotiating connections of place, identity and relations of power—in this analysis, gender relations in particular—highlights contradiction and ambivalence of positioning. For example, loss of 'public' identity or a devaluing of one's work may jostle with imagery of landscapes that are meant to offer spiritual nourishment, emotional protection and familial contentment. (The 'suburban dream' is not meant to be the 'suburban nightmare', if we are to believe the romance.) Meanwhile, spaces for pleasure are actively sought within the framework of this 'dream', despite, for women, the costs of its pursuit.

So, in a sense, these 'other' stories that I have discussed are stories of compensation. Here it is useful to ask: what meanings are encoded in these for building cities and suburbs of the future? From Sue's story, I might want to suggest that planning needs to take into account challenges to existing divisions of labour and to provide opportunities for satisfying work in which one's identity as a worker is confirmed and valued. In fact, we could speculate that, beyond a certain level of material comfort, consumer goods might become less important if identities within personal and work relations are nurtured and satisfied.[57] However, for feminist theory and politics, these 'other' stories—these attempts to seize moments of pleasure within existing social relations—are not sufficient.

Carolyn Steedman says:

> I refuse to say my mother's story, or my father's, or mine are perfectly valid stories, existing in their own right, merely hidden from history, now revealed . . . I think that the central stories are maintained by the marginality of others, but that these marginal stories *will not do* to construct a future by. They will have to be abandoned . . .[58]

According to Steedman, central stories of domination and 'other' stories of the search for agency within existing structural relations are part of the same dynamic. Simply privileging 'other' stories is an inadequate feminist project. Instead, the need for new feminist stories persists — not for comforting romances, but for discomforting challenges to power relations that underline the gendering of identities and places in ways that spell injustice for women. It is a continuing task of feminism to confront the 'other' of both women and suburbs, and to undo the construction of 'otherness' itself.

ACKNOWLEDGEMENT

Thanks are due to Carol Johnson for comments on an earlier draft of this chapter, and to the women interviewed for the project, especially to 'Sue McInnes'. To respect confidentiality, these women's real names have not been used.

NOTES

1. Wilson, E. (1991) *The Sphinx in the City: Urban Life, The Control of Disorder, and Women*, Virago, London, p.7, pp.105-106, p.111, p.114.
2. *ibid.*, pp.8-9.
3. *ibid.*, p.45.
4. Davidoff, L., L'Eperance, J. and Newby, H. (1976) 'Landscape with Figures: Home and Community in English Society', in Mitchell, J. and Oakley, A. (eds.) *The Rights and Wrongs of Women*, Penguin, Harmondsworth, p.175.
5. Game, A. and Pringle, R. (1983) 'The Making of the Australian Family', in Burns, A., Bottomley, G. and Jools, P. (eds.) *The Family in the Modern World: Australian Perspectives*, George Allen & Unwin, Sydney, p.83.
6. Boyd, R. (1961) *Australia's Home: Its Origins, Builders and Occupiers*, Melbourne University Press, Melbourne, p.6.
7. Gerster, R. (1990) 'Gerrymander: The Place of Suburbia in Australian Fiction', *Meanjin*, 49, 3, p.566.
8. Bedwell, S. (1992) *Suburban . . . Icons: A Celebration of the Everyday*, Australian Broadcasting Corporation, Sydney, pp.21-21, pp.44-46, p.137, p.147.
9. Laslett, P. (1969) *The World We Have Lost*, Cambridge University Press, Cambridge.
10. See, for example, Rowse, T. (1978) 'Heaven and a Hills Hoist: Australian Critics on Suburbia', *Meanjin*, 37, 1, pp.3-13; Gerster, *op. cit.*, pp.565-575.
11. Allport, C. (1983) 'Women and Suburban Housing: Post-war Planning in Sydney, 1943-61', in Williams, P. (ed.) *Social Process and the City*, George Allen & Unwin, Sydney, pp.64-87; Game, A. and Pringle, R. (1979) 'Sexuality and

the Suburban Dream', *Australian and New Zealand Journal of Sociology*, 15, 2, pp.4-15; Kingston, B. (1975) *My Wife, My Daughter and Poor Mary Ann: Women and Work in Australia*, Nelson, Melbourne; Watson, S. (1988) *Accommodating Inequality: Gender and Housing*, Allen & Unwin, Sydney.

12.	Samuel, R. and Thompson, P. (1990) 'Introduction', in Samuel, R. and Thompson, P. (eds.) *The Myths We Live By*, Routledge, London, p.21.

13.	Kass, T. (1987) 'Cheaper than Rent: Aspects of the Growth of Owner-Occupation in Sydney 1911-66', in Kelly, M. (ed.) *Sydney: City of Suburbs*, New South Wales University Press, Sydney, p.77.

14.	A series of interviews was carried out during 1988-89 with each of a small group of women who had married during 1955-65 and had had full-time responsibility for the care of their children born during this period. The women were living in adjacent northern Sydney suburbs, and identified themselves as either middle-class (as did Sue McInnes, whose story is discussed here) or respectable working-class.

15.	Modjeska, D. (ed.) (1989) *Inner Cities: Australian Women's Memories of Place*, Penguin, Ringwood, p.2.

16.	Interview 4 with Sue McInnes, Part A, pp.4-6.

17.	Interview 4 with Sue McInnes, Part A, pp.49-50.

18.	Gilding, M. (1991) *The Making and Breaking of the Australian Family*, Allen & Unwin, Sydney, p.111; Reiger, K. (1991) *Family Economy*, McPhee Gribble, Ringwood, p.44; Watson, *op. cit.*, p.7. Re interview responses see, for example, Interview 2 with Grace Farrow, p.33; Interview 2 with Helen Edwards, pp.144-145.

19.	Interview 5 with Sue McInnes, Part B, pp.38, 45; Interview 4 with Sue McInnes, Part A, p.49.

20.	Interview 5 with Sue McInnes, Part B, pp.37-38, 45; Interview 4 with Sue McInnes, Part A, p.50.

21.	Game and Pringle, *op. cit.*, p.96.

22.	Comments of Annear, H. Desbrowe and Wilkinson, L. are cited in Karskens, G. (1987) 'A Half World Between City and Country: 1920s Concord', in Kelly, (ed.) *op. cit.*, p.126, p.128.

23.	Boyd (1961) *op. cit.*, Preface.

24.	Spearritt, P. is cited in Karskens (1987) *op. cit.*, pp.128-129.

25.	Interview examples of Sue's preference for a productive garden or hobby farm will be discussed later in this chapter.

26.	A brief summary of these occurs in Reiger (1991) *op. cit.*, pp.36-39.

27.	Freestone, R. (1987) 'The Great Lever of Social Reform: The Garden Suburb 1900-30', in Kelly (ed.) *op. cit.*, p.58.

28.	*ibid.*, p.74. Freestone comments (p.66) in relation to Roseberry, a Sydney suburb, prior to the mid-1920s: 'Profit considerations doomed the more idealistic (and space-consuming) elements of Sulman's original design and Stanton [the developer] confessed that Roseberry had not "really reached the slum dweller".'

29. See, for example, MacKenzie, J. (1961) *Australian Paradox*, F. W. Cheshire, Melbourne, p.18, p.115, p.117, p.127.

30. Boyd, R. (1960) *The Australian Ugliness*, F. W. Cheshire, Melbourne, p.9, p.143.

31. *ibid.*, p.32.

32. The 'triple-fronted' house is one in which the building's longer side faces the street, rather than running the length of the block. This, Boyd ironically comments is a 'variation adopted by moderately successful men with wider building lots' (Boyd, (1961) *op. cit.*, p.11). An ordering of home building materials and construction methods by cost and status might rank 'full' or 'double' brick, brick veneer, timber and fibro in descending order (Pickett, C. (1993) 'Modernism and Austerity: The 1950s House', in O'Callaghan, J. (ed.) *The Australian Dream: Design of the Fifties*, Powerhouse Publishing, Sydney, pp.81-82). Sue McInnes uses the image of a timber house to signify modesty in dreams for 'the house', and a valuing of priorities other than more costly forms of building construction: 'There was a certain run of people who you knew were educated, but they were very happy to live in a timber house on a nice block of land and carry on their interests . . . and I very much want the same . . .' (Interview 5 with Sue McInnes, Part B, p.51).

33. Boyd (1960) *op. cit.*, p.143, p.152.

34. *ibid.*, pp.152-153. There are echoes of the garden suburb to be found in Boyd's proposals, though these are in the style of Walter Burley Griffin, with obvious attention to 'natural' space and contours and to native vegetation (Freestone (1987) *op. cit.*, p.64).

35. In 1964 Sue and Tom considered moving to the inner city to be closer to the college Tom was attending. However, Sue says, the city was 'all dirty and confined, and . . . we wanted gum trees. So we gave that away' (Interview 5 with Sue McInnes, Part B, p.45).

36. Interview 4 with Sue McInnes, Part A, p.3.

37. Boyd (1960) *op. cit.*, p.81.

38. Hunt, P. (1989) 'Gender and the Construction of Home Life', in Allan, G. and Crow, G. (eds.) *Home and Family: Creating the Domestic Sphere*, Macmillan, London, pp.75-76.

39. Segal, L. (1987) *Is the Future Female?: Troubled Thoughts on Contemporary Feminism*, Virago, London, pp.6-7.

40. Interview 5 with Sue McInnes, Part A, p.8.

41. Interview 5 with Sue McInnes, Part B, pp.37-38.

42. Allport, C. (1987) 'Castles of Security: The New South Wales Housing Commission and Home Ownership 1941-61', in Kelly (ed.) *op. cit.*, p.112; Boyd (1961) *op. cit.*, pp.91-92; Karskens (1987) *op. cit.*, p.136; Symons, M. (1982) *One Continuous Picnic: A History of Eating in Australia*, Duck Press, Adelaide, p.138, p.142.

43. Halligan, M. (1990) *Eat My Words*, Angus & Robertson, Sydney, p.15.

44. Allport argues that during the 1950s the availability of overtime meant that men were virtually absent from the home during the week, and that

responsibility for all domestic labour including child-care was shouldered by women (Allport (1983) *op. cit.*, p.84).

45. Harman, E. (1983) 'Capitalism, Patriarchy and the City', in Baldock, C.V. and Cass, B. (eds.) *op. cit.*, pp.114-116; Pringle, R. (1983) 'Women and Consumer Capitalism', in Baldock, C.V. and Cass, B. (eds.) *Women, Social Welfare and the State in Australia*, George Allen & Unwin, Sydney, pp.92-94.

46. Interview 4 with Sue McInnes, Part A, p.3.

47. Here I am arguing that 'present' constructions of the 'past' contain the filtering effects of ideas and experiences occurring since the remembered 'event', which itself is constructed in the first place. So remembered dreams of the early 1960s — here of a large garden with vegetables and ducks — may be overlaid by subsequent discourses and meanings, for example those of the 'earth mother', 'back to the land'.

48. Symons (1982) *op. cit.*, pp.251-253.

49. *ibid.*, p.252.

50. Delphy, C. (1984) *Close to Home: A Materialist Analysis of Women's Oppression*, Hutchison, London, pp.38-39.

51. A parallel example emerges in Game and Pringle's analysis of the 'breakdown' of the nuclear family in the late 1960s and 1970s: the middle classes, 'because of their material circumstances, are able to "escape" from the classical pattern, resolving the tensions they experience by moving outside of the family or by constructing new family forms. Contradictory forces in the working-class family cannot be so easily resolved. Thus it is the workers who are stuck with the "ideal middle class family", while the middle class moves on to bigger and better things.' Game and Pringle (1983) *op. cit.*, p.97.

52. Interview 4 with Sue McInnes, Part A, pp.32-33.

53. Interview 5 with Sue McInnes, Part B, pp.29-30, p.38.

54. Oakley, A. (1985) *The Sociology of Housework*, Basil Blackwell, Oxford, (2nd ed), pp.41-60.

55. It should be noted that here 'production' has a specific meaning — the creation of visible products. This is a narrower meaning than the usual one of household production referring to all household activities ('servicing' and 'productive') that are necessary to keep the household economy operational. For a discussion of this broader meaning of household production, see Ironmonger, D. and Sonius, E. (1989) 'Household Productive Activities', in Ironmonger, D. (eds.) *Households Work: Productive Activities, Women and Income in the Household Economy*, Allen & Unwin, Sydney, pp.18-32.

56. Prior to his marriage, Tom McInnes had qualified as a civil engineer. In considering the possibility of purchasing a house in a rural setting, the McInneses were assuming that Tom would continue in paid employment, and that their choice of location for home purchase was dependent on the availability of suitable work in that area.

57. This is the central argument of Lane, R. E. (1991) *The Market Experience*, Cambridge University Press, Cambridge.

58. Steedman, C. (1992) *Past Tenses: Essays on Writing, Autobiography and History*, Rivers Oram Press, London, p.46.

2

Suburbs of opportunity: the power of home for migrant women

Susan Thompson

Home to millions of Australians, the suburbs encompass the public sphere of neighbourhood and the private domain of domesticity. This is where most of us start and end the day, where familiarity and communion, freedom and creativity clash with loneliness, isolation and constraint.

The suburban setting as home is the context for this research with migrant women.[1] Through an interpretation of lived experience, I focus on the potential that the private dwelling and neighbourhood hold for the expression of personal power, both in the women's own communities and the wider Anglo society.

SUBURBAN DISCOURSE: FRACTURED TALES OF HOME?

The suburbs have long been a contentious issue. Lewis Mumford, a founding father of the planning profession, saw suburbia as a symbol of consumption, monotony, standardisation and assimilation: 'a low grade uniform environment from which escape is impossible . . . an asylum for the preservation of illusion'.[2]

In his expose of modern day Los Angeles, Mike Davis provides a more recent critique of suburban life. He talks of privatised neighbour-hoods where the affluent fortify their homes and create gated com-munities which deny public access to parks and other community facilities.[3] Similar patterns of social segregation are to be seen in other cities, with legislative sanctions encouraging the development of exclusive enclaves.[4]

Early feminist urban analysts viewed the process of suburbanisation as subjugating and controlling women, separating them from societal power and reinforcing their domestic position.[5] The suburb was seen to limit women's choices because of their dual roles. As paid workers outside the home and unpaid domestic workers within the home, women do spend considerable time travelling between their suburban residence, employment, childcare and retailing centres in order to fulfil their many duties. They make shorter and more frequent journeys than their male counterparts but their trips are fragmented and involve travelling out of peak hour when public transport tends to be sporadic. In addition, their destinations are typically not well serviced by major transport routes.[6] Such extended commuting characterises the far flung suburbs. Life spent combining paid employment with domestic responsibilities limits women's opportunities in full-time employment, education and recreation as well as participation in other aspects of community life and politics. It is not surprising that the suburbs are represented as feminised and a mechanism for constraining women in the private sphere, away from the masculine centres of production and power, a reinforcement of patriarchal relations in society.[7]

Contrasting this scenario are alternative, more favourable, per-ceptions of suburbia. Even within feminist theory, other voices challenge the notion that the suburb is 'all bad'. As Madigan and Munro state, 'no single environment, either suburban or urban, will provide an unambiguously best living environment'.[8] They question the degree to which the notion of suburb as a hated place relates more to its symbolic representation of respectability, family life and separation from the male world of power, than to the actuality of lived experience. The changing nature of the suburb is also raised here. Increasingly, jobs are being relocated to suburban locations with important implications for women's employment opportunities.[9] Similar trends are explored in Garreau's 'Edge City'.[10] Rather than abandoning the American suburbs, their continuation is being reinforced, initially by the movement of shopping centres and now, of major employment generators.

Hugh Stretton has been a long time advocate of the Australian suburb. He views its principle promise as that of self-expression in the form of one's own home. He criticises the suburb haters for their undervaluing of the potential freedoms, self-expression, comforting familiarity and mix of community and privacy that the suburb affords.[11]

Suburban discourse is indeed fractured and in spite of the breadth of this debate, the picture is incomplete. Cultural critiques are exposing the misrepresentations that have been wrought by both professionals and the media in stereotyping and patronising suburban life. Powell's study of Sydney's west allows the voices of its residents to be heard, so that they can claim their own truth and reality.[12] In a similar vein, the stories of non-English speaking background (NESB) women are presented here. Migration has dramatically altered the population base of the Australian suburb over the last 30 years. It is time to hear these, until now, largely silent voices.

Suburb as home, with its characteristic private dwellings and gardens, has profound implications for both individuals and communities. To understand the complex opportunities and constraints presented by suburbia, we need to return to an evaluation of what constitutes the deeper meaning of home for its inhabitants.

HOME: BEYOND THE TRADITIONAL CONCEPTUALISATIONS

The notion of home transcends the multitude of architectural forms which comprise the dwelling. It extends beyond the residence into the street and surrounding neighbourhood.[13] To begin to be a home, the physical qualities of the dwelling and its wider setting take on cultural and psychological significance. Inhabitants have a sense of belonging, a feeling that this is where they can seek refuge from the dangers and uncertainty of the outside world. Home is a symbol of personal identity, where the individual can exercise a degree of power and autonomy denied elsewhere. Important human relationships are central, as are significant events and memories. These serve to imbue the notion with a sense of permanence and continuity over time. Home represents the interface between public and private worlds, a place where cultural and societal norms are symbolically juxtaposed with expressions of individuality.

Until recently, housing studies tended to examine the household as a unit, rather than a collection of individuals each with his or her own distinctive roles and values. An important effect of seeing the household as one was the gender bias that entered into understandings of home. There has been a shift in the last decade, with research examining individual roles within the domestic sphere. What has emerged from this work is the realisation that for women, home can be a negative environment. The experiences of those subjected to violence, loss of freedom and personal power challenge the dominant discourse of home as haven and starkly illustrate a vision of home as nightmare, a prison of intolerability. Indeed for some women, the public realm can take on the connotations of safety normally reserved for the dwelling, as Ann, a survivor of incest, testifies: 'When I should have been my most vulnerable, walking all the way to town . . ., no one stopped me. That was all happening at home. It felt really safe out there — out on the streets, or out anywhere, away — but it didn't feel safe at home'.[14]

Ownership is an important element in shaping the meaning of home for many women. Of course this is significant for both sexes,[15] but the research on women has highlighted a profound sense of security springing from ownership, extending far beyond the financial consider-ations to emotional belonging, physical safety, security of tenure and a feeling of control.[16] Ironically, the realisation and maintenance of this security can be tenuous. Not only are women over-represented in low income households, they do not benefit equally from the potential of wealth accumulation from housing and frequently lose the ability to maintain a mortgage following divorce.[17] Ownership does not provide a 'safe haven' for women in violent relationships and if affordability is traded for accessibility, then home ownership may mean few nearby job opportunities.[18]

The physical form of housing has significant implications for women. Gender bias in design of both individual dwellings and the residential neighbourhood is discussed in many studies. Roberts identifies the need for spatial versatility given the range of households with which women are involved.[19] Madigan and Munro examine the connection between house designs and familial patterns, arguing that housing structures gender relations.[20] As the democratic model of the family has emerged, issues of privacy for women have increased in importance. The whole house is hers and yet she does not have her own space.

Craik provides an historical overview of the physical alterations to the kitchen and the accompanying changes to women's role within the domestic sphere. Following the demise of the servant, women took on the skilled tasks of household management. However, over time domestic work was devalued. This was accompanied by physical changes to the kitchen, which became smaller and part of the informal living room. Domestic work was reduced to a 'set of chores that anyone can do, but against a backdrop that promotes the ideal of mother in her domestic bliss'. It is this illusion, argues Craik, which is undermining and constraining for women.[21]

The meaning of home for women still needs further exploration. The voices of the displaced, those that have left one home to settle in another, are silent in this literature. As a planner working in a multi-cultural context, I found such a gap disturbing and decided to seek out some of the stories of migrant women. I interviewed 40 migrant and first generation Australian women from the Arabic, Greek and Vietnamese communities. I spoke with women who had established a home, taking from their own and the prevailing dominant cultures in the process of settling and creating their own special place.[22] With one exception, all the women are mothers, they either own or rent flats, houses or town houses, and are aged between 25 and 60 years. They come from a broad range of socioeconomic groups.[23] The Sydney suburban municipality of Canterbury is at the centre of my study area, where the Lebanese, Greeks and Vietnamese have established strong communities.

THE MEANING OF HOME FOR MIGRANT WOMEN: EMERGING THEMES

The stories migrant women told me reveal personal pictures of their homes — where they live now, the places they left behind and significant sites in transition. Common themes emerged from these stories suggesting that for these migrant women, home is a multi-dimensional concept and a powerful entity in their lives. Amongst other things, home is a site of power in an otherwise alien culture, a form of atonement for the losses associated with migration and a mark of success in the new world.[24]

Home as a Site of Power

What the women said about their homes challenges feminist notions of home as negative and oppressive. Within the wider context of an alien Anglo culture, the home has become a place where difference can be displayed and acted out. The performance of difference takes many forms. The domestic sphere is a safe place to speak one's first language, where encouraging children to study and speak their parents' first language is a high priority for the women. In this way control over language becomes a vehicle for claiming identity and reinforcing difference and separation:[25]

> That's why I'm trying to keep my home as I said, it's only Arabic
> . . . they can speak English with me in the car because I might

have others which they don't like hearing Arabic, or in the shopping centre we don't speak Arabic, but since we are in it's a rule, no more English, Arabic, because that's the only way to keep our culture . . .[26]

The physicality of the house is central to the migrant women and their appropriation of power. The dwelling facilitates the celebration of cultural festivals, religious practice and traditional entertaining. The formal dining and lounge areas are used on special occasions and display treasured furniture, ornaments and paintings. Throughout the rest of the house, internal decoration evokes cultural and religious heritage. I observed shrines in the houses of Vietnamese Buddhists and in others, pictures, statues and framed verses. Interestingly, the external appearance of the houses rarely reflect this heritage. The exceptions are new dwellings built by the women and their families where traditional plants and the organisation of external spaces facilitate particular activities.[27]

The desire for a house and garden is a recurring theme. Women speak of the powerful opportunities afforded by this residential form for cultural expression. A Vietnamese woman describes the role that her house and garden play in bringing a lost home closer:

We got . . . homesick so that we think that when we are here . . . when we settle down here, we want to have something just similar in my country so we want to have our own house, the house, so we set up everything looks like back home and also we need plants that remind us back home, remind us, a souvenir of everything back home. Sometimes my neighbour or my friend, they need some sound like a rooster . . . so they want to feed some roosters so that every morning they can listen, . . . you know different in here, different culture but you know remind you of your home, back home . . . your country. And also if you go out you look at your garden and you look at some tree and it's like palm tree and some plant that remind you of your home . . .

Privacy, freedom and comfort are other reasons for favouring the house and garden. This is well reported in other housing research.[28] What is not so common however, is the role of privacy in creating a climate of comfort to facilitate the expression of difference. The separate house maintains physical distance from those that might adversely judge such displays. The house and garden afford the freedom to do this in a culture that is not always accepting, in spite of the multi-cultural rhetoric.[29]

Confirming much of the mainstream literature, the meaning of home for these migrants extends beyond the dwelling into the neighbourhood. The women talk about the importance of having access to shops where they can buy specialist ingredients for traditional cooking. They also speak of their frequent use of social and religious institutions: 'I like it very much. I don't like to go very far, I mean far away because of the Mosque, we have the Mosque here. All the Muslim community and the Lebanese community . . . most of them live in this area. It's very social, very close to me, I can go any day I like, any time I like.'

The importance of access to ethnic community support networks is confirmed elsewhere.[30] My research indicates that physical proximity to family is also extremely important. Many of the women visit their mothers daily and do not want to spend vast amounts of time travelling. Others speak of the comfort they feel knowing that there are people in the street who come from their country. One Lebanese woman expressed her disappointment with the lack of neighbourliness in Australia, which reinforced her sense of loss.

> . . . in our country if you walk in the street which you grow up in, you know every single person living in the street. I've stayed here in the one street for seven years, believe it or not I hardly knew my neighbour in the same flat . . . because I was in Australian area . . . I did not know anyone and I tried to introduce myself with my little English when I came here but no-one would . . . accept me, take me as a neighbour or as a friend. After maybe six years I got one or two of my neighbours to be a good friend of mine. But otherwise there is no communication, there is no relation and it was *hard*.

Meaningful relationships are formed and/or maintained within the neighbourhood as the public realm of home. The importance of relationships with other community members is stressed in many of the stories. This is where cultural expression extends into the public realm, and from where a sense of communal belonging can emerge. It is also another important source of power for these women.

Home as Atonement

Throughout the women's stories, the pain of migration is evident. The realities of arriving and settling soon engulfed their initial perceptions of Australia as the land of opportunity. The road to material success was long and difficult, requiring considerable personal sacrifice and hardship. Reflecting on her contemporaries, a Greek woman put it this way: 'They expect something better. When they come here they find that it is just as hard here as it is there.' The exceptional hard work and self-sacrifice took their toll on both the women's and their children's lives. There was little time for sharing, helping with the homework or being together as a family.

Interspersed with stories of bereavement is an unfulfilled yearning for a lost home and denied culture. The belief that migration was only a temporary state, coupled with the promise to return one day, sustained many of the women and their families. However, as this dream slipped further from realisation the Australian home took on even greater importance. In the few cases where migrants did return, they found a changed countryside, friends gone and different cultural practices, which only served to consolidate their view of Australia as home. In turn, this enhanced its importance as a cultural representation.

Loss is further reinforced by the notion of home as a complex and shifting entity. 'Being at home' and 'belonging' are important feelings but they can be elusive when the deeper meaning of home is fragmented and disrupted. Even though the majority of women interviewed have links with present and former homes, there is still a degree of discomfort with their inability to define a single home. This unease can be seen in relation to their struggle within a culture which, until recently, denied any public acknowledgement of their difference:

> . . . put it this way, your roots are there but the trunk is here . . . you can say the tree is here because that's where your kids are . . . your life is here but your heart is there . . . and that's what makes it difficult because if I'm going there, there is nothing for me there . . . you are split up between the two countries.[31]

The women's stories suggest that their struggle in Australia enhances the importance of the physical house and neighbourhood in symbolising achievement and evoking 'another place'. Especially critical is the private component of home, the dwelling, as the controllable space afforded to the women by the dominant society. In established migrant areas, such as those being studied here, the neighbourhood can also take on these representations. It is in this way that home becomes a vehicle of atonement, although the pain of migration and loss of culture always remain.

Home as Success

Proving it in the new country is central to the women's stories. There is a need to demonstrate personal success that comes about from giving up a familiar way of life and suffering the consequences of self-sacrifice and denial. Many talked about their house and garden in terms of something to show for the hard work:[32] '. . . their home is their pride and joy. That's what they can show off. That's . . . the result of all their hard labour. And the cleaner it is, the more sparkling it is and the newer the things, or whatever, the prouder they get'.[33]

Nearly all of the women expressed a strong desire to own their homes. For them, ownership is linked to financial security and freedom to alter structures, decorate as they please and plant gardens unfettered by a constraining landlord. As previously discussed, the association of ownership with feelings of security is well documented. What is not evident is the relationship between ownership and success in a new country. The achievement of owning a house on a block of land is very tangible proof, to both their fellow migrants and those still living in the original country, that the sacrifice was, on one level, justified. It is also a demonstration to the wider society of their success, in a form that can be understood and potentially admired. It is interesting to note that in Australia, NESB people have a higher than average home ownership rate.[34]

CONCLUSION

> . . . we should be careful of a timid relativism which refuses to criticize suburban tackiness and the harmful social and gender effects of suburbanism. Like Australia itself, the suburbs have much to recommend and much to criticize. Either to dismiss them or only to laud them is to suspend our critical faculties.[35]

It is simplistic to discount the potential that the well-serviced neighbourhood and its dwellings hold for those who live there. For the migrant women represented here, there is the opportunity for the appropriation of personal power, both as women within a minority culture and as representatives of an ethnic group living in white Anglo Australia. The physical house is a tangible way of atoning for the losses sustained in the migration process. It serves as a symbol of success in the adopted country and a means of maintaining cultural, religious and personal links with the past.

My research indicates that we have to go back and look at the issues of diversity within suburban environments. We have to caution against imposing reform agendas from an ideological stance that alienates and denies the lived experience of those we are purporting to help. Home as both domestic dwelling and neighbourhood are central to the stories of the women discussed here. Their struggle is inextricably tied up with the notion of home as familiar territory and must be acknowledged in terms of the power that this provides. I am not suggesting that the established migrant woman can only be realised through her domestic setting, nor that this is an end in itself. What I am seeking is the valuing of lived experience, told through life stories, in any exploration of the complex and unique relationships between people and place. In the case of the migrant women here, this demands a thorough considera- tion of the opportunities afforded by the house and well-serviced suburb as representations of home.

NOTES

1. Pettman has alerted us to problematic constructions of the expression 'migrant women', particularly the tendency to make generalisations which disguise 'the variety of their backgrounds, identities and social interests' (Pettman, J. (1992) *Living in the Margins: Racism, Sexism and Feminism in Australia*, Allen and Unwin, North Sydney, p.42). My use of the term 'migrant women', does not imply homogeneous groups, categorised by their country of origin or stereotypical images of oppression, exploitation or disadvantage.

2. Lewis Mumford quoted in Short, J. (1989) *The Humane City: Cities as if People Matter*, Basil Blackwell, Oxford, p.16.

3. Davis, M. (1990) *City of Quartz: Excavating the Future in Los Angeles*, Verso, London, p.244.

4. Community Titles Legislation in NSW, for example, allows the construction of residential complexes with their own amenities. These include recreational facilities but can encompass child care and community centres. The legisla- tion enables private ownership of individual dwellings and common owner- ship of shared facilities. Enclosure walls and gated entrances are common, denoting exclusivity and a segregated community.

5. For example, McDowell, L. (1983) 'Towards an Understanding of the Gender Division of Urban Space', *Environment and Planning D: Society and Space*, 1, pp.59-72; and Women and Geography Study Group of the IBG (1984) *Geogra- phy and Gender: An Introduction to Feminist Geography*, Hutchinson, London.

6. Lang, J. (1992) 'Women and Transport', *Urban Policy and Research*, Vol 10, No 4, pp.14-25.

7. Short, J. (1991) *Imagined Country: Society, Culture and Environment*, Routledge, London, p.150.
8. Madigan, R. and Munro, M. (1991) 'Gender, House and "Home": Social Meanings and Domestic Architecture in Britain', *The Journal of Architectural and Planning Research*, Vol 8, No 2, p.118.
9. Van Vliet quoted in Madigan and Munro, *op. cit.*, p.118. Some commentators see the relocation of employment to the suburbs in a more sinister light. Employers are motivated by profit incentives to be gained through attracting well-qualified female workers forced to accept low-paid jobs because of proximity to home. See Monk, J. (1992) 'Gender in the Landscape: Expressions of Power and Meaning', in Anderson, K. and Gale, F. (eds), *Inventing Places*, Longman Cheshire, Melbourne, p.131.
10. Garreau, J. (1991) *Edge City: Life on the New Frontier*, Anchor Books, New York, 1991. See also Peter Murphy and Robert Freestone in this book.
11. Stretton, H. (1989) *Ideas for Australian Cities*, Third Edition, Transit Australia Publishing, Sydney, p.15.
12. Powell, D. (1993) *Out West: Perceptions of Sydney's Western Suburbs*, Allen and Unwin, St Leonards.
13. Hayward, G. (1975) 'Home as an Environmental and Psychological Concept', *Landscape*, Vol 20, No 1, pp.2-9.
14. Ward, E. (1985) *Father Daughter Rape*, Grove Press, New York, p.35.
15. See for example, Richards, L. (1990) *Nobody's Home: Dreams and Realities in a New Suburb*, Oxford University Press, Melbourne; and Thorne, R. (1991) 'Housing as "Home" in the Australian Context', *People and Physical Environment Research*, No 36, pp.54-64.
16. Barclay, L. et al (1991) *Speaking of Housing . . . A Report on a Consultation with Victorian Women on Housing for the Minister for Planning and Housing*, Ministerial Advisory Committee on Women and Housing and Women in Supportive Housing, Melbourne, p.39.
17. Madigan and Munro, *op. cit.*, p.117. Couple households are the most advantaged in entering and maintaining private home ownership because of their access to two incomes. See also Cass, B. (1991) *The Housing Needs of Women and Children*, Discussion Paper for the National Housing Strategy, AGPS, Canberra, p.20.
18. Cass *op. cit.*, p.4.
19. Roberts, M. (1991) *Living in a Man-Made World: Gender Assumptions in Modern Housing Design*, Routledge, London.
20. Madigan and Munro, *op. cit.*
21. Craik, J. (1989) 'The Making of Mother: The Role of the Kitchen in the Home', in Allan, G. and Crow, G. (eds.), *Home and Family: Creating the Domestic Sphere*, Macmillan, Houndmills, p.63.
22. The women I interviewed are English speakers and have been living in Australia long enough to have established relationships with both their own ethnic communities and the wider Anglo society.

23. The broad range of socioeconomic groups encompasses those owning businesses and holiday homes, with others depending on employment benefits and subject to the vagaries of the private rental market. I am aware that class is an issue in this type of research, but for my purposes here I discuss the commonalities that cross these divisions.

24. Important issues need to be articulated about the relationship between researcher and researched. There is an unequal sharing of power in my role as a university educated, Anglo woman interviewing NESB women, many with much lower levels of education. Also my use of English as a first language compared with my respondents is potentially problematic. There is also the issue of belonging/not belonging to the group. In some communities being an outsider can be an advantage in research. A member of the same community may be perceived as a potential informant to others within the group, resulting in the respondent being less open and honest. An outsider does not present the same threat. The fact that the women were able to speak about very personal issues, even though they often reminded them of painful experiences, indicated to me that a degree of comfort was achieved between us. The length of interviews and the empowering nature of the interview experience as expressed to me by the women, further reinforced my impression that the interview was not wholly for my benefit.

The interviews, lasting between three and eight hours, over several visits, were taped and transcribed. Focus groups were formed to further explore the issues raised and to verify my initial interpretations of the data.

In communicating the women's stories, I have not altered phrasing or grammar in an attempt to be true to them. I am aware however, that some readers could interpret this as patronising given that the respondents' use of English does not always fit within traditional grammatical constructions. This clearly is not my intention. As Susan Krieger affirms, 'We are encouraged to speak in generally acceptable styles, rather than to speak in ways that are our own. The ability to speak from within takes nurturance. It requires the use of one's own words . . .' (Krieger, S. (1991) *Social Science and the Self*, Rutgers University Press, New Brunswick, p.37). I also use the women's voices in an attempt to avoid the inherent dangers of outsider representations (Bottomley, G., de Lepervanche, M. and Martin, J. (eds.) (1991) *Intersexions: Gender/Class/Culture/Ethnicity*, Allen and Unwin, North Sydney, p.ix).

It should be noted that the methodology used in this study does not permit generalisations to be made in relation to other migrant women.

25. Daniel, J. O. (1992) 'Temporary Shelter: Adorno's Exile and the Language of Home', *New Formations*, No 17, Summer, p.26-35.

26. An Arabic speaking woman talks about the role that language plays within and outside the domestic sphere of her home.

27. The issue of external physical appearance is an interesting one. Apperly et al identify 'Immigrant's Nostalgic' as a distinctive architectural style in late 20th century Australia, predominantly found in domestic and religious buildings (Apperly, R. et al (1989) *Identifying Australian Architecture: Styles and Terms from*

1788 to the Present, Angus & Robertson, North Ryde). Whilst examples abound in my study area of the architecture they describe, the majority of the women interviewed did not live in these houses. The issue of physicality was nevertheless very important, albeit expressed in more subtle ways.

28. Ross Thorne, who has conducted significant research in this area, consistently reports that the freestanding house on its own block of land is the most desirable form of accommodation. It seems that flats are viewed as 'third class accommodation', with the house and land package offering '. . . privacy and control which no other house type can provide' (Thorne, *op. cit.*, pp.56-58). Perceptions of control, autonomy and privacy are closely linked to the ownership of private outdoor space. The usefulness of this is well documented in Halkett's study of Adelaide backyards. Rather than wasted spaces he found a multiplicity of utilitarian and recreation activities (Halkett, I. (1976) *The Quarter-Acre Block*, Australian Institute of Urban Studies, Canberra).

29. It can be argued that multicultural policy has essentially marginalised the expression of difference to the private sphere, with the exception of socially acceptable incursions—the 'interesting' ethnic restaurants, specialty food stores and colourful festivals.

30. Social Planning Consortium (1985) *Multicultural Housing Preferences: A Report on the Housing Preferences of Polish, Turkish and Indo-Chinese People in Melbourne*, Australian Housing Research Council, Canberra.

31. Greek woman who migrated to Australia in the 1950s.

32. The academic and social success of children is another important indicator of achievement. In one case, a Vietnamese woman linked the prosperity of home ownership with the attainments of her children: 'It's our house, we work hard, and we pay for it, and its where our children grow up and they're quite successful, they all have good jobs . . . it's our home really'.

33. Greek woman reflecting on her parents' house.

34. Housing Industry Association—National Homebuilders Council (1990) *Housing Towards 2000*, Housing Industry Association, Canberra, p.28.

35. Short *op. cit.*, p.151.

3

Colonising the suburban frontier: place-making on Melbourne's urban fringe

Louise Johnson

It was in 1901 that Australia gained formal independence from Britain, but the full meaning of being a postcolonial society is only now being realised. The form and timing of the postcolonial critique emerges from the particular history and demography of the country—as the term involves a questioning of Anglo-Celtic dominance by a resistant indigenous population and by those from non-English speaking backgrounds. It is a literature which owes much to oppositional discourses in the Third World and from minorities in other colonised and colonising countries.[1] In Australia it has been concerned with effacing silences within existing narratives of settlement, with recovering a neglected past, of articulating racial exclusion and ethnic difference and with giving a voice to those of Aboriginal or non-Anglo-Celtic descent to speak on their own behalf. Further, these literatures have begun to interrogate the whole question of identity and categorisation and to raise hard questions about who can speak for whom.[2]

This work affirms the prior occupancy of the continent and documents the many ways in which colonialism occurred. From it emerges a picture of colonisation as the exercise of state sanctioned force to secure property and to manage its occupants. As such it is ongoing, extending well beyond violent frontier conflict to encompass various forms of land acquisition and means of population negotiation, regulation and containment. It is a variegated process, perpetrated by a differentiated 'white' population which had various impacts on, and generated an array of responses from, women and men of the many indigenous tribal groups. But such regulation also occurred for those non-native populations defined as 'other' by the colonising powers. As such, colonisation is a notion which can also be extended to non-indigenous minorities, as they are constituted and managed as 'migrant' populations, different from an Anglo-Celtic norm.

Colonisation in Australia therefore is a dynamic and pervasive process, one which impacts on both the indigenous population and on those of non-Anglo-Celtic descent. The question thereby arises as to how such a concept can inform and transform studies of contemporary Australian cities. In particular, how can this notion of colonisation direct an investigation into a contemporary housing estate being developed by the Victorian Urban Land Authority, 20 kilometres north-west of Melbourne at Roxburgh Park?

Colonisation occurred here in the first few years of occupancy by the use of military and legal power to dispossess Aboriginal occupants of their land. The population was also constituted through the removal of Koori children and their education into gendered labouring tasks by 'Protectors' and mission schools. In such ways were Lots 1 and 14 in the Parish of Yuroke constituted and their original populations contained and regulated. Subsequent land and population management strategies have continued this process. Most recently, there has been an exercise of State financial and legal powers to acquire land and to delimit its population. While not without contestation, this place and its occupants are being constructed in terms of an ideal suburban environment — now named Roxburgh Park. Here there are a range of lot sizes, ample physical and social services and ecological sustainability all supported by a homogenous, if feminised, place-based community. Ethnic, racial and linguistic variations are subsequently either obliterated or subsumed by such definitions.

The colonisation of this part of Melbourne can therefore be seen as an ongoing process involving two main elements — place-making and the constitution of manageable populations. This proposition will be developed in more detail using the 1840s and the 1990s.

PLACE-MAKING ON THE SUBURBAN FRONTIER

Travelling as a scientific observer with the British explorer Captain James Cook, the botanist Joseph Banks observed in 1770 that there were 'very few inhabitants' on the eastern coast of Australia and, further, 'we may have liberty to conjecture however that [it is] totally [sic] uninhabited'.[3] The notion of an empty continent ripe for British settlement was contradicted soon after by the first sightings and continuing contacts with the indigenous population. Subsequently the concept of *terra nullius* was modified to include not only the occupancy of land but its appropriate use by those with acceptable racial and cultural characteristics.[4]

Despite the convenience of such ideas for land seizure, they were not without confusion, contestation or contradiction. Thus, in the years prior to British occupation, the land now called Roxburgh Park was but a small part of the tribal territory occupied by the Woiwurrung, Jajowrong or Wurundjeri—the spelling of such names varying markedly from account to account.[5] Numbering about 200, according to the anthropologist A.W. Howitt writing in 1904, Wurundjeri territory stretched from the junction of the Maribynong and Yarra Rivers to Mount Macedon, thence to the Dandenongs and back.[6] A sub-area between Kororoit Creek, the Maribynong River and the settlement of Sunbury—including what is now Roxburgh Park—was, according to historical research conducted for the Urban Land Authority, inhabited by a family clan of about 20 people.[7] In this small area, tribal and clan boundaries were drawn by a number of white observers over the years for a range of purposes, to subsequently enclose Koori groups of divergent name and number. Who occupied this site prior to European occupation is, therefore, confusing in the historical record.

The area's tussocky grasslands, swamps and water courses were surveyed by the British explorer William Hovell in 1824. It also fell within the region traversed by William Fawkner as he ventured from Tasmania in search of more pasture and was ultimately 'ceded' to the Port Philip Association in the *Batman Treaty* of June 6, 1835. The very existence of such a 'treaty' raised a number of dilemmas. For it recognised prior occupancy, gave some legitimacy to indigenous identity and land rights and secured a huge tract of land while, at the same time, also contravening official policy on settlement.[8]

In this 'treaty' and the exchange of trinkets for land which it documented, the notion of *terra nullius* was denied by both the assertion of British sovereignty and the assigning of common law property rights to the indigenous occupants. The denial of such a treaty in terms of usual practice did nothing to undermine this contradiction. This paradox of a formal agreement with an unrecognised people was to shape future population management at the site, especially by the Aboriginal 'Protectors' (see part two).

In the first census taken of the Port Phillip settlement in September 1838 the number of Koori inhabitants was not known or sought. Instead, it was recorded that there were 3511 (white) people, 3080 of these men, 310 946 sheep, 13 272 cattle and 524 horses.[9] In this, as with other regions, priority was given to land occupation and the generation of wealth from it. In this quest, the recognition of common law rights of prior occupancy was rare, as land was either squatted on under licence or sold for one pound an acre. One of the early occupants of the area now known as Sunbury included William Pomeroy Greene. Formerly of the Royal Navy, Greene chose his officer entitlement of 640 acres on the Moonee Ponds Creek. He arrived with full retinue of a wife and seven children, a governess, butler, carpenter, groom, cook, housemaid, nurse and two young men friends. Ann Greene took over the management of the property following her husband's death in 1845 and turned it into a model farm and centre of upper-class rural social life — complete with balls and steeplechases.[10]

Of the Wurundjeri, the young Mary Greene was to record: 'When we first took over our abode at Woodlands, a tribe of aborigines used to camp on the creek which ran through our property'.[11] Others apparently had different experiences. Thus John Aitkin, a Tasmanian sheep breeder, sought more grazing lands across Bass Strait. His boat ran aground and his party, including a large flock of sheep, had to be driven ashore and thence to land north of Melbourne. In this he was assisted by about 80 'natives'. In relating this story the local historian Allan Gross notes that, as a consequence, Aitken made a policy then and later of 'conciliating' Aborigines, mainly by giving them rations.[12]

A somewhat different story is told by another local historian — Ian Symonds — who notes how on April 15, 1838 John Aitkin's station was attacked by about 40 blacks armed with spears and three guns. Aitken managed to disarm two of the gunmen and narrowly missed being hacked to death by another black armed with a tomahawk.[13] The reasons why such an attack occurred and the retribution which followed are not mentioned by Symonds, whose story ends with the above description. However, the reconstructed experiences of the Greenes and Aitken point to some of the ways initial and ongoing land dispossession was effected.

The early colonisation of this area therefore involved its designation firstly as unoccupied land and then its steady and often violent occupancy by Anglo-Scottish land holders. While supposedly protected by common law prior occupancy rights, Aboriginal people were displaced by force, by official surveys which ignored their presence, and by land purchasers. These purchasers, both men and women, relied upon the might of the British legal and military systems to effect their settlements, remove the 'native' population from it and to turn a blind eye to their efforts to 'clear' their properties. In such ways the foundation was laid for the colony of Victoria; a place of rolling pastoral grassland inhabited by a unified and dominant Anglo-Celtic population. So too in these ways, were Lots 1, 14 and K in the Parish of Yuroke also created.

These blocks of land which now comprise Roxburgh Park were officially unoccupied from 1835 until 1848. While within the 'Settled District' of Melbourne, the catchment of the Baptist Mission School and encompassed by the North Western Aboriginal Protectorate, they only had European land holders adjacent to them, and on maps of the period they are shown as empty. In 1848 the southern portions were purchased by a Scottish family of sheep breeders—the Camerons—who held the property until the 1880s. After some speculative transfers, it was acquired by the flour miller and politician Thomas Brunton, after which it was used by a number of owners for sheep, cattle and horse grazing until purchased in 1950 by the Moonee Valley Racing Club. They sold it to the Urban Land Authority (ULA) in 1988.

Created in 1975, the aim of the authority has been to maintain a reasonable supply of affordable residential land in Victoria. This occurs through the use of Commonwealth loan funds to acquire, develop and resell large tracts in the market place. Since its creation, the ULA has disposed of between one fifth and one tenth of all urban land and in 1990 it handled 'more than half of all new development land in Melbourne, thus making it the State's largest and most influential developer'.[14]

If colonisation involves the exercise of superior, state sanctioned force—be it military, financial or legal—to acquire land and manage its occupants, then the history of these lots since 1988 continues the process begun in 1835. While not involving the imposition of a foreign sovereignty or driven by nationalistic or racialist ideologies, since 1988 the Urban Land Authority has used its financial and legal power to buy land from the Moonee Valley Racing Club, the Commonwealth government and from small landholders, who were ultimately subjected to compulsory acquisition orders.[15] Having secured the land through such means, the ULA has proceeded to mould it physically and socially. It is a more discreet, less violent but nevertheless potent exercise of state authority over resident populations, one which also has a long history.

COLONISING POPULATIONS

Having dealt with the dilemma of indigenous property rights by imposing a foreign system of land regulation and occupancy upon it, the management of Aborigines was officially dealt with through 'conciliation' programs in the 1840s.

'Conciliation'— or the systematic containment of the indigenous population through the use of persuasion, example, force and rations — had been tried in Van Diemen's Land and was seen by those in authority as a successful model to emulate on the mainland. It led to the creation of four 'Aboriginal protectorates' in the new Port Phillip colony in 1839. These joined with Christian missions and schools as key ways in which the Aboriginal population was constituted as a unified group, regulated and contained in this region until the 1850s. Adjacent to Roxburgh Park were two of these institutions—the North West Aboriginal Protectorate was ruled from 1839 to 1840 from Jackson's Creek and a Baptist mission school functioned at Merri Creek from 1846 to 1851. Both generated vectors of power which defined and were challenged by the Kooris in their charge. Their operation highlights some further dimensions and contradictions in the colonisation process.

Edward Stone Parker administered the North West Aboriginal Protectorate from Jackson's Creek. As an Assistant Protector, his brief was to:

> attach himself . . . to the aboriginal tribes . . . until they can be induced to assume more settled habits . . . teach them and encourage them to engage in the cultivation of their grounds, in building suitable habitations . . . watch over [their] rights and interests [and] defend them . . . from any encroachment on their property and from acts of cruelty, oppression or injustice; and faithfully represent their wants and grievances [and] promote [their] moral and religious improvement.[16]

In addition, he was to learn the native language, conduct a census and distribute rations. Parker quickly realised the ambivalence of his brief. Charged with protecting native rights and interests to their land and before British law, he constantly encountered the theft and occupancy of that land and violence towards native women and men. In particular, he noted the sexual violence towards Koori women, though he saw this as a result of female seductiveness rather than the product of male racism, and he explained conflicts between men and over land as a result of colonisation without compensation.[17]

Parker was also a Wesleyan minister and school master. With the assistance of his wife, he took to the task of bringing Christianity to his charges with enthusiasm. The number of pupils tended to be small, and attendance was related to the provision of foodstuffs. Some children refused to attend their school in 1842 with the ultimatum: 'No damper, no school'.[18] Parker wrote with dismay at how the children would be taken away with no notice by their kin and would not appear again for weeks. The attempt at moral regulation offered by the Protectorate school was therefore met with active resistance.

Despite the selective use and ignoring of English schooling, the idea of educating the native population persisted and was to receive a boost in this region by the establishment in 1846 of a Baptist boarding school at Merri Creek. The school was initially regarded as a success, with 20 pupils in its first year who read, sang hymns and displayed their handwriting and needlework to 250 townspeople.[19] The boys were schooled in carpentry and gardening and the girls in food preparation. While the boys excelled in literacy and numeracy, commentators were content to note the excellence of the girls at sewing. Success was measured by the number of pupils, the Christian principles which imbued the curriculum and the pattern of gendered skills which were taught. However, despite these 'achievements', in December 1847 tribal elders came and took the children into the mountains.[20] The problem of mass desertion was an ongoing one, such that the school had to be closed in 1851. Subsequently, the experiment in formally schooling the native population in Christian ways was declared to be futile by those whose opinions were recorded.[21]

The mission school and Protectorate represent just two of the means whereby colonisation continued in this region well after its first white occupation. From their scattered traces, a picture emerges of an area colonised by force and stealth — as the gaze of the British explorer was replaced by those men (and some women) who sought the physical containment and moral regeneration of its native population. The unification of tribal groups under racial categories, their physical containment and the imposition of gender stereotypes were critical to the land-use pattern and social character of this area. While an actively resisted process, the constitution of populations in these terms was integral to its colonisation.

This has again occurred, albeit in a very different way, in the most recent colonisation by the Urban Land Authority.

Administration of the 600 hectare site by the authority has involved a number of discourses which include elements — echoing the past — of containment, regulation and appropriate habitation. These planning, design, marketing and population regimes comprise four interrelated elements: affordability, ecological sustainability, comprehensive, co-ordinated and adequate servicing, and the creation of a community.

Affordability is achieved by the very means by which the land was acquired — through the exercise of state financial and legal powers which have also never involved the compensation of the original occupants — by the economies of scale in service provision, through balloted land sales and by an intensive pattern of land subdivision, so that up to 25 dwellings per hectare are built. These small lots are linked to the discourse of sustainability through their designation as *Smart Blocks*.

The ULA is intensively promoting the sale of land sized between 450 and 600 sq m — this in a city where 80 per cent of the housing is free standing on lots around 750 sq m.[22] On these blocks the house is designed and positioned so as to maximise privacy and minimise energy use and loss. This occurs through house positioning relative to the best aspect, through physical proximity to its neighbour on the south side, placement of windows along the north and east, and courtyard orientation.

The presssure on purchasers to agree to such an arrangement is profound and ranges from the financial to the regulatory and moral. For smaller house blocks are cheaper and houses built in 'Smart' ways will incur lower energy bills. Any house plan also has to be approved by the ULA before local government authorities view it, and must therefore conform to an array of setback, colour scheme, usage and building material requirements, many of which encourage its 'Smart' design. Added encouragement to be a 'Smart' (rather than a Dumb!) home owner is given through the ULA sponsored *Welcome Home* workshops for all new buyers and by having the well-publicised model *Green Home* on the estate.[23] The desire for ecological sustainability also permeates the layout of the streets, service centres and waterways.

Affordable and ecologically sensitive houses attract and create a suburban population of a particular class and income. But the design changes to support these objectives can also alter the ways in which these suburban houses are used. For many studies have shown the importance of outside private space to the male occupant of the suburb. It is here that he assumes a degree of household responsibility, engages in domestic labour and maintains the dwelling. Such yard space is also vital to the play needs of young children, within the boundaries set by fences and the gaze of the housebound mother. It is therefore ironic and perhaps challenging of existing domestic divisions of labour, that the most obvious feature of the *Smart Blocks* is the reduction in size of private open space, a shift to public open space provision and the relative increase in the scale of the house itself on the block. One therefore has to ask who these blocks are 'Smart' for: as the male occupant sees his traditional domain of work reduced and the woman her childcare responsibilities made more difficult and public, at the same times as the interior spaces she has to maintain are increased. [24]

The problems of existing suburbs which the planners of Roxburgh Park are trying to avoid through careful planning extend well beyond costliness and ecological wastefulness to those of servicing. The intention is to have the estate fully supplied with physical services — like power, roads, recreation reserves and walkways — before the blocks are sold and then to stage the provision of social services. Planning for these social facilities is comprehensive and codified in the 120 page (1991) *Community Plan*, put together by a team representing the ULA, the local council and relevant State government departments. [25] This sets down the ideal for suburban living in terms of public transport, health, education, sport, recreation and community services and links their provision to the development of town centres and population inflow. Services for women have been incorporated into general provisions while those needed for people of non Anglo-Celtic origin have been deferred, pending further knowledge of the population attracted to the area.

The conceptualisation and placement of services and the changing political climate make their provision problematical. In a state driven by cuts in the public sector any planned social service is under extra scrutiny. When women's needs are planned for, it is very much in terms of their domestic and childcare responsibilities. While embracing many of the demands long articulated by women, there is also a model family implicit in the plan. In these families, the young mother does not engage in paid work outside the home — so the community bus does not run regularly outside of peak hours — does not wish to go anywhere except the local town centre for her shopping or health needs and is not subjected to domestic violence or family breakdown. Her children also do not grow up. Thus, while there are elaborate plans for infant welfare centres and schools, there is nothing but ovals for older children. The daytime occupant of this suburb is therefore envisaged as mobile, a compulsive user of local shopping, recreation and health services and a perpetual mother of babies. It is a particular and outdated vision of womanhood and the family which is being provided for and constituted through the service inventory.

Those services which may be required by non-English speakers or non-Christians (land has been set aside for the Catholic and Uniting churches) are left undetailed — awaiting their articulation by the resident groups. For the moment, it is envisaged that Moslems in the estate will journey to a large mosque some five kilometres away, while the mix of Turkish (7.7%), Greek (3.2%), Italian (5.5%), Macedonian (1.2%), English (1.2%), Vietnamese (1.5%) and Filipino households have yet to offer their vision of alternative services.[26] How such an articulation is meant to happen relies on the forcefulness of the individuals and groups involved, the skills of the Anglo-Celtic and English speaking community workers and the success of the *Welcome Home* workshops in linking residents to service providers. An infra-structure and set of expectations have thereby been set in place for the expression of cultural difference. However, the ways in which such differences can be articulated means that they have to conform to a set of prescriptive planning guidelines. They can be articulated only within a unifying discourse of community.

The notion of community has been defined physically and ideologi-cally by the planners. Thus, the estate has been planned around a hierarchical series of service — or community — centres. These range from the corner store, through the neighbourhood centre — serving 6000 — to the regional shopping complex which will meet the needs of all 26 000 projected residents. These centres are the planned social hubs of the suburb and in them will be located all the retail, health, leisure and other services; while their siting adjacent to recreational areas and roadways, bike paths and walking tracks will ensure their utility and viability. Through such centres, especially their use by local women and their children, a community will be created. It is a feminised community — one built upon the anticipated usage patterns of women — and one constructed by propinquity. From it a localised identity is planned to emerge, one which is ultimately fixed in space. Other social dimensions constituting the identity of anticipated occupants are deemed to be either expressed in the choice of the area — with young, heterosexual, low to middle-income first home buyers of Melbourne's north-west suburbs the main target pur-chasers — or to be neatly subsumed by such considerations and the many opportunities for social mixing. The assertion of, for example, ethnic difference can thereby only occur within these boundaries.

An example of the tensions created in such boundary drawing was witnessed at the May 15, 1993 land ballot. For here, as the predominantly Anglo-Celtic, heterosexual young couples gathered to secure their building blocks, an extended family of Sikh Indians requested first to be able to purchase land on behalf of an absent brother, and to establish a medical clinic in one of the houses. At first politely listened to, it quickly became clear that such demands could not be accommodated. There were rules which meant that only those present could purchase property while zoning regulations meant that all service activity could only be located in the neighbourhood and regional centres. In choosing to make such a public statement this group of people—visibly different from the rest of the assembled bidders in their race, dress, family form, religion and language—presented a challenge to the smooth constitution of its community. In questioning the land disposal process and the zoning regulations of Roxburgh Park, some of the cultural and political assumptions informing its construction were exposed. The enforced physical and social separation of homes from work and services was thrown into question as was the assumption of the single family occupant. In offering these challenges, though, and in having them firmly rebuffed, the ultimate power of the newly colonising authority to define Melbourne suburban life was also revealed. In so appearing, the Sikhs disrupted the carefully orchestrated process of community creation, exposed its limits and the power of the Victorian state to colonise anew.

CONCLUSION

Postcolonial literatures in Australia—with their concern to retrieve an indigenous past, to document ongoing dispossession and to recognise the importance and complexity of racial and ethnic difference—have impelled a consideration of suburbanisation as a process of ongoing colonisation, of land and of peoples. Thus in the initial white occupation of the Port Phillip region, the presence of large 'empty' tracts of land belied its prior occupancy and the process of exclusion, containment and resistance which accompanied the maintenance of Aboriginal protectorates and mission schools.

More recently, suburbanisation has produced a different sort of colonisation as state power was exercised through a statutory authority with enormous planning and financial powers and an ideal suburban environment was constituted around affordability, service provision, community and ecology. The result, however, is a place in which ethnic diversity and the particular needs of women are subsumed by the techniques of place-making and homogenisation. Difference is obliterated in the quest for *the* suburban community.

NOTES

1. See, for example, Amos, V. and Parmar, P. (1984) 'Challenging imperial feminism', *Feminist Review*, 17, pp.3-20; Awatere, D. (1984) *Maori Sovereignty*, Broadsheet Publications, Auckland; Bhaba, H. (1983) 'Difference, discrimination and the discourse of colonialism', in Baker, F. et. al. (eds.) *The Politics of Theory*, University of Sussex, Colchester, pp.194-211; Bhaba, Homi (1990) *Nation and Narration*, Routledge, London; Hooks, B. (1982) *Ain't I a Woman?* *Black Women and Feminism*, Pluto Press, London; Hooks, B. (1990) *Yearnings: Race, Gender and Cultural Politics*, South End Press, Boston; Lorde, A. (1984) *Sister Outsider*, The Crossing Press, New York; Mani, L. (1990) 'Multiple mediations: feminist scholarship in the age of multinational reception', *Feminist Review*, 35, pp.24-41; Minh-ha, T. (1989) *Woman, Native, Other*, Indiana University Press, Bloomington; Mohanty, C. (1988) 'Under Western eyes: Feminist scholarship and colonial discourse', *Feminist Review*, 30, pp.61-88; Said, e. (1979) *Orientalism*, Vintage, New York; Spivak, G. (1988) *In Other Worlds. Essay in Cultural Politics*, Routledge, New York.

2. Within the academy, postcolonial work has emanated from: **sociology:** Bottomley, G. and de Lepervanche, M. (1984) *Ethnicity, Class and Gender in Australia*, Allen and Unwin, Sydney; Bottomley, G., de Lepervanche, M. and Martin, J. (1991) *Intersexions. Gender/Class/Culture/Ethnicity*, Allen and Unwin, North Sydney; Pettman, J. (1992) *Living in the Margins: Racism, Sexism and Feminism in Australia*, Allen and Unwin, North Sydney; **history:** Hunt, S. (1986) *Spinifex Fairies: Women in North West Australia*, University of Western Australia, Nedlands; Reynolds, H. (1972) *Aborigines and Settlers: The Australian Experience*, Cassell, Stanmore, N.S.W.; Reynolds, H. (1990a) *Frontier, Aborigines, Settlers and Land*, Allen and Unwin, Sydney; Reynolds, H. (1990b) *With the White People*, Penguin, Ringwood; Rowley, C. (1970) *The Destruction of Aboriginal Society*, Penguin, Harmondsworth; Rowley, C. (1971) *Outcasts in White Australia*, ANU Press, Canberra; Ryan, L. (1981) *The Aboriginal Tasmanians*, University of Queensland Press, St Lucia; **anthropology:** Bell, D. (1983) *Daughters of the Dreaming*, McPhee Gribble, Melbourne; Stanner, W. e. H. (1968) *After the Dreaming: Black and White Autralians — An Anthropologists View*, ABC Radio, Boyer Lecture Series, Sydney; **geography:** Gale, F. (1987) (ed.) *We Are Bosses Ourselves; The Status and Role of Aboriginal Women Today*, Australian Institute of Aboriginal Studies, Canberra; Gale, F. (1985) 'Seeing women in the landscape: Alternative views of the world around us', in Goodnow, J. and Pateman, C. (eds.) *Women, Social Science and Public Policy*, George Allen and Unwin, Sydney, pp.56-66; Jacobs, J. (1988), 'The construction of identity', in

Beckett, J. (ed.) *Past and Present: The Construction of Aborigines*, Australian Institute of Aboriginal Studies, Canberra; Jacobs, J. (1989) 'Women talking up big: Aboriginal women as cultural custodians', in Brock, P. (ed.) *Women's Rites and Sites*, Allen and Unwin, Sydney; and **cultural studies:** Carter, P. (1988) *The Road to Botany Bay: An Exploration in Spatial History*, Alfred A. Knopf, New York; Carter, P. (1992) *Living in a New Country*, Faber and Faber, London; Gunew, S. (1983) 'Migrant women writers: Who's on whose margins?!, *Meanjin*, 42 (1), pp.16-26, Gunew, S. and Yeatman, A. (1993) (eds.) *Feminism and the Politics of Difference*, Allen and Unwin, St Leonards.

Voices from the margins include Bandler, F. (1989) *Turning the Tide*, Australian Institute of Aboriginal Studies; Gilbert, K. (1977) *Living Black*, Allen Lane, Melbourne; Gunew, S. and Mahyuddin, J. (1990) *Beyond the Echo: Multicultural Women's Writing*, University of Queensland Press, St Lucia; Huggins, J. (1987) 'Firing on in the mind: Aboriginal women domestic servants in the interwar years', *Hecate*, 13 (2), pp.5-23; Huggins, J. and Blake, T. (1992) 'Protection of persecution? Gender relations in the era of racial segregation', in Saunders, K. and Evans, R. (eds.) *Gender Relations in Australia. Domination and Negotiation*, Harcourt Brace Jovanovich, Sydney, pp.42-58; Langford, R. (1988) *Don't Take Your Love to Town*, Penguin, Ringwood; Langton, M. (1988) 'The getting of power', *Australian Feminist Studies*, 6, pp.1-5; Morgan, S. (1987) *My Place*, Fremantle Arts Centre Press, Fremantle; Sykes, R. (1989) 'Blacks in the public sphere', *Hecate*, 17, pp.51-53.

3. In Beaglehole, J. (ed.) (1962) *The Endeavour Journal of Joseph Banks, 1768-1771*, Vol. 2, The Trustees of the Public Library of NSW in association with Angus & Robertson, Sydney.

4. Reynolds (1990a) *op. cit.*

5. Howitt, A. W. (1904) *The Native Tribes of South East Australia*, Macmillan, London; Symonds, I. W. (1985) *Bulla Bulla. An Illustrated History of the Shire of Bulla*, Spectrum, Melbourne; Urban Land Authority (1990) *Roxburgh Park: Local Structure Plan*, Urban Land Authority, Melbourne.

6. Howitt, *op. cit.*

7. Urban Land Authority, *op. cit.*; See also Wiencke, S. (1984) *When the Wattles Bloom Again*, S. W. Wiencke, Woori Yallock.

8. Wiencke, *op. cit.*, p.11.

9. *ibid.*, p.28.

10. Symonds, *op. cit.*, pp.35-41.

11. *ibid.*, p.38.

12. Gross, A. (1962) *History of the Shire of Bulla, 1862-1962*, Sunbury Shire Council, Sunbury, pp.26-27.

13. Symonds, *op. cit.*, p.16.

14. McLoughlin, B. (1992) *Shaping Melbourne's Future? Town Planning and Civil Society*, Cambridge University Press, Cambridge, p.125.

15. Moore, B. (1993) Project Manager, Roxburgh Park, interviewed March 2.

16. 'Sir George Arthur. Memo to Applicants for Assistant Protectors' (1982)

Historical Records of Australia, Vol. 2, Victorian Government Publishing Office, Melbourne, pp.32-33.

17. 'Parker to Robinson, April 1840. Being a Report for the period September 1839 to February 1840', *Historical Records of Australia*, Vol. 2, Victorian Government Publishing Office, Melbourne, pp.688-698.

18. MacFarlane, I. (Compiler) (1984) *Victorian Aboriginals 1835-1901*, Public Records Office, Victoria, p.43.

19. Christie, M. F. (1979) *Aboriginals in Colonial Victoria, 1835-1886*, Sydney University Press, Sydney, p.141.

20. Ramsey (1848) Forwarding a copy of the minutes of the Proceedings on the Aboriginal Mission Committees, *Merri Creek*, February 4. Victorian Historical Records Office, Transfer No. 1959/3, Series No. 11, pp.1847-1851.

21. Christie, *op. cit.*, p.144.

22. Moore, B. and Sadju, M. (1993) Project Manager and Community Development Officer, Roxburgh Park, interviewed December 14.

23. Moore, *op. cit.*; and Mitchell, B. (1993) 'Home of the future', *Sunday Age*, March 28, p.11.

24. Iremonger, D. (1989) (ed.) *Households Work*, Allen and Unwin, Sydney; Kathie Mee (1993) University of Sydney, Personal communication.

25. Urban Land Authority (1991) *Roxburgh Park: Community Plan*, Urban Land Authority, Melbourne.

26. Moore and Sadju, *op. cit.*

4

Dressing up the suburbs: representations of western Sydney

Kathleen Mee

For more than 20 years government agencies have had an interest in attracting economic development to western Sydney.[1] Local government involvement is justified by arguments such as the mobility of capital, federal policies which are too broad to encompass local interests, and appeals for the locality to be competitive.[2] This chapter examines the advertising material of a number of local councils and other government affiliated bodies used for attracting economic growth in western Sydney.[3]

A recurring feature of policy statements concerning economic development is the region's 'image problem'. As the Greater Western Sydney Economic Development Committee puts it: 'Greater Western Sydney has been plagued by *image* problems. Many beliefs and attitudes, both within and outside the region, are patently false. These misconceptions must be changed. A comprehensive regional marketing strategy is recommended to address this problem.'[4]

Regional marketing has been adopted to offer alternative images that counter these misconceptions about western Sydney. Local councils 'dress up' western Sydney to overcome their 'image problem'.[5]

In this chapter I consider some of the political implications of the new 'identity creation' strategies employed in western Sydney.

THE WEST AS 'OTHER'

In *Out West*, a history of western Sydney and a review of the media's treatment of the west, Diane Powell argues that western Sydney is treated as 'Sydney's other half'.[6] She asserts that the media have played a significant role in moving western Sydney to 'the "other side" of a social boundary'.[7] Negative incidents are often located by the press in the west but when similar incidents do occur in other parts of the city their location is not stressed.[8] The west: 'is seen as a repository for all those social groups and cultures which are outside the prevailing cultural ideal: the poor, the working class, juvenile delinquents, single mothers, welfare recipients, public housing tenants, Aborigines, immigrants from anywhere but particularly Arabs and Asians.'[9]

While other parts of the city represent the social norm, western Sydney is constituted as the 'other' as examples in Table 4.1 show.

Powell identifies several elements in the construction of otherness in western Sydney. First there is the nature of language used when speaking of the region. It is associated with lack and its residents are denied a speaking position and put into the position of 'them'. The western Sydney environment is described as alien, and the physical environment derided as a wasteland, sprawling, ugly, and homogeneous. Its people are characterised by a collection of negative epithets, a selection appear in Table 1. Their bodies are considered sick, they lack taste and education.[10]

Symonds makes a similar argument, noting that in comparison to Sydney proper, western Sydney: 'is *all* to be spurned. There is no fascination, no sense of the exotic or of sexual attraction.'[11] Indeed, he positions it as a colony of Sydney, something which can be other without being desired.[12] Alternatively western Sydney could be seen as containing some desirable elements, in representations of its Anglo-Australian culture, multicultural places and undisciplined bodies.[13]

Western Sydney is negatively positioned by a process which positively defines the parameters of a Sydney identity. Western Sydney becomes excluded from the totality of Sydney, and the differences between the two take on greater importance. Meanwhile the internal differentiation and diversity of western Sydney is ignored. As Young notes: 'Any move to define identity, a closed totality, always depends on excluding some elements, separating the pure from the impure.'[14]

In this case western Sydney has been excluded as impure, because its

Table 4.1
Western Sydney as other

Category	Western Sydney	Sydney
General	lack	excess
	outer	inner
	bad	good
	them	us
Physical environment	homogeneous	heterogeneous
	ugly	beautiful
	frontier	centre
	flat	hilly
	hot	temperate
	dry/dusty/treeless	coastal/leafy
	sprawling	compact
	new	old/mature
	violent	tranquil
People	ignorant	intellectual
	poor	wealthy
	tasteless	trendy/fashionable
	uncultured	cultured
	criminal/violent	law abiding
	passive	active
	indolent	ldynamic
	neglectful	concerned
	ugly	beautiful
	despairing	hopeful
	aimless	purposeful
	working-class	mixed/middle-class
Body	sick/alcoholic	healthy
	overeater	thin
	mentally ill	balanced

Source: Derived from a range of sources, especially Powell, D. (1993) *Out West: Perceptions of Sydney's Western Suburbs*, Allen and Unwin, Sydney.

existence threatens representations of Sydney as affluent, coastal and at the core of Australian life. If negative elements can be confined to the western fringe, then Sydney can have a uniformly positive identity. Designated as 'other', western Sydney is placed outside the boundaries of conventional definitions of Sydney.

Economic development strategies adopted by authorities in the west must continually negotiate this othering of western Sydney. The images used in promotional literature seek to place western Sydney *inside* notions of Sydney, rather than asserting a separate existence with different values. Western Sydney's *physical* boundaries are notoriously fuzzy.[15] In advertising, local councils exploit this fuzziness and seek to transgress the rigidities of Sydney's *social* boundaries. They claim for western Sydney desirable characteristics thought to belong exclusively to 'Sydney'.

CREATING A NEW VIEW OF THE WEST

Local economic development strategies have been the subject of significant interest in geography in recent times.[16] Such local initiatives have been inspired by broader economic stresses in advanced capitalist countries. Cox and Mair regard the problem for straitened localities as one of local dependence.[17] People, local State authorities and some capitalists are locally dependent and suffer when more mobile capitals relocate.[18] Some fractions of capital may over emphasise their mobility in order to gain concessions from locally dependent states.[19] One political consequence of these events, although there are other possible outcomes,[20] is that the locality may engage in regional competition, an element of which is 'boosterism'.[21]

An important part of the strategy is the creation of a saleable community identity. One way of doing this is an appeal to patriotism.[22] Cox and Mair claim: 'The nationalistic impulse is appropriated in the idea that the locality is worthy because it is an exemplar of national ideals.'[23] Thus western Sydney advertising attempts to appropriate positive aspects of the 'Australian' and 'Sydney' identities from which it has been excluded.

Promotion of the local area is not without internal contradictions. Taking on these identities involves participating in the processes of exclusion by which western Sydney itself has been excluded. While councils seek to project a prosperous and united regional image for the purpose of local booster campaigns, they also need to seek funding from State and federal government for local area projects. To gain this funding local government must highlight local needs. As the Greater Western Sydney Economic Development Committee notes: 'The region is undervalued as merely the hinterland of Sydney . . . This has often been emphasised by local interests in their arguments for more equitable funding for the region.'[24] The various political strategies of each council may therefore be in conflict.

There is also a conflict in the scale of regional initiatives. Western Sydney councils compete with each other for new investments at the local government level, sometimes making obvious references to the inadequacies of their neighbours in their advertising.[25] In other arenas regional committees and advertising strategies concentrate on development of the region as a whole, and council officials seek greater regional cooperation. While employment creation might be generally welcomed, residential proximity to a factory may well be opposed, both by residents and council regulations.

The next sections focus upon three strategies followed by government advertisers and consider the politics of exclusion and inclusion which characterise the discourses created.

LIVING IT UP IN WESTERN SYDNEY

Ubiquitous advertisements promoting the lifestyle benefits available to investors in western Sydney attempt to appropriate dominant images of what the 'Sydney' lifestyle essentially involves. But in presenting western Sydney as a place that offers the 'Sydney' lifestyle its working-class image must be addressed. While working-class culture and spaces have been considered attractive by the middle class in their move back into the inner city,[26] in western Sydney the community ideals inherent in working-class inner-city locations are not perceived to exist.[27] Councils have chosen to counter the stereotyping of western Sydney as working-class space by representing the region as a middle-class space. Constituting this image are pictures of large two-storey houses surrounded by trees, suggesting this is the accommodation desired by the executive (Figure 4.1). Only occasionally is diversity stressed, showing that workers and managers can *both* find a place in western Sydney and can coexist happily. Judging by the imagery the house is the essential centre of the executive lifestyle. By displaying such houses, the boundaries of middle-class space in Sydney are moved to include western Sydney without challenging the denigration of working-class suburban spaces.

Linked to images of the executive house is that of the 'happy family life' based on the heterosexual couple. Women are seen with children, or reclining in the luxury of the home which the man's shrewd investment decisions have fortuitously provided. Children playing are key to this image. Providing for children and their needs is an essential element in the construction of masculinity.[28] Thus, says the advertising, the male executive who moves to western Sydney will have his masculine identity affirmed by success in the public world of business and the attainment of an ideal family life. The home is presented as the site of male relaxation from the stresses of

Figure 4.1
Large houses and happy children: some lifestyle images of western Sydney

Source: Liverpool City Council (1990) *Industrial Development in Liverpool*, Economic Development Unit Liverpool City Council; Business Land Group (1991) *Macarthur: Perfect for Business and People* Campbelltown.

business. Female desires are assumed to be subsumed under those of children and mate.

This construction of the socially sanctioned nuclear 'happy family' needs to be seen against the backdrop of the denigration of family life in western Sydney. The region is stereotypically represented as the home of 'single mothers'.[29] In the working-class in general and in western Sydney in particular, family life is popularly portrayed as dysfunctional.[30] The promotional content thus seeks to move the boundaries of socially acceptable family life to include western Sydney.

Large houses, happy children, and finally, 'the good life'. In Australia, this final drawcard usually focuses on the outdoors: the bush and the beach. Local government areas on the urban fringe of Sydney usually concentrate on the bush. The images suggest executives can be close to their factories, have all the comforts of inner-city living and still attain an idyllic rural lifestyle. Romanticising the bush and mythologising a past when life was slower and simpler is a common technique in Australian advertising. Here the imagery replaces associations with ugliness and pollution of the physical environment in western Sydney with more positive images of the peace and tranquillity typically associated with middle-class suburbia.[31] It attempts to move the boundaries of 'beautiful Sydney' around western Sydney.

We are all familiar with the ways in which Sydney is represented by its harbour and its beaches.[32] The west is stigmatised by the physical lack of a beach. 'Westies' are out of place when they arrive at the beach because of their supposed unfamiliarity with beach rituals. They are criticised for wearing inappropriate clothes and weekends, when 'westies' have a day out, are said to be a hard time for life-savers.[33] Yet Powell argues that: 'The beach is something all people of Sydney feel they own, whether they come from Dee Why and Cronulla or Campbelltown and Penrith'.[34]

Given the importance of the beach to Sydney culture, it is not surprising that beach images are also to be found in western Sydney advertising, both in text and image. The beaches shown and referred to are most likely to be around Wollongong. For example Liverpool's advertising places proximity to water as a high priority: 'If you like to spend your leisure time outdoors, Liverpool provides — water sports on Georges and Nepean Rivers, Chipping Norton Lakes and Bent's Basin State Recreation Area; the South Coast's unpolluted beaches are only 35-40 minutes away.'[35] Beach alternatives such as rivers and theme parks are also portrayed.

In presenting all these images of lifestyle, promotional advertising attempts to move the boundaries of a Sydney lifestyle around western

Sydney. Local government projects challenge dominant representations of the west as a working-class area, made up of dysfunctional families inhabiting an ugly and unstimulating physical environment. It seeks to have western Sydney associated with what is considered valuable. By championing conventional lifestyle features western Sydney advertising merely tries to make the boundary between 'Sydney' and its other disappear.

CONSTRUCTING A WORKFORCE

The presentation of an attractive workforce is vital to an economic development strategy. Like all other images, representations of the workforce do not exist in a vacuum but are conditioned by notions of work and views of what constitutes 'Australian workers'. Attitudes to work according to Rowe are ambivalent.[36] One dominant image of the Australian worker is that of an indolent, lazy, leisure-oriented individual who lacks: 'the almost obsessive work orientation frequently asserted as being essential for economic survival'.[37]

The latest buzz-words, 'microeconomic reform', posit the inefficiency of the Australian labour market and work practices as impediments to the international competitiveness of Australian industry. Western Sydney, where large numbers of 'workers' are understood to live, is again popularly constructed as other in terms of its workforce. Powell notes how in media images: 'The westie body is thought to be undisciplined in its eating and exercise habits. The westie mind is also seen as undisciplined.'[38] Thus 'westies' become an undisciplined potential workforce, unable to develop a level of physical fitness appropriate for work, lacking mental discipline and an interest in education,[39] and therefore insufficiently skilled to become an active workforce.[40]

The popular impression is of western Sydney as a potentially bad investment choice. In contrast, Asian economies are represented as being able to successfully compete for investment.[41] The Greater Western Sydney Economic Development Statement notes that Asian manufacturing has been more efficient in implementing structural change particularly by the adoption of advanced technology, development of a highly skilled work force and growth in the knowledge-intensive service industry.[42] Hence the Asian economies have attained a more favourable balance of trade and regional development than western Sydney in particular, and Australia as a whole.[43]

In combating negative stereotypes of the western Sydney work force, advertising sidesteps the large pool of unemployed and highlights the pool of potential workers. In repeated publications the large size of the western Sydney workforce is stressed.[44] Often this is noted in combination with workforce age, and the rapidly growing population. Images conjure a bright future both for workers and for business in western Sydney.

The economic development advertising of Asian countries in the early 1980s also emphasised these characteristics. Two countries specifically mentioned in the Greater Western Sydney Economic Development Committee as industrial successes, Thailand and South Korea, have used the quantity of labour in their countries as a selling point. In a 1975 advertising campaign Thailand claimed: 'One of the major factors which recommends Thailand to the investor over other countries is its *abundant* supply of cheap and trainable labour'.[45] Similarly South Korea asserts: 'Korea's labour force is one of her primary resources'.[46]

In Western Sydney the stereotypical images of indolence and irresponsibility are countered by representation of workers as 'willing and able', 'stable' and industrially responsible.[47] Liverpool's advertising describes: 'A large skilled local labour force with an excellent industrial relations record. (In fact, the South West Sydney region has the lowest number of strike days per capita in Australia).'[48]

Advertising of the work force in this way is a common feature of economic development promotion according to Cox and Mair: 'good labour relations and a generally quiescent local population are viewed as important elements in a locality's business climate and hence its attractiveness to outside investors'.[49] Thus in western Sydney promotions, local workers are portrayed as less prone to transportation problems, more likely to develop employer loyalty reinforced by the local location and, as younger home buyers, having a vested interest in the economic health of the region.[50] In the light of the clever country discourse there are repeated references to worker skill, diversity and the broad range of occupations they represent.[51]

Labour force representations are also gendered. While images of women and men are almost equal in the 'lifestyle' sections of advertising (there are slightly more women), men usually outnumber women two to one in workforce representations.[52] The occupation groupings dominated by men are more heavily stressed: 'Our population has a broad cross section of skills. Liverpool can provide your organisation with resident professionals and administrators as well as tradespeople and labourers.'[53]

Liverpool Council's advertising narrative *includes* 85% of all jobs men do in Liverpool, and *excludes* 58% of all jobs women do, because it fails to mention the non-manual non-professional jobs women usually perform. These advertising images reinforce a conception of women workers as unskilled[54] and therefore women remain ineligible to be foregrounded in the promotion of a skilled workforce.

These representations seek to move the borders of a stable, hard working, efficient work force to include western Sydney. In this case the boundaries are not necessarily moving from other parts of Sydney. Advertising attempts to challenge work values in general, moving Australian workers into competition with those overseas. In seeking to alter the perceived social geography of workers held by potential employers it largely ignores the availability of female labour and thus does not target the region's full potential for industrial expansion.[55]

Council officers pointed out that industrial advertising was important to provide jobs for 'their people' but this involved a narrow view of who the people were, and what roles it might be desirable for them to perform. In attempting to join the international community of skilled and attractive workers, western Sydney councils continue to under represent the value of women workers potentially to their region's economic detriment. Such exclusions reinforce dominant ideologies of the role of women in the public and domestic sphere. Dressing up the work force involves representing the men of western Sydney as docile, compliant and efficient while the women of western Sydney largely remain invisible in the home.

LOCATING WESTERN SYDNEY—A MOVE TO THE CENTRE

Characteristic of the othering of western Sydney is the stress on the region as peripheral. As Powell notes: '[western Sydney] does not *belong*, it is not part of the totality . . . The suburbs are constructed as exterior to the city, outside it'.[56] In a similar vein, Symonds has argued that western Sydney is treated by the metropolis as a colony. He draws an analogy between the treatment of Australia by Britain, and western Sydney by Sydney: 'The western suburbs were cast in the same way by the Sydney centre as Botany Bay had long been by London'.[57] He argues that an increasing perception of cultural sophistication in Australia by an inner-city elite has relocated the Australian yobbo image to western Sydney: ' "the west" is what "the centre" considered *it* was'.[58]

Both Powell and Symonds recognise that the separation of the perceived 'centre' from western Sydney is crucial to the region's cultural depiction. It is not surprising therefore that conveying a sense of centrality is an important selling point in regional marketing strategies. Given that locational centrality is frequently mapped onto economic and political power, centrality has played an important role in advertising regions elsewhere.[59] Government agencies have identified the problem of western Sydney thus: 'The region is undervalued as merely the *hinterland of Sydney*, a flat hot dry dusty plain with inadequate resources, insufficient skills and bad transport'.[60] The potential of business to profit from a central location, of course, is a belief founded in classical economics.[61]

Hence the following examples from local government image makers in western Sydney:

> Let your business benefit from Parramatta's *central* location.[62]
>
> Liverpool's place is in the *centre* of Sydney's future.[63]
>
> Penrith is rapidly emerging as the commercial, cultural and recreational *centre* of western Sydney.[64]
>
> As well as being close to the demographic *centre* of Sydney, Blacktown is in the *heart* of Sydney's Greater West — the largest market of families, households and buying power in Australia. It is also *centrally* located between Newcastle and Wollongong.[65]
>
> Although Macarthur is essentially open spaces, it is surprisingly *central*, an easy 80 minute drive from Sydney's Central Business District.[66]

The councils focus on various features to highlight their particular centrality; one concentrates on the distribution of population, another on market accessibility, while Blacktown and Macarthur include access to Wollongong to support claims that make the urban fringe central. Access to Sydney (the traditional centre as Powell and Symonds demonstrate) is an essential element.

The key visual image of the centre is the map, drawn with the place in question in the centre of a series of concentric circles (Figure 4.2). Note how Wollongong is included in Macarthur's circle, but several northern Sydney suburbs are not. Parramatta includes most of the city, but highlights Sydney city, North Sydney, Chatswood and Hornsby in locating itself, referring only to Liverpool in the rest of western Sydney.[67]

As councils in western Sydney claim centrality they sometimes deliberately set out to convey the impression that such is not the case for other parts of the west.[68] Competition is fostered among the western regions. As each centre requires the inclusion and exclusion of some

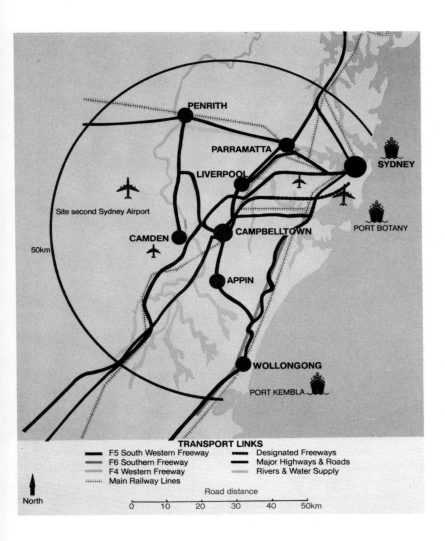

Figure 4.2
Representing centrality: mapping western Sydney in the centre

Source: Business Land Group (1991) *Macarthur: Perfect for Business and People*, Campbelltown.

parts of the whole, the tradition of exclusion which has marginalised western Sydney continues within.

Symonds suggests that focusing on the centrality of the area is an important step in overcoming the otherness of western Sydney: 'The west should itself be recognised as a "centre" or a place with many centres. Parramatta and Penrith have many "centre-like" qualities — high-rise office blocks, huge malls, theatres. But they still exist only as a pale reflection of Sydney centre's glory . . . And so postmodern notions of a decentred geography in Sydney appear, mostly, inappropriate.'[69]

Claiming the central ground is consistent with the political strategy adopted by councils in attempting to attract economic development. Sydney has been the symbolic centre of economic vitality and health, the point from which others define their position. In order to attract the attentions of investors western Sydney councils seek to usurp this central position. Alternative strategies of presenting western Sydney as part of a decentred city remain unexplored.

CONCLUSION

The advertising of western Sydney challenges the position of west as other, by claiming that western Sydney is in fact *Sydney*. It attempts to show how, despite considerable myth making to the contrary, the dominant features of Sydney centre life are also part of western Sydney life.

The presentation of a middle-class lifestyle rebuts a homogeneous working-class image. The happy nuclear family counters images of family dysfunction. Presentation of the good life confronts the exclusion of western Sydney and its residents from environmental amenity and enjoyment. Advertising of the labour force counters images of Australian workers as unsatisfactory and the characterisation of 'westies' as lazy and indolent. Claiming a central position that is efficient and functional for industrial location counters the placement of western Sydney as marginal and peripheral compared to the centre of Sydney's concern.

Advertising texts are one of many resistance strategies through which western Sydney residents and their representatives confront stereotyping and marginalisation.[70] The campaigns to alter the regional image are funded to encourage economic development. The scope of the campaigns is small, generally relating directly to business. However the strategy of regional boosterism also penetrates the print media in Sydney. Local mayors make statements to the media consistent with a more positive regional image,[71] thus spreading a discourse of redefinition (the west as Sydney) beyond business people alone. Dressing up the suburbs involves a number of problems. The exclusion of others is unchallenged by a discourse which merely attempts to gain access to social norms. As Young notes: 'If the only alternative to the oppressive exclusion of some groups defined as Other by dominant ideologies is the assertion that they are the same as everybody else, then they will be continue to be excluded because they are not the same'.[72]

An alternative strategy might claim that excluded other groups are valuable in their own right, but such a politics of difference is often rejected by marginalised groups who feel it has the potential to continue a pattern of marginalisation and exclusion.[73] Such a strategy is also inconsistent with the political context of local development. Local economic policies are based on regional acceptability to mobile capital, and as such are more likely to appropriate dominant discourses than challenge them.

Nevertheless by unsettling some of the negative stereotypes of life in western Sydney, local advertising creates initial conditions for the valuing of difference. Perhaps if western Sydney can secure a place *within* dominant discourses as a legitimate citizen of Sydney, then the other within western Sydney will have a better chance of asserting its diversity and value.

NOTES

1. Fulop, L. and Sheppard, D. (1988) 'The life and death of regional initiatives in western Sydney: the case of the Local Government Development Programme', *International Journal of Urban and Regional Research*, 12(4), pp.609-626.
2. Blacktown City Council (1992) *Local Economic and Employment Development in Blacktown*, Town Planning Report No. 019 (P), pp.27-29.
3. As western Sydney lacks a rigid definition, for the purposes of this study I adopted the definition of the Greater Western Sydney Economic Development Committee and contacted the local government areas of Auburn, Blacktown, Baulkham Hills, Blue Mountains, Campbelltown, Camden, Fairfield, Hawkesbury, Holroyd, Liverpool, Parramatta, Penrith and Wollondilly Councils. I also contacted the Western Sydney Regional Organisation of Councils (WSROC), the Macarthur Regional Organisation of Councils (MACROC), western Sydney regional promotion groups funded by the state

government such as the Business Land Group, the Western Sydney Chamber of Commerce and several tourist information services.

4.   Greater Western Sydney Economic Development Committee (1992) *Greater Western Sydney Economic Development Statement*, Parramatta, Chairman's Introduction.

5.   In variation on the 'mutton dressed up as lamb' theme, in western Sydney it is not age which is the barrier to attractiveness but youth and a sense of otherness.

6.   Powell, D. (1993) *Out West: Perceptions of Sydney's Western Suburbs*, Allen and Unwin, Sydney, p.5.

7.   *ibid.*, p.xviii. Pettman argues that there exists a 'politics of boundary making which assumes only particular groups have an ethnicity and the others are part of some social norm' (Pettman, J. (1992) *Living in the Margins: Racism, Sexism and Feminism in Australia*, Sydney, Allen and Unwin, p. 13).

8.   Powell (1993) *op. cit.*

9.   *ibid.*, p.xviii.

10. Powell (1993) *op. cit.*, pp.1-17.

11. Symonds, M. (1993) 'Imagined Colonies: On the social construction of Sydney's western suburbs', in Hage, G. and Johnson, L. (eds.) *Communal/ Plural: Identity/Community/Change*, Research Centre in Intercommunal Studies, University of Western Sydney.

12. *ibid.*

13. Powell (1993) *op. cit.*, p.32, pp.134-139, pp.140-147.

14. Young, I. (1990a) 'The Ideal of Community and the Politics of Difference', in Nicholson, L. (ed.) *Feminism and Postmodernism*, Routledge, New York, p.303.

15. Department of Planning (1993) *Sydney's Future: A Discussion Paper on Planning the Greater Metropolitan Region*, New South Wales Government, Department of Planning, Sydney, p. 6.

16. See for example Cox, K. (1993) 'The local and the global in new urban politics', *Environment and Planning D*, 11(4), pp.433-448; Cox, K. and Mair, A. (1988) 'Locality and Community in the Politics of Local Economic Development', *Annals of the Association of American Geographers*, 78(2), pp.307-325; Cox, K. and Mair, A. (1991) 'From localised social structures to localities as agents', *Environment and Planning A*, 23(2), pp.197-213; Eisenschitz, A. and Gough, J. (1993) *The Politics of Local Economic Policy: The Problems and Possibilities of Local Initiative*, Macmillan, London; Harvey, D. (1989) *The Condition of Postmodernity: An Enquiry into the Origins of Cultural Change*, Basil Blackwell, Oxford; Jackson, P. (1991) 'Mapping meanings: a cultural critique of locality studies', *Environment and Planning A*, 23(2), pp.215-228; Watson, S. (1991) 'Gilding the smokestacks: the new symbolic representations of deindustrialised regions', *Environment and Planning D*, 9(1), pp.59-70.

17. Cox and Mair (1988) *op. cit.*

18. *ibid.*

19. Cox (1993) *op. cit.*, pp.440-442.

20. Eisenschitz and Gough (1993) *op. cit.*

21. Cox and Mair (1988) *op. cit.*, pp.315-320.
22. *ibid.*, pp.315-318.
23. *ibid.*, pp.317-318.
24. Greater Western Sydney Economic Development Committee (1992) *op. cit.*, p. 14.
25. Liverpool City Council (1990) *Industrial Development in Liverpool: Proud of Our Past — Confident in Our Future*, Economic Development Unit Liverpool City Council.
26. Symonds (1993) *op. cit.*, p.66. For examples of this elsewhere see Burgess J. and Wood P. (1988) 'Decoding Docklands: Place Advertising and the Decision-making strategies of the Small Firm' in Eyles, J. and Smith, D. (eds) *Qualitative Methods in Human Geography*, Polity Press, Cambridge.
27. Symonds (1993) *op. cit.*, pp.65-66.
28. Donaldson, M. (1991) *Time of our lives: Labour and love in the working class*, Allen and Unwin, North Sydney, p.65-70; Segal, L. (1990) *Slow Motion: Changing Masculinities, Changing Men*, Virago, London, p.297-298.
29. Powell (1993) *op. cit.*, p.xviii.
30. *ibid.*, p.91-97.
31. Powell (1993) *op. cit.*, p.33-35; Symonds (1993) *op. cit.*, p.66-69.
32. Game, A. (1991) *Undoing the Social: Towards a Deconstructive Sociology*, Open University Press, Milton Keynes; Ryan, B. (1990) 'The "Official" Image of Australia', in Zonn, L. (ed.) *Place Images in Media: Portrayal, Experience and Meaning*, Rowman and Littlefield, Maryland.
33. Powell (1993) *op. cit.*, pp.114-118. Ann Game makes a similar argument about perceptions that overseas tourists are out of place at the beach (Game (1991) *op. cit.*, p.174).
34. Powell (1993) *op. cit.*, p.115; Dee Why and Cronulla are Sydney beach suburbs. Campbelltown and Penrith are western Sydney suburbs.
35. Liverpool City Council (1990), *op. cit.*, p.8.
36. Rowe, D. (1993) 'Leisure, tourism and "Australianness"', *Media, Culture and Society*, 15(2), pp.253-269.
37. *ibid.*, p.258.
38. Powell (1993) *op. cit.*, p.33.
39. *ibid.*, p.33. Note that Iris Marion Young claims that groups often suffer from 'stereotypes [that] confine them to a nature which is often attached in some way to their bodies' (Young, I. M. (1990b) *Justice and the Politics of Difference*, Princeton University Press, Princeton, p.59). In this context it is not surprising that the 'westie' body should be vilified as being other.
40. The perception of the inappropriate nature of the western Sydney workforce has been challenged in other ways. WESTIR commissioned Horvath, R., Mills, C. and Mee, K. (1989) *A Skills Atlas of Western Sydney* WESTIR, Sydney, in order to highlight both the skills deficits and potential of the western Sydney workforce. Elsewhere the perception of western Sydney as 'educationally challenged' has resulted in the inadequate provision of educational services to western Sydney (Hodge, S. (1993) 'Reading the landscape of Western Sydney

for disadvantage', Paper Presented at the Institute of Australian Geographers Conference, Monash University, 27-30 September).

41. Greater Western Sydney Economic Development Committee (1992) *op. cit.*, p.8-14. The western Sydney economy is compared with the economies of Thailand, Malaysia, Singapore, Taiwan, Hong Kong, and South Korea.

42. *ibid.*

43. *ibid.*

44. Blacktown City Council (undated) *Blacktown*, p.8; Blacktown City Council (1984) *Blacktown: City on the Move*, p.7; Liverpool City Council (1990), *op. cit.*, pp.1,4; Macarthur Development Board (1985) *Share the Vision of Macarthur*, Campbelltown, p.13; New South Wales Planning and Environment Commission and Western Sydney Regional Organisation of Councils (1978) *Western Sydney Investment Prospectus*, Blacktown, pp.6-7; Western Sydney Regional Organisation of Councils (1986) *Sydney's Greater West Investment: The WHERE, WHY and HOW of Developing with Sydney's Greater West*, Blacktown, p.4.

45. The Office of the Board of Investment (*15 Powerful Reasons Why You Should Invest in Thailand*, p.13) cited in Frobel, F., Heinrichs, J., and Kreye, O. (1980) *The New International Division of Labour: Structural Unemployment in Industrialised Countries and Industrialisation in Developing Countries*, Cambridge University Press, Cambridge, p.342.

46. Economic Planning Board (*Guide to Investment in Korea*, pp.45-46) cited in Frobel et al (1980) *op. cit.*, p.342.

47. Blacktown City Council (1984) *op. cit.*, p.8; Business Land Group (1991) *Macarthur: Perfect for Business and People*, Campbelltown; Liverpool City Council (1990) *op. cit.*, p.1,4; Macarthur Development Board (1985) *op. cit.*, p.13; Wollondilly Shire Council (1992) *Business and Industry in Wollondilly Shire*, Picton, p.3.

48. Liverpool City Council (1990) *op. cit.*, p.4.

49. Cox and Mair (1988) *op. cit.*, p.314.

50. Blacktown City Council (1984) *op. cit.*, p.8; Liverpool City Council (1990) *op. cit.*, p.1; Macarthur Development Board (1985) *op. cit.*, pp.13-17; Wollondilly Shire Council (1992) *op. cit.*, p.3.

51. Blacktown City Council (1984) *op. cit.*, p.3,8; Business Land Group (1991) *op. cit.*, p.2; Liverpool City Council (1990) *op. cit.*, pp.1,4,9; Macarthur Development Board (1985) *op. cit.*, p.13; Macarthur Development Corporation (1991) *Annual Report*, Campbelltown, p.3; New South Wales Planning and Environment Commission and Western Sydney Regional Organisation of Councils (1978) *op. cit.*, pp.6-7; New South Wales Planning and Environment Commission and Western Sydney Regional Organisation of Councils (1982) *Western Sydney Investment Prospectus*, Blacktown, p.19; Western Sydney Regional Organisation of Councils (1986) *op. cit.*, p.4; Wollondilly Shire Council (1992) *op. cit.*, p.3.

52. The two to one ratio is an average from all photographs portraying paid work. In *Macarthur: Perfect for Business and People* the ratio is 1 to 1, but of the three

women presented, one is engaged in child care, and another is a graduating student rather than the qualified doctor which a male represents (Business Land Group (1991) *op. cit.*).

53. Liverpool City Council (1990) *op. cit.*, p.9.
54. See for example Game, A. and Pringle, R. (1983) *Gender at Work*, George Allen and Unwin, Sydney, pp.7-9, p.18; Pocock, B. (1988) *Demanding Skill: Women and technical education in Australia* Sydney, Allen and Unwin, pp.10-17; Segal (1990) *op. cit.*, p.297.
55. Hanson, S. (1992) 'Geography and Feminism: Worlds in Collision?', *Annals of the Association of American Geographers*, 82(4), pp.569-586, p.580. This strategy contrasts that of the Asian countries mentioned earlier who specifically mention the skills of their female labour force, Frobel et al (1980) *op. cit.*, p.347.
56. Powell (1993) *op. cit.*, p.150.
57. Symonds (1993) *op. cit.*, p.68.
58. *ibid.*, p.70.
59. Burgess and Wood (1988) *op. cit.*, p.95.
60. Greater Western Sydney Economic Development Committee (1992) *op. cit.*, p.14.
61. Although Blacktown City Council notes that location may be of decreasing importance to some industries (Blacktown City Council (1992) *op. cit.*).
62. Parramatta City Council (undated) *Your Welcome at the Centre*, Connex West, Toongabbie.
63. Liverpool City Council (1990) *op. cit.*
64. Penrith City Council (1992) *Penrith: growth City of Sydney's West*, Penrith.
65. Blacktown City Council (1992) *Blacktown: Fastest growing city in Australia's premier state*, Blacktown.
66. Macarthur Development Board (1985) *op. cit.*
67. Parramatta City Council (undated) *op. cit.*, front cover.
68. Liverpool City Council refers to the end of pioneering conditions in Liverpool experienced in other areas (Liverpool City Council (1990) *op. cit.*, p.1).
69. Symonds (1993) *op. cit.*, p.71.
70. For others see Powell (1993) *op. cit.*, p.4, p.34, pp.157-159.
71. For example, Willis, R. (1993) 'Mayors hit at "Westies" slur', *Sun Herald*, September 12, p.7.
72. Young (1990b) *op. cit.*, p.168.
73. *ibid.*, p.169.

5

Acts of enclosure: crime and defensible space in contemporary cities

George Morgan

In big cities in the Western world there is a widespread fear of threat to property and person. In Los Angeles wealthy suburbanites live in walled estates, modern day fortresses, with perimeters patrolled by armed guards. In Australian cities the gulf between rich and poor, insiders and outcasts, is not so great but moral panics around crime surface with alarming frequency, skewing public support away from the civil libertarian and 'bleeding heart' liberal politics and towards strong state solutions—greater police powers, stiffer sentences and more restrictions on prisoners. Gruesome stories of strangers assaulting, raping, robbing and murdering their victims in public places are the stock in trade of the tabloid press and television. Residents gather regularly in local halls to be advised by police on how to protect themselves from crime and how to identify potential perpetrators. This paper will explore the origins of the popular desire to enclose and defend territory in cities. It will examine a shift in the form of respectable fears of urban crime.

Historically the overcrowded and insanitary residential areas were the focus of middle-class fears. Respectable people were concerned that the vigorous street life would spill over and undermine the moral and physical health of all inhabitants. The city was frequently described in organic terms with 'diseased' areas having the potential to 'infect' other more affluent areas. Suburbanisation, with its norm of the privatised nuclear family, was seen by policy makers as the antidote. Yet the form of low density urban development which has been adopted in Australia's cities has encouraged a very different moral panic around crime.

Cities are now viewed as dissipated rather than organic. Fragmented private spaces are interwoven with dangerous and impersonal public space. The archetypal folk devil has simultaneously shifted from being the dubious immoral figure plying vice on street corners, to the anonymous and inconspicuous stranger who lurks in public space. This man (for it is predominantly men who are dangerous) may well be known to his acquaintances as a family man, or a prominent community figure. The practices of 'defensible space'— by which buildings and landscapes are designed to be amenable to surveillance— have emerged on the contemporary landscape: where home, work and city/shopping centres have been separated, where car access is given highest priority and where the forms of gregarious social life of the old inner city have been replaced by a much more privatised existence.

THE ORGANIC CITY

Threatening, disruptive and ungenteel behaviour in city streets was in the past a source of considerable concern within the urban middle classes. In Sydney during the 1890s depression young men known as larrikins gathered in gangs called Pushes and attacked, robbed and insulted passers by. Each Push was in a specific neighbourhood— for example Glebe, The Rocks and Waterloo. Although radical nationalist writers like Henry Lawson depicted the larrikin as a romantic knockabout figure, this view was not shared by the main opinion makers of the time, whose pronouncements were more characteristic of the class bound rhetoric and censorious tones of the English establishment.

The potential for the corruption of respectable young people in public places was the cause of several moral panics around the turn of the century. Prison administrator Frederick Nietenstein argued in the 1890s that the lack of an orderly and secure home life led young people to seek out diversions like 'unsavoury literature, dancing halls and gambling establishments present in the city.'[1] Middle-class parents feared the indiscriminate mixing of social groups in public places.

Public figures inveighed against the opening of a Palais de Danse in Melbourne in 1913, declaring that they would never let their daughters attend such an establishment.[2] The Royal Commission into Chinese Gambling (1891) had found that gambling and opium smoking were common practices in Sydney. The figure of the Chinese opium peddler seeking to entice unsuspecting young passers-by into dens of iniquity became a racist stereotype in the popular press.[3] Such perceived threats prompted calls from pillars of society for the redevelopment of cities. The desire to confine the leisure of young people to the circumscribed safety of the suburban block informed the designs of urban redevelopers from the 1920s onward.

The conditions of the 1890s depression provoked fears of disease as well as those of crime. These fears were mapped onto city spaces. A torrent of moral indignation followed the outbreak of bubonic plague in The Rocks in 1900.[4] Public figures blamed the moral hygiene of the Rocks inhabitants rather than the pestilential rats, which came off ships at nearby wharves. NSW parliamentarian WJ Spruson called for the area's houses to be completely demolished and for the 'sweaters and toilers to go elsewhere'.[5] The body was the metaphor for descriptions of the city. The criminal quarters of the city had the capacity to infect respectable areas, and were responsible for the ills of the city as a whole.

The 1890s depression produced a popular reaction to laissez faire philosophies and an understanding that poverty was a social, not simply an individual, concern. Yet most of those who advocated Fabian or New Liberal state strategies wished to distinguish the victims of economic decline from those whose indolence and vices were deemed to be the cause of their situation. They saw urban reform as a necessary antidote to the spread of rough habits into respectable areas. Planning strategies from the early 20th century were designed to minimise the potentially corrupting gregarious street culture of inner-city areas. An ironic contrast can be drawn between the fear of a dense and public sociability at the turn of the century and the contemporary fear of urban crime which is based on lack of sociability in street spaces that are not occupied or controlled.

Australian cities were among the first in the world to move towards suburban solutions. Garden suburbs like Daceyville in Sydney were intended to produce an ordered and harmonious civic culture to replace the disorder of working-class areas of the inner city. The Great Depression slowed urban reform initiatives as public funding dried up. As in the 1890s the social conditions of the 1930s sharpened popular awareness of the need for the state to take a more proactive role. Fears of urban infection were stronger than ever. The Housing Improvement

Board of NSW, 1937 Report stated: 'It is almost an axiom that a slum district eventually spreads and engulfs adjoining areas. Unchecked, the blight can spread with a rapidity that often astonishes.'[6] In their *Housing the Australian Nation* (1942) Oswald-Barrett and Burt called for public finance for housing to stem slum expansion: 'Better homes make better citizens and better citizens inevitably raise the standard of social and national life.'[7]

At the close of World War II conditions were ripe for the expansion of the social welfare activities of the state. Fifteen years of economic hardship and war had created popular support for reformist politics. Urban reform was high on the agenda.

The postwar reconstructing state took up the cause from 1945. The Commonwealth and State Housing Agreement led to the construction of 96 158 new dwellings in Australia up until it was terminated in 1957. Large blocks of inner Sydney were earmarked for slum clearance by the State Housing Commission. While some of the inhabitants of the redeveloped areas were rehoused in new dwellings in the same neighbourhoods, most were encouraged to take up Housing Commission places in the suburbs. The broadacre estates offered the promise of clean middle-class living and an escape from noise and squalor. Of 288 families who lived in the redeveloped Devonshire Street area of Surry Hills in inner Sydney only 43 were rehoused in the new Housing Commission flats built there.[8]

Suburban living was an alluring option to many who had lived in the inner city through the Great Depression, but the process of outward movement of population undermined local culture and community in the centre. Many of those who moved to the suburbs were young couples who left ageing parents behind in the inner cities. This middle generation might have sustained the neighbourhood culture and developed contacts with the new social groups moving into the inner city (migrant groups, the bohemian fringe, gentry). Most members, however, shared Stretton's view that suburbia was the most appropriate place to bring up children.[9] The closure of much established manufacturing industry in central Sydney and the location of what new investment there was in the suburbs, particularly from the mid 1960s, further encouraged the outward shift of population. The resultant generational dislocation, coupled with the destructive impact of mass car ownership on street life, undermined the local ecology of the inner city.

From the 1890s respectable people in Australia were concerned that the habits of the rough working class would be transmitted across permeable neighbourhood boundaries to infect the respectable districts, particularly through the agency of young people. Many believed that suburban life would permit the confinement of many of those social activities which in the overcrowded inner cities spilled out into the streets. Yet the destruction of semi-public local zones paradoxically laid the ground for a new moral panic around crime in which the problem was the lack of social life.

MODERNISM AND THE ERASURE OF LOCAL CULTURE

The material preconditions for urban redevelopment—population increase through higher birthrates and immigration levels, the long economic boom and the restructuring of capital across urban space— converged with the ideology of modernism as forces informing professional practice and state policy during the 1950s and 1960s. Those who planned urban areas along modernist lines envisaged utopian landscapes, and also attempted to predetermine the ways in which life was lived, the ways in which public space was used, the forms of community which emerged and the moral economy of urban populations. The ideal, imaginary citizen who moves in an orderly and predictable way along specified urban pathways is the normative figure of modernism.

Modernism projected a future which denied those aspects of traditional urban life which were seen as dissonant and unacceptable. The notion of progress is central here. Only those parts of history which lead up to the shining modern present are acknowledged. If the nuclear family, neatly contained in a suburban block, is an operating norm of modernism, then the prior existence of extended kinship and other communal networks, and associated vigorous street culture in the inner city, is erased from the official memory.[10] Public housing authorities allocated dwellings according to rational criteria of equity—those in the most need or who had been on the list the longest got preference—rather than seeking to transplant existing neighbourhood networks into new suburban settings.

Those who moved from inner-city terrace to broadacre block never completely accepted the life patterns expected of them by the social engineers. They brought with them the memory and experience of local culture and an inclination to reclaim some of its best aspects. The patterns of gregarious association which characterised the old neighbourhoods were not totally discarded. Those who experienced life in such a setting retained a desire to establish local networks. Where the modern landscape frustrated those impulses by making it difficult for networks to form and for local cooperation to take place around domestic tasks and the care of children, there was fertile ground for political movements to emerge to counter these isolating effects. The desire to reclaim indigenous street culture can be a subversive force. Holston described how Brasilia was designed as a modernist abnegation of the street life of other big Brazilian cities.[11] The way in which its inhabitants have come to use public space, to reimpose gregarious traditions on a hostile terrain, has cut across the privatising suburban vision of the city's planners.

In Australian cities economic and social forces have in recent times worked against the formation of active neighbourhood networks. The decentralisation of manufacturing, commerce and retailing has meant that most working people no longer live close to where they work and shop. The cross fertilisation of occupational and local networks which was possible in the old inner city is therefore less likely. In addition the central role which women play in traditional local culture has been eroded in the modern city. The networks and forms of mutual assistance which develop around childcare, housework and shopping are important in sustaining that culture. Yet the erosion in the real wage levels of male breadwinners since the early 1970s has meant that two incomes are needed for most families to meet mortgage repayments. The expansion of the service sector over the last 30 years has led to the recruitment of large numbers of women into the work-force. Although they generally still shoulder the burden of housework, women on average spend less time in the home, and are less able to sustain relationships with neighbours than previously.[12]

The problems that postwar metropolitan architecture in Western cities has posed for women indicates that those responsible for it were both ignorant of the rhythms of women's lives and of the ways in which they occupied and moved through public space.[13] The norm of the stay-at-home wife and mother informed modernist urban designs of the '50s and '60s. Yet how housewives without cars in outer suburban areas were going to perform tasks like shopping and picking up children from school was not an issue high on the agenda for planners and architects. Moreover, both in the inner city, at suburban shopping centres, and wherever modernism has left its mark on the built up environment, hard edged, impersonal, poorly lit and dangerous public spaces placed many more restrictions on women's lives than those of men.

CREATING THE PURIFIED COMMUNITY

Sennett (1973) wrote a stinging critique of modernism and its effect on American cities.[14] He saw postwar town planning as involving the creation of purified communities. These suburban enclaves embodied an attempt to fix an image or identity in advance and to prevent the difficult encounters with disparate individuals which inner-city life can involve. The extreme form of this trend can be seen in Los Angeles today[15] where walled suburban communities are policed by armed guards who exclude 'undesirables' (see Hillier and McManus in this book). Those who can afford to live in such communities are shielded from the problems of the modern world. In the traditional neighbourhoods with their higher population densities, no such domestic and neighbourhood insulation could be guaranteed. Housing, workplaces and leisure facilities were located close together without the compartmentalisation which occurs in suburbia. For Sennett, suburban community is not a positive and empowering force but a restricting force in which a purified local identity is set up and the only forms of neighbourly association are based on enforcing that identity. Those who do not conform to its features are ostracised.

Sennett also argues that the gregarious street life of the traditional neighbourhoods has been replaced in the suburbs by an intensified family life. He observes that modernism has made public places more impersonal: 'There has been a destruction of arenas for social interchange — little bars, shops and pool halls — because of the middle class vision of what a comfortable and secure place should really be.'[16] Leisure facilities in modern cities are not mixing places in which one can expect to encounter people of all colours, classes and creeds, but places in which we expect to be left alone — to eat our fast food fast and hurry off home to our families.

A dichotomy has been set up between the very private realm of the suburban house and the very public realm of the city, particularly the inner city. Because we travel large distances in sprawling cities to work, to shop and to enjoy ourselves, we encounter vast numbers of people whom we have no knowledge of. Even workmates are less familiar than they were when home and workplace were dovetailed as in the old inner cities. This dichotomy fosters a socio-psychological division between public and private personas: the man who is indifferent to the beggars on the streets of the city, who abuses the other driver out of the car window, who cruises in search of prostitutes in the red light district, can be the very epitome of caring family virtue and morality in the home. Tabloid newspapers will always seize on the macabre irony of murderers and rapists who are known only as loving and caring fathers, husbands and sons by their families. It is this dangerous anonymity which is at the heart of the moral panic around crime. While in the past it was the territory which was too heavily controlled by the local people which generated most public alarm, today it is the lack of control of those public spaces which modernist design has bequeathed us which is at the heart of the moral panic around urban crime.

DEFENSIBLE SPACE

The undermining of urban village culture has profoundly altered popular attitudes to crime. Gruesome crimes have always been part of urban life. Yet the moral panics which flow from child abductions, murders and rapes in public places are based not only on revulsion but on the sense of vulnerability which many city dwellers feel. We sense that public space is not sufficiently controlled. The diverse and complex nature of contemporary city life means that we are no longer so familiar with those we encounter every day. Stories and experiences of burglaries in local areas tend to engender a fortress mentality. Large numbers of people are resorting to barred windows, large and vicious dogs and all of the other accoutrements of the security industry to protect their property.

Valentine's research demonstrates that women feel particularly vulnerable.[17] Crime statistics reveal that they are much more likely to suffer violent attacks within the home but that there is a 'mismatch between the geography of violence and the geography of fear'.[18] The women from Reading, UK who were the focus of Valentine's study felt themselves to be highly constrained in their movements in public but were relatively blase about the threat of domestic violence. The ideologies of private safety and public danger which are a feature of modern life clearly have a greater hold on the consciousness of women than do statistics which point in the opposite direction.

The notion of defensible space was formulated out of the belief that the failure to define territories was at the heart of the problem of urban crime.[19] The advocates of this approach argue that criminals make rational calculations about potential risks of surveillance and capture. Where public space is open, well lit and prone to observation from those inside the private space of homes and workplaces, this has a deterrent effect. Panoptic architecture is central to the defensible landscape in which private space is synonymous with surveillance and public space with movement. Such architecture maximises the field of vision of the concealed observer. The only respectable thing to do in much public space in our cities today, particularly in residential areas, is to walk, to move on.

Various strategies are advocated in order to make space more defensible.[20] These include:

- delineating public spaces from private spaces in aesthetic terms;
- providing visual buffers between private spaces and public pathways, courtyards and streets;
- using materials like mirror glass to permit looking out but not looking in;
- clustering dwellings such that public space is claimed as the territory of each cluster;
- erecting real or symbolic barriers to discourage strangers from entering such territories;
- setting up good lighting and even security cameras in unobservable areas;
- removing obstacles to observation like trees and shrubs;
- personalising the exteriors of dwellings;
- minimising hiding places for criminals;
- designing public facilities to discourage loitering. For example making bus seats which can be sat upon but not slept on.

A paradoxical consequence of all of this is that, where there is a stated commitment to creating a more friendly communally controlled environment through defensible space, the environment is necessarily stark. Foliage is an obstacle to observation and public facilities like parks signify openness and potentially attract outsiders. So defensible space is essentially about securing a buffer zone around private spaces.

Defensible spaces are also associated with strategies of social control. Perlgut advocates tenant screening by housing estate management committees and the eviction of 'seriously disruptive families'.[21] Geason and Wilson argue that the 'formation of some degree of homogeneity within the community' serves to counteract crime.[22] The implicit aim here is to create respectable privatised residential communities. 'Strangers', like wandering vagabonds in feudal times, are driven out of the parish. There is no sense of where urban outcasts might go, no commitment to an overall civic responsiblity. The effects of defensible space are to divide cities between the vastly impersonal transit corridors, central and commercial areas, and the controlled territory of residential suburbs.

NEIGHBOURHOOD WATCH AND THE QUESTION OF COMMUNITY

The formation of neighbourhood networks to counteract crime is a vital part of defending space. Neighbourhood Watch (NW) groups are active in most areas of large cities in Australia. They are coordinated through local police stations. Beat constables attend regular gatherings to inform residents about reported crime in the area, how to protect their property, what warning signs to look out for and how to identify potential offenders. The rhetoric of community control is used by the police. It is, however, a very particular form of community which is being constructed here. The bureaucratic rational state is calling forth the forms of democracy which it requires. A community of surveillance is being officially encouraged, where people peep out with a suspicious gaze from behind net curtains. This is a far cry from the more inter-active local cultures of the old neighbourhoods. The vigilant citizenry which informs police of actual or potential crime makes the task of policing, which is so difficult in the fragmented modern cities, so much easier. Foucault observed that the passage from feudal to modern society saw state power shift from a visible form in which punishment was a spectator sport to an invisible form in which discreet surveillance and observation were more important. [23]

There has been considerable debate over whether NW is an entirely reactionary force or whether there are some potential progressive consequences of the scheme. Wilson argues that NW is an instrument for convincing members of the view of reality presented by the police and the tabloid media and for winning support for conservative law and order politics. [24] The community is defined as necessarily pure and the threat as external to it. This, as Wilson correctly observes, precludes acknowledgement of crimes like domestic violence which take place within the home. The scheme is undemocratic, with priorities being set by police and the stereotypes and scapegoats (e.g. ethnic minorities, homeless youth) which inform their work being transmitted to NW members. Yet it is possible, as Hurley, a NW coordinator, suggests, for the links which are forged through the scheme to develop beyond the surveillance function which is antici-pated by the police, and potentially improve community relations. [25] I would therefore support Brown who argues that there is no pre-constituted community to which NW, in spite of the police rhetoric, gives expression especially in those diverse and multicultural inner city areas where burglary rates are among the highest. [26] He advocates moving beyond the official parameters of NW to develop democratic policing:

> NW schemes [should] be one element in a pluralist cultural resurgence attempting to rebuild civic trust and constitute a sense of pride and community. But this requires going far beyond the exhortations in the NW pamphlet to 'become the eyes and ears of the Police'. For NW is as much about reconstituting

current forms of policing. Away from the emphasis on detective superiority . . . to a preparedness to respond to more mundane and localised concerns: noise, vandalism, pollution, danger spots, traffic hazards, dangerous environments, domestic violence etc. . . . Issues of policing policy and priorites should not be the sole preserve of the police but matters of public debate in the same way as health, welfare or town planning. [27]

As O'Malley argues, however, that there is a concerted move by police to minimise their responsibility and involvement in those everyday law and order areas which Brown describes. [28] He claims that the encouragement of NW members to engage in 'target hardening'— making their dwellings and cars more secure — and to insure themselves against property theft is more significant than the surveillance function. This effectively amounts to a privatisation of domestic security in which the insurance industry is a force of social regulation. O'Malley cites the sponsorship of NW schemes by insurance companies as evidence for his claims and asserts that responsibility for domestic security is being passed over by the police to the investigators and assessors employed by these companies. NW therefore magnifies fears of crime in order to encourge domestic protection.

CONCLUSION

Prior to World War II there was a deep historical concern about high density areas of big cities. The potential for the morality, habits and ways of life of the inhabitants of these areas to spill over into the respectable streets was viewed with some alarm by the middle classes. Calls for urban redevelopment schemes were associated with strategies of containment and regulation. The move to suburbanisation involved the development of utopian visions of ordered city spaces in which the disorderly and interactive street culture of the old neighbourhoods was denied. The designers and developers of suburbia have paradoxically created its shadowy obverse in public space. In the modern city the dissipated character of everyday life has produced a fear of the stranger who haunts public space with malevolent intent. This fear cuts across class divisions and has produced a widespread support for Neighbourhood Watch and the ideas of defensible space. At the heart of these moral panics is a sense that the protective fabric of local life, of supportive forms of community, is disappearing.

NOTES

1. Grabosky, P. (1977) *Sydney in Ferment: Crime, Dissent and Official Reaction 1788-1973*, Australian National University Press, Canberra, p.89.
2. Clark, C. (1981) *A History of Australia: The People Make Laws 1888-1915*, Melbourne University Press, Melbourne, pp.357-358.
3. Manderson, D. (1993) *From Mr. Sin to Mr. Big: A History of Australian Drug Laws*, Oxford University Press, Melbourne.
4. Grace, H. (1987) 'A New Journal of the Plague Year', *Cultural Studies*, 1(1), pp.25-38.
5. Roddewig, R. (1978) *Green Bans: The Birth of the Australian Environmental Politics*, Hale & Iremonger, Sydney, p.22.
6. Housing Improvement Board (1937) *NSW Parliamentary Papers 1937*, cited in Barrett-Oswald and Burt (1942) *Housing the Australian Nation*, Ruskin Press, Melbourne, p.16.
7. Oswald-Barrett and Burt (1942) *op. cit.*, p.5.
8. Allport, C. (1989) 'The Human Face of Remodelling: Postwar "Slum" Clearance in Sydney', *Urban Policy and Research*, 6(3), pp.106-118.
9. Stretton, H., (1970) *Ideas For Australian Cities*, Georgian House, Melbourne.
10. Boys, J. (1989) 'From Alcatraz to the OK Corral: Images of Class and Gender', in Attfield, J. and Kirkham, P. (1989) *A View from the Interior. Feminism, Women and Design*, The Women's Press, London.
11. Holston, J. (1991) *The Modernist City*, Columbia University Press, New York.
12. Richards, L. (1990) *Nobody's Home*, Oxford University Press, Melbourne.
13. Matrix (1984) *Making Space: Women and the Man Made Environment*, Pluto Press, London.
14. Sennett, R. (1973) *The Uses of Disorder: Personal Identity and City Life*, Penguin, Harmondsworth.
15. Davis, M. (1990) *City of Quartz: Excavating the Future in Los Angeles*, Vintage, London.
16. Sennett (1973) *op. cit.*, p.69.
17. Valentine, G. (1989) 'The geography of women's fear', *Area*, 21 (4), pp.385-390.
18. Valentine, G. (1992) 'Images of danger: women's sources of information about the spatial distribution of male violence', *Area*, 24 (1), pp.22-29.
19. Newman, O. (1972) *Defensible Space: Crime Prevention Through Urban Design*, Macmillan Architectural Press, New York.
20. Daley, P. (1987) *The Neighbourhood Crime Prevention Handbook*, Angus & Robertson, Sydney; and Geason, S. and Wilson P. (1989) Designing Out Crime, Australian Institute of Criminology, Canberra.
21. Perlgut, D. (1981) 'Crime Prevention for Australian Public Housing', *Forum: Australian Crime Prevention Council Quarterly Journal*, No.4, pp.16.
22. Geason and Wilson (1989) *op. cit.*, p.252.
23. Foucault, M. (1977) *Discipline and Punish: The Birth of the Prison*, Allen Lane, Harmondsworth.
24. Wilson, L. (1987) Neighbourhood Watch: A Reply', *Community Quarterly*, No.10.

25. Hurley, A (1986) 'Security: The Neighbourhood is Watching', *Community Quarterly*, No.7, pp.40-45.

26. Brown, D. (1987) 'Fear and Loathing in Darlinghurst: To Neighbourhood Watch or Not', *Legal Services Bulletin*, 12 (6), pp.251-4.

27. *ibid.*, pp.251-254.

28. O'Malley, P. (1989) 'Redefining Security: Neighbourhood Watch in Context', *Arena*, No.86, pp.18-23.

6

Pull up the drawbridge: fortress mentality in the suburbs

Jean Hillier and Phil McManus

It is the . . . partition that . . . I heard discourse[1]

The erection of new, walled elite suburban developments as enclaves that penetrate or gentrify areas of existing lower or middle-class residences represents a violation of those areas. These developments force existing residents into a condition of otherness,[2] excluded, outside of the macho bastions of capitalist power. These new exclusive residential ghettos are characterised by hilltop sites and special statements of design. They are a commodified expression of the search for personal and collective identity, 'the search for secure moorings in a shifting world'[3] of economic recession, Royal Commissions and so on. In order to provide some form of certainty within contingency, as Harvey suggests, place-identity becomes an important issue, with the traditional connection between place and social identity being strongly reinforced.[4] The construction of such places represents the creation of a 'localised aesthetic image', according to Harvey, which allows people to construct some limited sense of identity for themselves in a confusing and confused world.[5]

In Perth, Western Australia, the development of Buckland Hill and
the redevelopment of St John's Wood/Mount Claremont, are similar to
processes of gentrification in that they involve the movement of high
status residents into, or adjacent to, an area of lower status residents.
However, in both cases this movement has been openly supported by
the state, and has occurred en masse in a large development rather than
through individual purchase and renovation as mostly occurs with
gentrification. The development of Buckland Hill and the redevelopment of St John's Wood/Mount Claremont has enabled the developers
to include in the initial design alienating aspects, such as walls and
dense or high vegetation, between segments of the subdivision and
between the subdivision and adjacent, lower status residential areas.

Buckland Hill is being developed on open space near former
stevedores' cottages and factories. St John's Wood/Mount Claremont is
an instance of wealthy people taking control of a former public housing
area called Graylands (which became notorious in Perth because of its
mental hospital). The change of suburb name is important. Where
'Graylands' was associated with insanity and deviance the new name,
St John's Wood, conjures images of that essentially English, discreet,
genteel and affluent London suburb. These two Perth developments
are designed to reflect both the personal identity and status of their
inhabitants. Both enclaves enable access only to the privileged few
whilst closing out Others.

In this chapter we attempt to demonstrate, using these examples
from Perth, WA, how the practice of town planning exemplifies
Foucault's ideas of the interconnections between power and space.
These new residential areas, with their walled fortress-like appearance,
offer exclusivity and inwardness, a respite and h(e)aven from the other
world of contingency, disruption and disadvantage outside.[6]

We treat the notions of difference and otherness as essential to an
understanding of the dialectics of space.[7] We demonstrate how image
and place-identity are used by the wealthy to mirror us-them difference. We explore how safety becomes 'security' and is commodified as a
personal good defined by income, access to private protective services
and membership in some hardened residential enclave or restricted
suburb:[8] a haven where urban design, architecture and the police/
security apparatus have merged to ensure personal insulation from 'unsavoury' groups and individuals.

TERRITORY AND IDENTITY

Two of our basic human needs are for self-evaluation and self-
estimation. These are mediated by the evaluations of others; evalua-

tions based, among other things, on income, or material commodities purchased through income. Status and identity are endowed particularly when specific material commodities are relatively scarce and appreciated by others. The search for financial self-sufficiency in order to own objects and the expression of self through objects have become 'the marks of identity in capitalist society'[9] and ownership becomes an authentic metaphor for identity.[10] Home ownership thus offers a major physical object of exchange-value, being a commodity that can be bought and sold while also being an indicator of status and source of personal autonomy.

As Cooper states, 'the house nicely reflects how man (sic) sees himself with both an intimate interior . . . and a public exterior . . . the self we choose to display to others'.[11] The house is often the largest and most expensive private object whereby individuals can assert their identity. It is used to display to others who one is, what one's class, lifestyle, and tastes are.[12]

Landscapes, and particularly elite landscapes may be regarded as cultural productions, a 'signifying system through which . . . a social order is communicated'.[13] Suburban landscapes do more than fulfil simple functional requirements. As Duncan indicates, by encoding signs of social status and group membership within a landscape, individuals tell morally charged stories about themselves and the social structure of the society in which they live.[14]

The erection of elite, walled enclaves has much to do with identity and image, or 'sign-value'. These new enclaves are classic cases of territories which satisfy basic human needs for security and identity.[15] Territorality provides a culturally derived means of both enhancing and impeding social interaction. The main benefits of territorality are diminished randomness, increased order and thus predictability in the environment.[16]

Traditionally one of the main ways to demonstrate territorality is through the erection of containing walls. From ancient times people have surrounded their settlements with walls, which were often associated with symbolic spiritual ideas of harmony and cohesion, both between the residents within the walls and between the residents and the cosmos above. In the Middle Ages in Europe 'when the portcullis was drawn and the town gates were locked at sundown, the city was sealed off from the outside world'.[17]

However, the ineffectiveness of walls as a means of defending territory in modern society, and the developments in transport technology (used skilfully by land developers to 'open up' their land)[18] informed the development of suburbs in 'modernist' cities, initially based on trams and later on the automobile. Despite their many limitations suburbs represented, until recently, the most egalitarian form of land-use distribution achieved under capitalism — where everybody lived outside the castle walls. Within suburbia 'territories' were established without recourse to physical boundaries.

The situation is changing now. Instead of one large medieval castle in the town centre there are many castles being built in the suburbs. The notion of castle is reinforced by 'the moat', the distributor road or regional highway which forms the boundary between territories or kingdoms, or alternatively there may be a buffer area of low density or the strategic use of 'public' open space. Safety, prestige and nomenclature have in this way been commodified and legitimated by the supposedly technical plans of urban planners and designers. Suburban planning still implies a conservative vision of family and community life. Similar to medieval architects who believed that the built environment could reform and regularise human behaviour, the providers of today's fashionable solutions, the walled enclaves favoured by up-market private housing schemes, also make explicit the reinforcement of privacy.

There are thus striking territorial oppositions in today's suburbia between those within the walls and those without, between us and them, rich and poor, men and women, empowered or capacitated and disempowered/incapacitated. Such oppositions in contemporary society exist less as overt repression, but rather as avoidances, aversions and separations enacted by the privileged in relation to the oppressed.[19]

Kristeva offers us the useful concept of abjection; the feeling of loathing and disgust on encountering the other.[20] The abject, however, resides only just on the other side of the border. It is therefore not directly opposed to and facing the subject at a distance, 'but next to it, too close for comfort'.[21] Today these abject others are blacks, the unemployed, gays, disabled people, who are not so unlike the wealthy enclave inmates as to be obviously 'different'. Residents living in the 'freedom' of their exclusive walled enclaves are constantly reminded of the presence of the abject other only a few metres away. The other intrudes within their lounges via television, a representation of what lies just beyond the borders of the self.

What does it matter if the rich and aspiring rich isolate the other outside of their walled kingdoms? Why should we care? Certainly, in Perth, those of us living in parts of the city without the design features of a latter day castle are not at the mercy of invading hordes. Why not simply let everyone enjoy/suffer each other's company?

We think there are numerous reasons why planners, sociologists, and so on, should be concerned about the proliferation of walls and gated communities.[22] First, in the eyes of the residents in these areas, 'we' are the hordes. Second, the creation of a walled suburb is encouraged through clever marketing which creates the 'need' for such a facility by establishing fear of 'the other'. The drawbridge mentality is particularly evident in the process of gentrification, where wealthier individuals conquer space traditionally (though often not originally) occupied by poorer people, and place grills over windows, additional locks on doors and a wall or gate separating the house and yard from the other people and the street.

Walled suburbs then, represent both fortresses to which the drawbridge can be raised, cutting off contact with those outside, and asylums, segregated communities in which difference is reduced and irregularity eliminated. In both representations we are confronted by an image of physical and ideological power.

OF POWER AND PANOPTICONS

But what is this power? How does it work? What are its spatial effects? Michel Foucault has suggested that 'a whole history remains to be written — which would at the same time be the history of powers — from the great strategies of geo-politics to the little tactics of the habitat'.[23] It is these 'little tactics of the habitat' in Buckland Hill and St John's Wood about which this chapter tells its stories.

Foucault argues that power and space are intertwined, as 'space is fundamental in any exercise of power'.[24] To illustrate this argument he cites Bentham's plan of the panopticon. Bentham's original Panopticon was an architectural structure, an annular building surrounding a central tower. Both building and tower were pierced with corresponding windows enabling constant surveillance: 'the panopticon mechanism arranges spatial unities that make it possible to see constantly and to recognise immediately'.[25]

Through spatial ordering, the panopticon brings together power, control of groups and knowledge. It locates individuals in space, in a hierarchical and efficient organisation. Davis demonstrates how modern urban security logic, which echoes that of the panopticon, finds its most popular expression in the efforts of Los Angeles' affluent neighbourhoods to insulate home values, privacy and lifestyles.[26] He illustrates how new upper-class developments have become fortress neighbourhoods, complete with encompassing walls, restricted entry points with guard posts, overlapping private and public police services and privatised roadways. Within the fortress suburbs, the rich live in high-tech castles, protected by security system 'packages' which include alarm hardware, monitoring, watch patrols, personal escorts and 'armed response'. As Davis writes, 'anyone who has tried to take a stroll at dusk through a strange neighbourhood patrolled by armed security guards and signposted with death threats quickly realises how merely notional, if not utterly obsolete, is the old idea of the "freedom of the city"'.[27]

The discipline of urban planning operates in ways similar to the panopticon (see also, Huxley's chapter in this book). New suburban enclaves are often built on hilltop sites with particular street and lot configurations which not only enable surveillance of those within the walls, but especially those without. At the same time then, not only do some of the new suburbs physically represent Foucault's ultimate model of power as an 'observatory' (the military camp or fortress, employing architecture not simply built to be seen but to observe in hierarchised surveillance), they also ideologically represent Foucault's model of power as discipline, using procedures of partitioning and verticality (the construction of walls) to introduce as solid a separation as possible between different economic, cultural and spatial elements. The walled enclosure not only gives physical and ideological protection from those outside, it maintains freedom within.

In the Buckland Hill and St John's Wood/Mount Claremont developments, stone walls, wrought-iron gates, burglar alarms and armed response systems are landscape signifiers which define membership in a social group to the exclusion of non-members. Minute attention has been paid by the various developers to signage and furniture (notice boards, street signs, lamps) which all stress the exclusivity of the estate. In the St Johns Wood development each cul-de-sac unit has its own demarking wall and entry statement, further fragmenting the landscape and segregating the residents into a social order of hierarchy within the elite estate itself. The development philosophy was one of 'elegant' residential. Promotional literature uses phrases such as 'investment strategy', 'not inexpensive', 'Perth's most elegant', 'at the heart of Perth's blue ribbon western suburbs', 'Perth's finest assets', 'exclusive shopping', 'top schools and colleges'.[28]

This is somewhat ironic in the case of St John's Wood where development was made possible by the decommissioning of the old Graylands public mental hospital. The site has had to be 'enhanced', transforming its image from that of a lunatic asylum, with adjacent defence force and public sector housing, to that of an exclusive upper-middle, aspiring upper-class area. Landscaping 'philosophies'[29] reflected this objective.

The practical application of this 'philosophy' has been to turn the backs of the new houses onto the main road adjacent to the public estate and to construct a three metre high 'security screen' between them. This process thus renders the excluded others less visible from the direct sight of the elite (on the outside of gates and walls) but conversely *more* visible (through unsleeping electronic eyes) should they stray out of their 'proper place'. Space thus represents power—the power to exclude.

The development of walled suburbs in Australia is occurring predominantly in new areas where there is an opportunity to limit access to an exclusive feature, e.g. high terrain, beach, etc and in older locations that are being comprehensively redeveloped (Table 6.1).

Table 6.1
Schematic development of a walled suburb in a new area

The site as	Becomes a site as
communal reserve	private reserve
landmark	vantage point
natural feature	commercial opportunity
historical continuity	present opportunity
public asset	private commodity
inclusive	exclusive
shared	protected
open	closed
accessible	inaccessible
for everyone	for me and mine, but not for them

Source: After Farrant, G. (1991) 'Case notes, Planning Practice 212', (Unpublished) Department of Urban and Regional Planning, Curtin University, Perth, p.5.

Walled or gated developments are often cited as 'cutting-edge' examples of contemporary planning but it is only a matter of time before aspects filter into the fabric of established suburbs. The process of filtering can be observed in Los Angeles, where gated communities have moved from being the exclusive domain of the very privileged few into being the expectation of the privileged many. Developers are quick to provide for this expectation because the economy enables them to charge high prices for what is perceived and presented as an area of higher amenity. Urban design has often been used as a tool in the sublimination of what were once public spaces to the will of private capital.

Areas that are not gated are advertised as semi-gated in the real estate pages of the *Los Angeles Times*. In Mt Claremont in Perth, Urban Concepts, the marketing arm of Homeswest (the State's public housing authority), has simulated the urban design of the private developers in order to provide higher amenity (partly because of the intention to sell most of this housing into the private market) and to physically and psychologically separate this new area from the older public housing. Steep slopes of hilltop sites, together with high walls, fences/stockades, surveillance systems and often blind house walls reinforce the image of home as haven, refuge and castle. Restrictive covenants contain landscaping constraints, protecting mature trees as screens and buffers to protect privacy and lot sizes.

What of women in these new estates? Many are in paid work, others are not, virtually all are unseen except to emerge through wrought-iron gates or entry statement cocooned in the privacy of a hermetically sealed car. Women survey and their movements are surveyed. A small community, such as the cul-de-sac unit or the estate itself, is often strictly surveyed and controlled. It offers 'none of the opportunities for escape, anonymity, secret pleasures'.[30] Do Richards' 'Little Boxes made of Ideology'[31] simply reflect a paternalistic form of planning and architecture in which regulation and surveillance have played a key role? But how different are his dream and hers? her security and his? her home and his haven?

The traditional slight movement of net curtains suggesting women's eyes covertly surveying the street has been replaced by the automated movement of overt electronic eyes. In many ways this symbolises the failure of trust that neighbours will perform the basic functions of community.[32] Perhaps the neighbours are too busy maintaining/ enhancing their own material lifestyle. The movement of women into the workforce, while increasing individual independence and self-fulfillment in many cases, has left the material possessions of each household vulnerable. This trend is reinforced by possession of commodities such as the telephone, television and video recorder which reduce the need to know neighbours, thereby also reducing trust and accountability.

Into this void come land developers with walled suburbs and security companies with products and services. However, as the tragic case of James Bulger in Liverpool[33] demonstrates, electronic security is not an adequate substitute for human interaction; 'it was the cold eye of commerce protecting its own, and into its field of vision strayed an innocent child whom no one protected at all'.[34]

CONCLUSIONS

The urban design of new, walled elite suburban developments in the midst of existing middle-class residential areas would appear to be more a function of marketing and ideals of the newly created communities rather than based on other processes of design in response to a site's individual characteristics. The image and discourse of landscape and architecture in such enclaves signifies a particular way of life, ideas, values and beliefs and level of economic power.

The capacitated few, generally men, work elsewhere in the city, then escape to their fortified suburbs in search of certainty in their contingent world. These fortress-like bastions of power admit only Us, the empowered wealthy. As one enters, the drawbridge is pulled up against the abject others who reside outside. In turn, individual houses look inwards, excluding the outside world unless viewed through hermetically-sealed glass or an electronic surveillance system. The physical manifestation of bi-polar fragmentations of the social body into us/them, in/out, rich/poor, empowered/disempowered men/ women in these enclaves is legitimised by the discipline of planning. Power and space have intertwined and become physically manifest in suburban fortress planning.

'Haven is an illusion
so please leave before checkout time
and don't forget to lock the door'.[35]

NOTES

1. Shakespeare, 'A Midsummer Night's Dream', Act V, Sc I, L165-6.
2. Originating in de Beauvoir, S. ((1953) The Second Sex, Knopf, New York) and developed by Derrida, J. ((1972) Dissemination, University of Chicago Press,

Chicago) and Irigaray, L. ((1977) *Ce Sexe qui n'en est pas un*, Minuit, Paris), the Other reflects the idea of an excluded object. The Other is always seen as not, as a lack or as lacking in the valued qualities of society.

3.   Harvey, D. (1989) *The Condition of Postmodernity: An Enquiry into the Origins of Social Change*, Oxford, Blackwell, p.302.
4.   *ibid.*
5.   *ibid.*, pp.303-304.
6.   Wilson has called this Other world the 'infernal urban space' (Wilson, E. (1991) *The Sphinx in the City: Urban Life, the Control of Disorder, and Women*, Virago, London, p.6).
7.   'Dialectics' is a term which suggests that thought and the development of ideas proceed through a process or pattern of contradiction and the reconciliation of contradiction.
8.   Davis, M. (1992) *City of Quartz: Excavating the Future in Los Angeles*, Vintage Books, New York.
9.   Agnew, J. (1992) 'Place and politics in post-war Italy: a cultural geography of local identity in the provinces of Lucca and Pistoia', in Anderson, K. and Gale, F. (eds.) *Inventing Places*, Longman Cheshire, Melbourne, p.62.
10.   Wikse, J. (1977) *About Possession: The Self As Private Property*, Pennsylvania State University Press, Pennsylvania.
11.   Cooper, C. (1974) 'The house as symbol of the self', in Lang, J., Burnette, C., Moleski, W. and Vachon, D. (eds.) *Housing and Identity*, Croom Helm, London, p.131.
12.   Duncan, J. (1985) 'The house as symbol of social structure', in Altman, I. and Werner, C. (eds.) *Home Environments*, Vol 8, Plenum Press, New York, p.135.
13.   Williams, R. (1982) *The Sociology of Culture*, Schocken Books, New York, p.13.
14.   Duncan, J. (1992) 'Elite landscapes as cultural (re)productions: the case of Shaughnessy Heights', in Anderson, K. and Gale, F. (eds) *Inventing Places*, Longman Cheshire, Melbourne, pp.37-51.
15.   'Territories' or the phenomenon of 'human territorality' has been defined by Walmsley and Lewis as a learned response to small scale environments which satisfies basic human needs for security and identity (Walmsley, D and Lewis, G. (1984) *Human Geography: Behavioural Approaches*, London: Longman, p.41).
16.   Sack, R. (1983) 'Human territorality: a theory', *Annals of the Association of American Geographers*, Vol.73, pp.55-74.
17.   Mumford, L. (1961) *The City in History*, Penguin, London, p.350.
18.   'Opening up' land could be seen as analogous to the rape of greenfield sites, destroying virgin bush and the habitats of flora and fauna.
19.   Young, I. M. (1990) *Justice and the Politics of Difference*, Princeton University Press, Princeton.
20.   Kristeva, J. (1982) *Powers of Horror: An Essay in Abjection*, Columbia University Press, New York.
21.   Young, I. M. (1990) *op. cit.*, p.144.
22.   Davis, M (1992) *op. cit.*; Greinacher, U. (1994) 'The new reality: media technology and urban fortress', Paper presented to International Making

Cities Liveable conference, San Francisco, California; McManus, P. (1994) 'Beyond suburban sprawl and apple pie community', Paper presented to International Making Cities Liveable Conference, San Francisco, California.

23. Michel Foucault as quoted in Gordon, C. (ed.) (1980) *Michel Foucault: Power/Knowledge*, Harvester, Brighton, p.149.

24. Rabinow, P. (1984) *The Foucault Reader*, Pantheon, New York, p.252.

25. Foucault, M. (1977) *Discipline and Punish: the Birth of the Prison*, Allen Lane, London, p.200.

26. Davis, M. (1992) *op. cit.*

27. *ibid.*, p.250.

28. Melsom, C. (1991) 'Case notes, Planning Practice 212', (Unpublished) Department of Urban and Regional Planning, Curtin University, Perth, p.5.

29. *ibid.*, p.5.

30. Wilson, E. (1991) *op. cit.*, p.154.

31. Richards, L. (1990) *Nobody's Home*, Cambridge University Press, Melbourne.

32. McManus, R. (1994) *op. cit.*; and Richards, L. (1990) *op. cit.*

33. James Bulger was a toddler abducted from his mother in a shopping mall in Liverpool, England in 1993 by two primary school aged boys. He was led to a railway line where he was murdered by being beaten up and then left on the tracks to be run over by a train.

34. Barrett, G. (1993) 'Boys Charged for a crime that sickened a nation', *Melbourne Age*, 22nd February, p.1 and p.7.

35. From an unpublished poem of McManus, P. (1993).

7

Cultural continuity in multicultural sub/urban places

Helen Armstrong

Australians tend to live in a few large cities scattered around the coast. The largest and oldest city, Sydney, is a multicultural city whose inner-city suburbs contain complex mixes of ethnic groups. The history of ethnic groups in Sydney reflects the challenges of making one's way in a new country. Urban immigrant groups have tended to live in concentrated clusters with others of the same country of origin, creating places which reflect their culture. With rising economic strength the second and third generations disperse into outer areas, possibly away from strong ethnic bonds. This process is played out over and over again in inner-city suburbs resulting in changes and possible loss of valued places for different ethnic groups.[1]

In New South Wales, the current method of assessment of culturally valued places is through Heritage Studies. These are undertaken by a small group of heritage professionals, predominantly middle-class and eurocentric, who derive their assessment of places from field observation and archival research. Culturally valued places in ethnic neighbourhoods, however, are not readily accessible through such techniques. More commonly the meanings attached to places lie in ideas, stories and folklore associated with the immigrant experience. The conservation of valued places can be described as cultural continuity, a concept which has arisen within heritage planning despite its obvious associations with the sociological aspects of culture. The concept of cultural continuity in Australia, however, is complex in that all Australians are dealing with an underlying cultural discontinuity.

Contemporary Australia is a multicultural population with every one of its multicultural groups in varying degrees of disconnection with its past. For Aboriginal Australians the disconnected past is related to the ancient landscape. For Anglo-Celtic Australians the disconnection is with a middle distant past, and for the wide spectrum of recent immigrant groups there is a disconnection with their recent past. Added to underlying cultural disconnections, the rich and diverse qualities of Australian cities in the 1990s are such that the prevailing Anglo-Celtic culture is receding to become just one of many urban cultures. How does this pervasive disconnectedness affect Australian communities' relationship to cultural continuity and the project of Heritage Studies in sub/urban places? Questions arise about con-nectedness to place and cultural continuity when faced with a kaleido-scope of cultures which become manifest and then change at an increasingly rapid rate. Such a fluid and changing environment has curiously led the prevailing Anglo-Celtic Australian bureaucrats into attempts to create a sense of a coherent past.

The concept of heritage in Australia has followed the pattern of a number of 19th and 20th century nation states whose emerging legitimacy has been fostered by a sense of national heritage closely associated with a sense of identity.[2] In Australia this was particularly evident in the 1890s and continued into the mid 20th century. It was not until the 1970s that heritage assumed the specialised meaning of 'things we want to keep'[3] in response to the rapidly changing urban fabric of Australian cities. By the late 1970s the concept of heritage and cultural continuity had become highly bureaucratic under the various Acts at federal and State level, and a growing body of heritage professionals had emerged. This continued into the 1990s. Meanwhile in the 1980s the push for tourism generated a 'heritage industry'[4] which appropri-ated the concept of heritage through numerous marketable icons and nostalgic representations of Australianness. Thus cultural continuity in Australian multicultural sub/urban places today is being constructed largely by a professionalised Anglo-Celtic interpretation of the past, while a burgeoning 'heritage industry' serves up trivialised 'ethnic places' for tourist consumption. In both processes of place-making a mythic groundedness is generated to paper over underlying cultural discontinuity.

It is interesting to consider the increasing professionalisation of heritage practice and how this applies to the interpretation and management of cultural continuity in multicultural sub/urban places in Australia. In this chapter a case study of Marrickville, one inner-city area of Sydney, is used to explore the disparity in perceptions of cultural continuity between urban planners and the different immigrant groups who live in the area.

CULTURAL HERITAGE PRACTICE

Urban planners in Australia conserve urban places through statutory systems. In New South Wales, State and local government planners interpret cultural heritage places through processes devised under the Heritage Act (NSW) and the Environmental Planning and Assessment Act (NSW). Within the terms of these Acts cultural heritage places are considered to be those places which have aesthetic, historic, scientific or social significance for future generations as well as the present community. Planners invite heritage professionals to undertake heritage studies of places as precursors to planning controls for conservation.

The heritage study has become a highly developed methodology for identifying, analysing and assessing the cultural heritage of an area. Heritage professionals are required to develop a thematic history for the area which is then used as a framework for analysis of places considered to be part of the cultural heritage. When such places have been identified, they are further tested against a set of criteria in order to evaluate their heritage significance. After this rigorous system of assessment conservation practices are determined.

The Marrickville heritage study was considered to be a thoughtful and reflective study.[5] It identified the thematic history of the area as 'the theme of change', change which was directly attributed to changes in the demography of greater Sydney, including the more recent changes which reflect the immigration policies of the last 50 years. Marrickville has an extensive range of immigrant groups as well as Kooris (Aboriginal Australians). Immigrant groups include Anglo-Celtic Australians, Chinese-Australians, Greek-Australians, Lebanese-Australians, Yugoslav-Australians, Vietnamese-Australians and Portuguese-Australians,[6] to name the main groups who live in the area.

Although a theme of change is appropriate for Marrickville, it is problematic in terms of defining cultural heritage conservation parameters. In highlighting change as a heritage theme there is a high risk that conservation practices will fix on manifestations of particular cultural groups which stereotype and thus trivialise aspects of that culture. This is true of the heritage industry's activities in terms of the Anglo-Celtic culture, but it is also true of multicultural groups where aspects of say 'Greekness' are conserved to provide the sense of 'exotic other' for people in the greater urban environment.

For many people in Sydney the 'exotic other' is an important aspect of the richness of places not only for the prevailing Anglo-Celtic culture but for multicultural groups as well. The commodifying of 'Italianness' in Lygon Street, Melbourne, which is resulting in ethnic stereotyping and commodification of sense of place is accepted as much by the ethnic groups as others.

Authenticity is one of the casualties of contemporary conservation planning.[7] Such commodification and stereotyping not only undermines authenticity, it also interferes with any depth of understanding about valued places. In a multicultural New World, depth of understanding about the relationship to place is complex and continually evolving.

While the Kooris are working towards a contemporary understanding of their culture in an urban environment, Anglo-Celtic Australians reveal that they are unsure about their values in relation to urban places. This is most evident in the Commissions of Inquiry under the Heritage Act (NSW) where people voice their objections to heritage constraints.[8] Meanwhile, so called 'multicultural Australians' have not had an opportunity to discuss and consider what is their heritage within Australia. Is it their Greekness, their Italianness, their Vietnameseness or is it something less obvious and yet profoundly important to these groups, something that is related to the migrant experience in Australia?

Questions also need to be asked about what in the urban landscape multicultural groups would like to see conserved. Do such groups want evidence of their presence to persist as traces or do they want a more robust Anglo-Celtic Australianness to be crystalised, something to replace the culture they have left? Do migrant groups want the sense of cultural continuity to be the persistence of a New World ideology — Australia as a land of opportunity where cultural values privilege the future rather than the past?

Current heritage practice has not addressed such issues. Instead it has been concerned with objectifying heritage so that it is presented as 'fact', that is 'real' history verified through scientific objectivity. Contrary to perceptions of heritage practice, which sees itself as professionally objective, all interpretations of cultural heritage are narratives whether they are derived from heritage professionals or from other groups in the community. In the light of this, two cultural heritage narratives for the same urban place, Marrickville, are contrasted—the professional heritage narrative which represents a particularly influential group and an immigrant narrative where the voices are subordinate and rarely heard in planning.

TWO CULTURAL HERITAGE NARRATIVES FOR MARRICKVILLE

Conservation policy tends to reflect the values of the prevailing Anglo-Celtic Australian culture. Conservation policy in turn facilitates the form of cultural continuity in sub/urban places. This dominant heritage narrative focuses on built form as the reflection of cultural history, such built form being evaluated in a thematic context. In the case of Marrickville, the narrative focuses on buildings which reflect the different periods of residential, retail and industrial history.

In terms of the (Anglo-Celtic) heritage narrative—the official narrative—the most significant *residential heritage* in Marrickville today belongs to the building boom period of the 1870s and 1880s. It consists of narrow grid-patterned streets, back lanes, large elaborate villas and terraces on the high land and crowded single-storey terraces in creek valleys. Associated with the predominant 1880s residential character are some modest Federation cottages in small unified groups. There are also areas of 1930s and 1940s bungalows and 1930s blocks of flats with intricate brick detailing.

The *retail heritage* identified by the heritage professionals focuses on the shopping street in Newtown which is considered to have outstanding examples of Sydney's retailing history including details and fixtures which are now rare examples of past retailing practices. In the suburb of Marrickville there are also many corner shops which were rare in high income areas, but were frequently part of speculative low-cost developments in the 1890s. The heritage study does not investigate the rich lived meanings associated with the shopping streets over the last 40 years.

The *industrial heritage* of the area had a major impact on the character of Marrickville, with the employees living in close proximity to the factories and the employers living in large houses on the surrounding slopes. The industrial areas were also a major reason for the influx of the Mediterranean communities in the 1950s which changed the character of Marrickville. The heritage professionals did not investigate the meanings associated with the industrial areas; their interest was predominantly archeological. The narratives associated with the large factories are yet to be told, particularly the migrant stories of the 1950s and the 1960s.

The heritage narrative focuses on built form and does not consider cultural heritage that is manifest as a way of life. Planning codes which can facilitate the continuity of a way of life are particularly challenging and to be meaningful require a deep understanding of 'ways of life'. This is not just customs and folkloric festivals. It might be the right of small business to continue, which requires planning codes capable of preventing large internalised shopping franchises in the area. It might be the protection of existing hospitals in the area. It might be the acknowledgement of the importance of the local libraries and their supply of books in many languages. These aspects are not covered in local planning conservation. To understand heritage as ways of life requires contemporary community input, but professional heritage processes do not allow for this. Community values are included only as they are expressed in published histories and archival newspaper reports. Thus community responses are only allowed to enrich the history if they are history themselves. Contemporary discourse is treated with suspicion, being subjective, emotive and therefore unreliable. However the notion of the only true assessment of a place as one which comes from an objective outsider (outside in place and outsider in time) is to privilege a distorted narrative.

The professional heritage narrative (Anglo-Celtic) can be contrasted to the multicultural heritage narrative constructed to facilitate a deeper understanding about multicultural heritage in one place. Indepth discussions were held with different ethnic groups in Marrickville as part of a research project investigating different heritage values in inner suburbs of Sydney.[9] Only the Greek discussions are included here, but similar values have emerged in other immigrant groups.

The Greek group consisted of ten men and women over 65 years of age who had come to Marrickville in the 1950s directly from Greece. Some of the group had come from Athens and others from small villages; but all had left Greece after a period of civil war. The group felt that their heritage was related to their immigrant experience: the hardship and humiliation, the language barrier and how much Marrickville meant as a place where they could speak Greek, and their experiences under assimilation policies. The relinquishing of their own culture was seen as very painful, particularly as Anglo-Celts were considered to be free to: 'remember the stew of Mum; of great, great grandmother from Ireland and to celebrate everything that is important to the English — but we had to forget'.[10]

Discussion centred on what expectations the Greek group had of Australia before they arrived. Such expectations are interesting in that they set a framework for the first relationship with a place. The fact that Australia was seen as 'a paradise in terms of making money' implies that the notion of hard work and the pioneering spirit were part of the early relationship with place, despite the obvious dispelling of the paradise myth soon after arrival. It also implies that each immigrant group saw Australia as a land of opportunity.

The concept of a Greek-Australian heritage emerged when the group was asked what they did to settle in and thus make Marrickville feel familiar. The responses came in a particular sequence: namely food and shops, plants in the gardens, places of worship, the houses and then the recreational facilities and folk rituals.

In order to contrast the Greek narrative, perceptions of heritage are separated into *residential, retail and industrial heritage* which allows a comparison with the heritage narrative and *cultural practices* or ways of life which highlight the missing components of the heritage narrative.

RESIDENTIAL HERITAGE

The Anglo-Celtic official heritage narrative stated that the most significant residential heritage in Marrickville belongs to the boom period of the 1870s and 1880s.

There is an interesting difference between the Greek perception of residential heritage and the heritage professional assessment. The Greek group agreed with the heritage professionals' assessment but added their own particular history in terms of the housing stock. Part of the immigrant experience is clearly a need to change the houses. The Greeks changed the houses initially. They painted the guttering blue and the walls white. They modernised the houses by putting in aluminium windows and opening up the interiors. They did this in the 1950s because they felt they were improving the houses by making them more airy and increasing the accommodation. As one of the group stated: 'When I came to Marrickville in the 1950s, I was used to white houses, straight lines, not fussy. [I thought] why all these decorations? [referring to the Victorian terraces] They seemed so anachronistic.'[11]

The group pointed out that the arches, balustrades and colonnades on housing stock today are not Greek details from the 1950s. Instead they are the alterations done by more recent immigrant groups from the Mediterranean. The Greeks commented that altering houses to reflect the country one has left is a phase. When asked what the group would like to keep as housing which reflects the cultural heritage in the areas, it was felt that the 'Australian character' was important to conserve. One member of the group pointed out: 'I didn't understand the houses when I first came; but over the years I got used to it or came to appreciate it and sometimes I think this is the personality of Australia.'[12]

In terms of the Greek character which had been added to the housing, the group did not feel it was important to conserve it as their heritage because it was a phase they went through as part of the settling in period. It is interesting to speculate at what stage in the immigrant experience evidence of early attempts at settling in would be seen as the cultural heritage of the group.

RETAIL HERITAGE

The retail heritage identified by the heritage professionals focused on the shopping street in Newtown which is considered to have outstanding examples of Sydney's retailing history including details and fixtures which are now rare examples of past retailing practices.

The Greek group did not relate to the academic interpretation of retail heritage in the heritage narrative, but they felt very strongly about the role of the Greek shops in Marrickville as part of their settling in process. Being able to eat the food with which they were familiar was extremely important. This was not easy in Sydney in the 1950s where olive oil could only be purchased in small phials in pharmacies. The Greeks were enterprising in finding fresh olives and fresh herbs and in creating food shops which serviced their needs. The Marrickville shops became the focus for the Greek community in Sydney. The Greek signage, the way produce was displayed, delicatessens rather than Anglo-Celtic general stores all added to the vitality of Marrickville shops. The generic Greek cafe appeared alongside the tea shops. Less obvious to the Anglo-Australians were the cafe neros, Greek coffee clubs where men could gamble and drink coffee.

During the 1980s the supermarkets started to sell specialty goods so that so-called 'ethnic food' was now widely available. Also by the late 1980s the Marrickville food shops had become predominantly Vietnamese. Cultural continuity in ethnic retail areas is important to understand. There is a certain dynamic in such areas. When a particular ethnic group establishes their shops they are not only providing goods and services that are relevant to their cultural practices, they are also creating small business opportunities. This is characteristic of the enterprising ethos of immigrant groups. Over time the members of the immigrant group consolidate their economic base and move on to other enterprises. Meanwhile new ethnic groups come into the area. Often the first indication of changing ethnic demography is in the shopping areas. Such local shopping areas are now under threat by the new large regional shopping complexes.

In a city with such diverse, dynamic and locally specific ethnic shopping centres, it is important to recognise the heritage significance of these places and their role in the cultural continuity of sub/urban places. It would appear that these centres need planning protection if they are going to survive the trend towards large internalised supermarket complexes containing franchise shops which rarely reflect the culture of the local community. The challenge of holding small scale and marginal activities is as much an issue of heritage planning as the designation of conservation items.

INDUSTRIAL HERITAGE

The industrial heritage of the area had a major impact on the character of Marrickville, with the employees living in close proximity to the factories and the employers living in large houses on the surrounding slopes. The industrial areas were also a major reason for the influx of the Mediterranean communities in the 1950s which changed the character of Marrickville.

The Greek group could not understand why the industrial areas were considered heritage and yet the industrial areas are rich in social heritage significance in terms of the stories told by the Greeks. They spoke of the hardship and humiliation associated with factory work. The stories need to be documented so that future generations of Greek-Australians can understand the heritage value of these places. The thin line between history and heritage is interesting. It would appear that to have worked in such conditions is too recent to be romanticised as heritage. The industrial heritage at present is valuable to the Anglo-Celtic outsider and even then only the heritage professionals. This is not to deny the significance of the heritage professionals' expertise and their custodial role.

HERITAGE AS CULTURAL PRACTICES

The orthodox heritage narrative focuses on built form and does not consider cultural heritage that is manifest as a way of life. In contrast, the Greek narrative spoke strongly of heritage as cultural practice. Plantings, places of worship and recreational places were all suggested as important aspects of the Greek cultural heritage in Australia, most of which do indeed persist as a form of cultural continuity in sub/urban places today.

Plantings

The use of plants by different cultural groups is an interesting aspect of cultural continuity in urban places. The heritage professionals identified the street trees, in particular the avenues of brush box and palms, as part of the Anglo-Celtic cultural heritage. Such trees, which are rainforest trees, reflect the British settlers' ideal, namely of Australia as an antipodean Garden of Eden.[13] The Anglo-Australians realised that such visions were far from reality but sustained the myth in urban places by continuing to plant Australian rainforest trees. The Greeks talked about planting grapevines, olive trees, figs, lemon trees and jasmine in their gardens soon after they arrived in Australia. They stated that a Greek presence in an urban place in Australia can always be recognised by particular plants in the gardens.

Places of worship

Although there are a number of fine church buildings in Marrickville reflecting aspects of Anglo-Celtic heritage, all of which are listed as having been constructed in the 1880s and 1890s, they are not privileged as part of the heritage professional's narrative; the listings merely refer to the churches as part of the suburban expansion in the 1880s. The Greek group felt that the Greek church was the main focus of Greek life, however they considered the big churches in Darlinghurst and Chippendale were their heritage. They were surprised that the heritage professionals had identified the Greek church in Marrickville as part of the cultural heritage of the area because they did not think it was good architecture (apparently because it was designed by the priest rather than an architect). It would appear that this particular Greek group had evaluative criteria which privileged the aesthetics of design.

Recreational places

Different ethnic groups highlight recreational places as part of the process of settling in. The Greeks revealed that there have been some significant losses of valued recreational places in their urban environment in Australia, many of which would not have been known to the wider community.

The Greek cinema had been an important focus for the Greek community in Sydney. The best known cinema was the Lawson at Redfern. The Greek group spoke warmly about their experiences in the Lawson on Saturdays and Sundays. They described it as being 'like a festival' where extended families came with prepared picnics and watched Greek films. There were other strong expressions of Greek culture such as the Greek dances, the clubs and the Greek theatre which helped the community settle in Sydney. Many of these activities were related to particular places which may have been considered important to conserve had the Greek community values been part of the heritage professional's narrative.

Discussions about the process of settling into a new country reveal valued places unknown to outside groups. As decisions about the conservation of such places rest with the local planners who are advised by heritage professionals and other planning professionals, it is important to involve immigrant groups. To date ethnic communities have rarely been involved in planning decisions.

HERITAGE AND CULTURAL DIVERSITY

Cultural continuity in sub/urban places in multicultural Australian cities is highly complex. The prevailing conservation and planning practice follows a method derived from the Anglo-Celtic Australians' perceptions of heritage planning situated in an objective scientific methodology. Such urban planning practice ignores the many different cultural heritage narratives existing in multicultural urban places and ignores its own inherent subjectivity.

Interestingly cultural continuity in multicultural urban places is most threatened by the Australian development agenda, not by the new waves of immigrant groups who tend to reinforce existing land use patterns, while using them in their own way. Multicultural urban places such as Marrickville provide a unique opportunity to understand cultural diversity and to facilitate its continuity without commodifying it or stereotyping it. Planning codes need to recognise the strength of the existing built fabric, allow for difference at a small scale and understand the dynamics of ethnic retail centres.

When the most unifying attribute of a nation is cultural discontinuity, cultural continuity assumes profound importance. The Aboriginal-Australians are starting to reconstruct connections to their culture and the Anglo-Celtic Australians are deepening comprehension of their culture. The multicultural Australians need to be part of the many narratives about places and in the process of understanding their culture in this place, become empowered to participate in the continuity of cultural diversity in sub/urban places.

NOTES

1. Lee, A. (1987) 'Discovering Old Cultures in the New World: The Role of Ethnicity', in Stipe, R. and Lee, A (eds.) *American Mosaic*, US/ICOMOS publication.
2. Davison, G. and McConville, C. (1991) *Heritage Handbook*, Allen and Unwin, Sydney.
3. Hope, R. M. Chair. Australia Committee of Inquiry into the National Estate (1974) *The National Estate: Findings and Recommendations*, AGPS, Canberra, pp.334-349.
4. Hewison, R. (1987) *The Heritage Industry*, Methuen, London.
5. Marrickville Municipal Council (1986) *Marrickville Heritage Study*, Marrickville Municipal Council.
6. The notion of the hyphenated Australian is one result of the cultural diversity and hybridisation now occurring under multicultural policies in Australia (Zubrzycki, J. (1991) 'Ethnic Heritage in a Multicultural Australia', in *Proceedings of Council of Australian Museum Association Conference*, Canberra, No.1990).
7. Authenticity in this context is used to contrast processes which create facsimiles or reproductions created by others in order to commodify place. See Goodwin, R. (1991) 'A Green Theory of Value', in Mulvaney, J. (ed.) *Humanities and the Australian Environment*, Occasional Paper 11, Australian Academy of Humanities, Canberra, pp.66-69; and Wright, P. (1985) *On Living in an Old Country*, Verso Press, UK.
8. Armstrong, H. (1991) 'Environmental Heritage Inconsistencies in a Multicultural New World', Unpublished Occasional Paper, Faculty of Architecture, University of NSW.
9. The research used the qualitative focus group technique where there is emphasis on the understanding individuals develop about the project and each others' responses. The project seeks to understand personal, social and cultural meanings as expressed in ordinary conversation (Burgess, J. Goldsmith, B. & Harrison, C. (1990) 'Pale Shadows for Policy', *Studies in Qualitative Methodology*, Vol.2, pp.141-167).
10. Greg, 14/10/92, as cited in Armstrong, H. (1993) Draft Report on Greek Cultural Heritage in Marrickville, Unpublished.
11. Greg, 21/10/92, as cited in Armstrong (1993), *op. cit.*
12. *ibid.*
13. Armstrong, H. (1990) 'Australian Cities and their Past', *Landscape Australia*, Vol.2. pp.143-148.

8

Towards edge city: business recentralisation and post-suburban Sydney

Peter Murphy and Robert Freestone

David Harvey has written of the 'restless formation and reformation of geographical landscapes' under capitalism.[1] There is evidence from many quarters that perhaps an epochal phase of restlessness in the built environment is upon us in response to new financial, technological and social forces but with economic power providing the fundamental underpinning.[2] New metropolitan forms and patterns of employment distribution are crystallising that represent a significant departure from the modernist city. 'Beyond the central city', writes Knox, 'suburban strips and subdivisions have been displaced as the conventional forms of new developments by exurban corridors, office parks, business campuses, privately planned residential communities and outlying commercial centers big enough to be called "edge cities"'.[3]

The latter label was coined by Joel Garreau. A senior writer for the *Washington Post*, he was nominated for a Pulitzer Prize for his newspaper reports on American suburban development that form the basis of his best-selling *Edge City: Life on the new frontier*.[4] In a 1988 article that encapsulates the argument in the larger work he described these new suburban agglomerations as 'high-rise, semi-autonomous, job-laden [and] road-clogged'.[5]

Garreau's edge cities have several defining characteristics. Most obviously they are large: at least 450 000 square metres of leaseable office space and at least 55 000 square metres of leasable retail space. They are usually sited at the intersection of major suburban 'beltways', they evince a greater attention to landscaping and nature conservation than old downtowns and they are increasingly sophisticated and cosmopolitan places. They are more commercially-created than publically-planned and tend to be neither distinct political entities nor officially named localities.

Edge cities are portrayed as the product of the third wave of suburbanisation. The first was population decentralisation; the second was 'the malling of America'; the third is bringing the 'world of work' to suburbia which has traditionally been 'a place apart'. Garreau whips this latest wave into a veritable tsunami representing 'the most radical change in a century' in how Americans build their cities. He notes that this latest form of suburban development is 'being copied all over the world'.[6]

The two most active agents shaping the new landscape are identified as developers and the automobile. Planners don't get a look-in ('there is no zoning, only deals'). If anything, edge cities are explained as the positive, putatively democratic product of a kind of ecological sifting as 'individuals [seek] out the best combinations of how and where to live, work and play'. Garreau's populist appreciation sails past the restlessness inherent in the capitalist space-economy or even the triumph of recent development trends. His main interest is in the psyche of American culture, a realm of almost metaphysical inquiry into national character and manifest destiny.

Garreau has written a book about a phenomenon which is not, however, an overnight sensation.[7] From the 1960s, and especially since the 1970s, the changing scale and structure of American metropolitan areas has meant that central cities have become increasingly peripheral to the day-to-day lives of many suburbanites. The acceleration of the rates of suburbanisation of business and cultural activity 'pushed' and 'pulled' from traditional downtown locations has helped create a new suburbia quite different from the predominantly homogeneous residential communities of the postwar years. 'Accidental' suburban agglomerations of offices, retailing and other commercial activities represent a manifestation of the recentralising metropolis. They are changing metropolitan areas 'into something much more difficult to understand, use, or plan'.[8]

What, then, of evidence for spatial concatenations in the Australian suburban landscape comparable to the North American experience? Although deconstructions of the postmodern urban landscape tend towards caricature,[9] the rapid restructuring of capital in recent years has led to particularly distinctive spatial consequences.[10] There are many signs of restlessness now registering in the Australian urban landscape comparable to those described in North American cities.[11] This chapter attempts a preliminary exploration and conceptualistion of new suburban business agglomerations in metropolitan Sydney in the light of Garreau's American work.

BUSINESS RECENTRALISATION AND THE SHIFTING URBAN LANDSCAPE

The urban built environment in Australia is being remade on several fronts with new patterns of growth, decline and stagnation, often in close proximity to one another. The signatures of change are numerous: design of self-conscious new 'postmodern' buildings; renaissances of old waterfronts; redevelopment of inner-city factory sites abandoned by deindustrialisation; upgrading and up-marketing of older industrial areas; new mixed use developments; exurban and sunbelt migration; security residential estates; infill, recycling and renewal of historic fabric; and new leisure and tourist-based land-scapes. These hallmarks of change are paralleled in the 'shifting landscapes' of the American metropolis.[12]

New-look suburban employment zones have arisen, variously but often erroneously labelled 'industrial', 'business', 'office', 'technology', 'science' or 'hi-tech' parks. There are also larger agglomerations which might be regarded as evolving toward 'edge city' status, these being significant functional clusters of offices, retailing and other land uses which have arisen over the last 20 to 30 years outside of long-established suburban activity centres.

To some extent, these new clusters are not so much the result of some sudden and miraculous suburban spawning, but rather the inevitable products of metropolitan economies and populations grown too large to contain most activity in their traditional cores. They reflect a market equilibrium between centrifugal (high central land prices, congestion etc) and centripetal (consumer demand, employee location, lower land prices, prestige location etc) forces, accentuated directly or indirectly by public policy. In this sense, the work on office suburbanisation trends in the 1970s and early 1980s still has some explanatory power.[13]

However, over the last decade, the impress of larger factors on the economic landscape of suburbia has become more pronounced. Financial deregulation, accelerated tertiarisation and internationalisation of the economy, continued decline of traditional secondary industry, growth in the hi-tech industrial sector, increased competition between localities for growth, and so on, have added up to a sea change in the forces shaping metropolitan economies. These are not unique forces, but at the same time there are distinctive characteristics of Australian cities which may peculiarise the spatial manifestations of economic change. There are several factors which might well mitigate the emergence or rapid development of large-scale suburban employment centres. They include lack of truly dynamic hi-tech growth industries, dependence on imports and branch plants, relatively vigorous central cities and poorly developed intra-metropolitan freeway networks which might otherwise help to reduce their primacy,[14] and stronger State and local planning controls.

DOWNTOWN SUBURBS

> Sydney, Australia, even without a beltway, is seeing Edge Cities emerge. The largest is North Sydney, the fourth largest office market in Australia, marked by Amdahl, Arthur Anderson, Mobil Australia, and Qantas. It is across the Harbour Bridge from downtown.[15]

This reference in Garreau's own world survey of edge cities illustrates the point made by American critics that Garreau applies the term far too loosely for its own good.[16] He does not identify the others in Sydney, but seldom has North Sydney — effectively an extension of the CBD[17] — been conceptualized in such terms.

The growth of North Sydney clearly registers the impact of economic restructuring in the form of sustained office-based employment in finance, property and business services (Table 8.1). But more clearly in line with the phenomenon documented in *Edge City* is the intensification and diversification of office-based employment opportunities in the suburbs (Figure 8.1).

The growth of the suburban marketplace has taken several forms. The emergence of business clusters based on hi-tech industry or office parks has already attracted interest in planning,[18] employment,[19] design,[20] and metaphorical terms.[21] More rare has been the development of freestanding corporate estates, with the notable exception of the IBM bushland campus at West Pennant Hills. Through the late 1980s, there was also strong commercial development in suburban

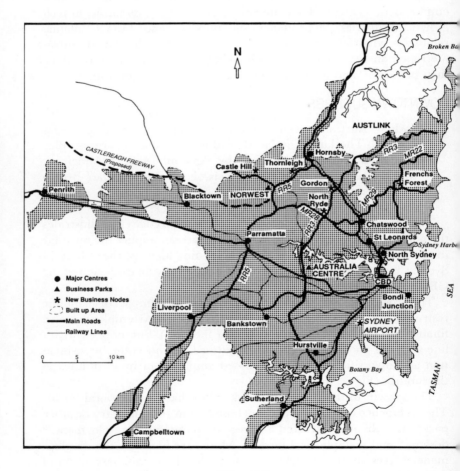

Figure 8.1
Major centres in Sydney metropolitan region

Table 8.1
Sydney metropolitan workforce, 1971-91

Industrial category	1971 ('000)	%	1991 ('000)	%
Manufacturing	370.0	29.6	264.5	15.8
Wholesale/retail	254.9	20.4	351.2	21.0
Community services	133.2	10.6	309.9	18.5
Finance/property	124.3	9.9	276.5	16.5
Transport/storage	100.5	8.0	128.9	7.7
Construction	90.1	7.2	105.4	6.3
Recreation	69.2	5.5	133.4	8.0
Public administration	71.3	5.7	60.5	3.6
Total	1250.8	100.0	1672.9	100.0

Source: Australian Bureau of Statistics (1971 and 1991) *Census of Population and Housing*, ABS, Sydney.

centres in accordance with State government policy, without any individual centre challenging the pre-eminence of the CBD.[22] The strongest growth axis has been up the north shore railway line beyond North Sydney from St Leonards through Chatswood to Gordon.

The Chatswood skyline created in the office boom of 1988-90 is reminiscent of the suburban skyscrapers of the classic edge city.[23] Its history has similar connotations too, with major retail development following population decentralisation in the early 1960s and subsequent office development outstripping effective integration of land use and transportation planning.[24] While Chatswood could well count as what Garreau might call an 'uptown' edge city, there are still significant departures from the archetypal American prototypes. Chatswood enjoys good bus and train access, has been designated by State planning authorities since the late 1940s as a sub-regional centre, and has benefited crucially from the planned decentralisation of public sector employment.

More spontaneous has been the commercial growth which has taken place outside of established centres. A major trend confounding local planners in 1980s was the increasing volume of office space in industrial zones.[25] This blurred traditional land-use classifications and called forth the need for more flexible local planning instruments,[26] and created *de facto* rather than planned office-based nuclei, with several established and emerging centres now falling into this category in Sydney.

NORTH RYDE

Postal authorities and street directories call the area Macquarie Park, but this is not a label in common popular or bureaucratic use. The core is the North Ryde Industrial Area, lying near the intersection of two major arterial roads: Epping Road (MR 28), a key route to the northwestern suburbs, and Lane Cove Road (RR 3), Sydney's only real outer 'ring road', linking the northern beaches with the southern suburbs. Other core land uses are Macquarie University, Macquarie Shopping Centre, the Australian Film, Television and Radio School, Ramada Resort Hotel, and neighbourhoods of medium density housing. The regional significance of the general locality is enhanced by the proximity of the CSIRO research laboratories, Hoyts Television studios, the Lane Cove River State Recreation Area, Northern Suburbs Crematorium, and the University of Technology's Ku-ring-gai Campus.

Figure 8.2
The Thomas Holt Drive development at North Ryde

Photo: Peter Ward

Note: This development has three signature buildings comprising 40 000 square metres of floorspace over a landscaped four hectare site, formerly a drive-in theatre. Prestige tenants include the Sydney headquarters of Honeywell, Memorex and Canon Australia.

Figure 8.3
The Macquarie View estate at North Ryde

Photo: Peter Ward.

Note: This estate consists of smaller business units leased to a variety of computer, medical, telecommunications, and electronic equipment companies. Macquarie University is planning its own technology park opposite. View from the roof of the Macquarie Regional Shopping Centre.

Thirty years ago this was a semi-rural area, with green belt designation under the County of Cumberland Planning Scheme 1951. The initial impetus for development came with selection of the site for Sydney's third university in 1963, four years after State government planners sought reservation of the site for 'a campus and industrial park on the North American pattern'.[27] The State Planning Authority remained responsible for initial development of the area.[28]

The first stage of Macquarie Shopping Centre was developed in 1979-81 by leading retail developer Grace Bros which had acquired the greenfields site in the early 1960s. It has been expanded and refurbished into a major centre, taking on a quasi-community centre role. The adjoining land was zoned light industrial in the 1960s and attracted older-style factories and assembly plants. Remnants of this past remain, but the visual accent now is on high quality multinational corporate offices/R & D complexes with specialisation in computers, electronics, pharmaceuticals, cosmetics, and publishing.

North Ryde now seems more commercial than industrial, a prestigious 'hi-tech' area commanding high land values and rentals. It is a dynamic landscape, with factories no more than 20 years old now being demolished and their sites redeveloped. A former drive-in has been transformed into a landscaped office precinct. While zoning as a Special Industrial (University) Zone and rigorous development controls on site coverage, setbacks and parking provision have helped unify development, there has been no master plan. Sites are in separate ownerships. The new signature developments are low slung corporate headquarters and architect-designed 5-6 storey buildings in land-scaped surrounds. Open space (in temporary use for agistment) is private land awaiting development. The locality is totally car-oriented, and suffers from peak hour traffic congestion.

An indication of the scale of development at North Ryde is provided in Table 8.2. In December 1990, total commercial/industrial space in North Ryde was just under 490 000 square metres, with an estimated 60% of this in offices — three times as high as any other major 'in-dustrial' area in Sydney. Local planning controls stipulate a 'research' component to floorspace. 'Industrial' employment excluding the university and the Macquarie Centre is in the vicinity of 12 000, making it the fourth most important employment node on the north shore behind North Sydney, St Leonards and Chatswood.[29]

Table 8.2
North Ryde: floorspace and employment, 1990

	Floorspace (sq metres)	Employment (head)
Occupied office/industrial	412 100	11 554
Retail/services	n/a	165
Macquarie Centre retail	63 220	1 700
Vacant office/industrial	75 600	2 055*

Note: * = potential.
Source: NSW Department of Planning (1991) *Employment Monitoring of Commercial Centres and Industrial Areas*, Department of Planning, Sydney, p.ii.

Incredibly, North Ryde has become the most important head office location in Sydney outside the central city for businesses serving statewide or national markets.[30] Multinationals headquartered here include American Express, Elizabeth Arden, Canon, Kodak, Memo-rex, Microsoft, Rockwell, Sandoz and Sony. By any criterion, it has emerged as an important economic agglomeration.

WARRINGAH ROAD

The corridor of new commercial development stretching from the Wakehurst Parkway (MR 22) east along Warringah Road (MR 29) towards Beacon Hill comprises freestanding office buildings, business park complexes, and leased office/warehouse units or 'corporate centres'. Key developments are the Forest Corporate Park boasting Apple, NEC and Dow, Pacific View Business Park (Gestetner), Forestridge Business Park (Mitsui), and the Allambie Business Park (Alcan, Warner Music).

The Forest Business Park off Skyline Place is on the site of Sydney's first drive-in theatre (1955), giving a clue to the early recognition of the accessibility of the locality for large scale land uses on the north shore. Other established functions in the locality are the Forestway shopping complex, an ABC Studio, a hotel-motel, Forest High School, the Warringah Aquatic Centre, and the Spastic Centre. These uses add to the regional importance of the locality.

Not all that long ago both the Warringah Road corridor and North Ryde would have been discussed solely as important locations within an industrial sub-market concentrated on 'hi-tech' products — electronics, data processing, computer software, bio-technology.[31] Shifts in the economy and corporate reorganisation allied to established locational advantages such as accessibility and prestige have seen them evolve into commercial areas.[32] It is when viewed in wider perspective with contiguous or nearby non-residential land uses that they take on greater metropolitan interest and importance.

SUNRISE CLUSTERS

There are no *bona fide* Australian versions of post-fordist hi-tech growth centre axes like Boston's Route 128.[33] But as a ring road studded by new corporate or technologically oriented complexes, RR 3 is perhaps the closest equivalent in Sydney. As Lane Cove Road it provides the main circumferential access to North Ryde Industrial Area. Four kilometres away is another new office cluster at its junction with the Pacific Highway at Gordon, intersecting with the main spine of north shore office suburbanisation. Anchored visually by 3M, a pioneering corporate decentralist which developed its Australian headquarters here in the late 1960s, the significance of this employment node has been augmented with the addition of the twin towers of the Pymble Corporate Centre and the head offices of Bayer Australia and Harper Collins.

On the other side of the Parramatta River where RR 3 becomes

Concord Road, a new office zone has arisen based on the Australian headquarters of Digital and a speculative low-rise building (PPK Consultants).

At the southern end of the Homebush Bay deviation in the heart of Sydney's most restless landscape zone, where the public and private sectors joined forces to gear up for the city's successful Olympic 2000 bid, is The Australia Centre, a joint venture between the state government and Lend Lease. Several major multinational electronics corporations have facilities here.[34] The Australia Centre is one of three large-scale planned technology parks in the metropolitan area.[35] The other two, at Terrey Hills and Castle Hill, while at present lacking the scale of development, land use diversity, and multiplier impacts of the North Ryde and Warringah Road centres, are further manifestations of the new suburban landscapes of capital.

The Austlink Business Park at Terrey Hills, named because of proximity to the Aussat telecommunications facility, is the fourth significant new business cluster on MR 33. Designed and developed by the Dainford group, its master plan also envisages development of a golf course and country club, retail and other ancillary services. Considerable road construction and other infrastructural works have been undertaken, although to date only two office buildings have been developed—both are hi-tech postmodern statements for Bull Information Systems and Panasonic. The Norwest Business Park at Castle Hill is even more ambitious although again there was little actual development in the recessionary economic climate of the late 1980s and early 1990s. The master plan for the 377 hectare site contains planned office, industrial, commercial, retail, hotel, leisure and residential components.[36] Both are set pieces, bearing the imprimatur of the NSW Department of Planning as the only genuine master-planned business parks in Sydney because of the 'special' business requirements involved, their location in professional-managerial commuter zones, and poor public transport provision.[37]

Closer to the landscape and functional dynamism of the Warringah Road and North Ryde kind is Pennant Hills Road (MR 55) between Pennant Hills and Thornleigh. Proximity to Sydney's most prestigious urban release areas, and upgrading of the road which provides one of the two main links to the central coast, has seen the remaking of the roadscape into what Garreau might call a nascent 'pig in the poke boomer'. (Despite road improvements, a notorious traffic congestion problem remains.) At the northern (Thornleigh) end, quality office space is concentrated in a development corridor which boasts McDonalds' Australian headquarters. The southern (Pennant Hills) end is dominated by the City View Office Park (A V Jennings; NSW Forestry Commission) and the 3 star Country Comfort Inn with obligatory conference facilities.

THE NEW FRONTIER?

The landscape of postmodern suburbia is registering the impacts of economic restructuring, technological changes, speculative development, new modes of cultural life, and government entrepreneurialism in various ways. The rise over the last three decades in the United States of new downtowns — major car-dependent agglomerations of office-based employment, retailing and ancillary land uses — has been one of the more dramatic manifestations. The bigger spatial picture is accentuation of the trend toward cities 'multi-centred around information-based industries'.[38]

Over the same period Australian cities have experienced a related restructuring of traditional city-suburban relations.[39] There are now diversified employment centres in the suburbs which have grown up almost despite, rather than because of, traditional land-use planning policies. They similarly have given substance to the inexorable evolution towards genuinely multi-nucleated metropolitan areas predicted by Logan on the basis of much less evidence in the 1960s.[40]

The label, edge city, while obviously masking great diversity in the patterns of office-led suburbanisation,[41] does appear to have some relevance to Sydney in offering a fresh reconceptualisation of suburban development trends in Australian cities but also raises questions about their real nature, meaning and comparative significance.

We know of nothing resembling Garreau's archetypal edge cities of Tysons Corner, Virginia and Dallas Galleria, Texas on a post World War II greenfields site in any Australian metropolitan area. Factors highlighted earlier (city size, economic mix, nature and degree of socio-spatial polarisation, constraints on intra-urban accessibility etc) undoubtedly go some way to help explain why Australian cities have not experienced the same scale of centrifugal forces as in American cities, especially in regard to jobs, in the same way as they are suggestive of why the impacts of economic restructuring 'have not been so dramatic' as in other urban capitalist space-economies.[42]

In Sydney, in terms of Garreau's criteria, North Ryde would be the leading contender as an 'edge city' in terms of its land use mix, amount of business floorspace, orientation to hi-tech industry and information services, appeal to major corporations, prestige premises, 'unoffical' status and amorphous boundaries, auto-dependence, peak-hour gridlock. However, the scale of this development is insignificant compared to the American prototypes. While it may be the oldest and most important new office/technology suburban precinct in Sydney, its 130-odd companies scarcely compare to, say, the 1200 plus in California's Silicon Valley.[43]

To the extent that the non-planning documented by Garreau in the United States is not an overstatement, there are contrasts in the Sydney experience. The State has actually played a significant role in the making of North Ryde, despite its challenge to the orthodoxy of the 'centres policy' favouring office development in established rail-serviced town centres implicit in strategic metropolitan planning since the late 1960s.[44] The NSW government was instrumental in setting the direction of North Ryde towards clean light industry and scientific research. And strict local design controls have helped consolidate the area's prestige.

North Ryde is also not quite the siliconised technopole on the North American or Western European model.[45] There actually appear to be few significant linkages between constituent firms or with the university.[46] This may well change with development of a projected 'research and development park' for Macquarie University and the CSIRO's proposal for a 'science and technology park'. But for the time being it is a high technology-oriented precinct which has arisen more as an amalgam of independent preferences for a prestige address[47] as opposed to the inter-industry linkages and agglomeration economies characterising genuine global 'new industrial spaces'.[48]

From here, of course, more detailed questions can be raised about the actual functioning of such a complex. Just what is the breakdown of floorspace between office, warehousing, assembly, and production functions in individual premises? What precisely happens in each of these? Does the preponderance of foreign-owned businesses indicate minimal on-site production and product development and thus explain the few apparent functional linkages within the cluster? How different or distinctive is the blurring of office and industrial space in North Ryde compared to other industrial spaces in Sydney?[49] Are firms as labour-orientated as they seem to be? Are they essentially footloose? What are their trading links? Can we quantify the impact on cross-commuting and labour shed formation? How significant are their links with the CBD? Are they helping to create a virtually independent metropolitan sub-system, as the classic edge city thesis implies?

Our tentative discussion inevitably raises the need for more research on the characteristics and functioning of these areas in the context of general metropolitan development. The distributional implications of these post-suburban employment and activity trends already seem clear in that they bear out the realities of uneven development. The most prestigious development has overwhelmingly favoured the middle-ring northern and northwestern parts of Sydney in centres easily accessible by car from the most affluent belt of suburbs and executive residences. Largely excluded from the phenomenon has been the outer western and south-western suburbs where growth in the labour force continues to far outstrip growth in employment opportunities.[50] Thus, the status quo of the north shore as a preferred sector for suburban office development has been entrenched. Remote from the vast majority of the workforce and job-hunting population, access can be difficult without a car and anecdotal evidence from North Ryde suggests that some employers have had difficulty recruiting junior clerical staff.[51]

In this respect the Sydney experience conforms to something which Garreau makes no reference to: the upper middle-class area bias of most American edge cities.[52] While lacking the same racial and segregationist logic, there are perhaps not dissimilar processes at work entrenching privilege, social homogeneity, and high property values. The domination of the new suburban business nodes by multinationals further underscores the creation of what Zukin would term a 'landscape of power'.[53]

A qualification to this interpretation of edge cities comes from considering the feminisation of the workforce. In the US, for example, work by Nelson focused on the suburbanisation of low-wage office work.[54] These jobs have decentralised to suburban centers to the cost of — usually minority — women workers living in the inner city. But the middle-income women of the suburbs are not necessarily hugely advantaged. They have jobs which suit their needs to supplement household incomes but the jobs are usually dead end. Nelson argues moreover that this labour supply is captive to employers and thus likely to be stable and non-unionised. The extent to which parallel processes operate in Australia is worthy of research.

ENVOI

While far from definitive, Joel Garreau's account of one feature in the restless landscape of post-industrial suburban America has helped bring to popular attention the restructuring of urban business space which has been of increasing academic interest. Edge City and its reception in North America make it timely to look afresh at the Sydney scene. While raising more questions than can be immediately answered, some of these appear to be worth pursuing if one accepts the broader proposition that cities are essentially structured by their workplaces. [55]

NOTES

1. Harvey, D. (1985) *The Urbanization of Capital*, Basil Blackwell, Oxford, p.150.
2. Knox, P. (1992) 'Facing up to urban change', *Environment and Planning A*, 24, pp.1217-1220.
3. *ibid.*, p.1218.
4. Garreau, J. (1991) *Edge City: Life on the New Frontier*, Doubleday, New York.
5. Garreau, J. (1988) 'In search of a sense of place', *Landscape Architecture*, December, p.51.
6. The words and phrases quoted in this and the following paragraph are scattered throughout Garreau (1991) *op. cit.*
7. Freestone, R. and Murphy, P. (1993) 'Review of a debate: edge city', *Urban Policy and Research*, 11, pp.184-190.
8. Barnett, J. (1992) 'Accidental cities: the deadly grip of outmoded zoning', *Architectural Record*, February, p.94.
9. Bourne, L. S. (1991) 'Recycling urban systems and metropolitan areas: a geographical agenda for the 1990s and beyond', *Economic Geography*, 67, p.191.
10. Stilwell, F. (1992) *Understanding Cities and Regions: Spatial Political Economy*, Pluto Press, Sydney, p.184.
11. e.g. Knox, P. (1991) 'The restless urban landscape: economic and sociocultural change and the transformation of Washington DC', *Annals of the Association of American Geographers*, 81, pp.181-209.
12. Zukin, S. (1991) *Landscapes of Power: From Detroit to Disneyland*, University of California Press, Los Angeles, p.20.
13. Alexander, I. (1979) *Office Location and Public Policy*, Longman, Melbourne, and (1982) 'Office suburbanisation: a new era?', in Cardew, R. V., Langdale, J. V. and Rich, D. C. (eds.) *Why Cities Change: Urban Development and Economic Change in Sydney*, George Allen and Unwin, Sydney, pp.55-76.
14. Fishman, R. (1987) *Bourgeois Utopias: The rise and fall of suburbia*, Basic Books, New York, p.192.
15. Garreau (1991) *op. cit.*, pp.235-236.
16. e.g. Ford, L. K. (1992) 'Reading the skylines of American cities', *Geographical Review*, 82, p.195.
17. Daly, M. T. (1982) *Sydney Boom Sydney Bust*, George Allen and Unwin, Sydney, p.65.
18. Spearritt, P. and DeMarco, C. (1988) *Planning Sydney's Future*, Allen and Unwin, Sydney.

19. Cardew, R. (1989) 'Retailing and office development', in Langdale, J. V., Rich, D. C. and Cardew, R. V. (eds.) *Why Cities Change Updated: Urban Development and Economic Change in Sydney in the Late 1980s*, Conference Papers No 7, Geographical Society of NSW, pp.34-55.

20. Lukovich, T. and Colman, B. (1992) *Industrial Parks: An Overview of Site Planning and Design*, Environmental Planning and Management Series 92/3, School of Town Planning, University of NSW.

21. Watson, S. (1991) 'Gilding the smokestack: The new symbolic representations of deindustrialized regions', *Environment and Planning D: Society and Space*, 9, pp.59-70.

22. NSW Department of Planning (1988) *Sydney into its Third Century: The Metropolitan Strategy*, Department of Planning, Sydney.

23. Luscombe, R. (1987) 'Chatswood: the changing face of a commercial centre', *Planner*, 5, pp.20-26.

24. Westerman, H. L. (1984) 'Managing transport and environmental planning', *Planner*, 2, pp.4-10.

25. Cardew (1989) *op. cit.*, and Cardew R. V., and Rich D. C. (1982) 'Manufacturing and industrial property development in Sydney', in Cardew, Langdale and Rich (eds) *op. cit.*, p.133.

26. Western Sydney Regional Organisation of Councils (WSROC) (1989) *Non-retail Commercial Uses in Industrial Zones*, Report prepared by Hirst Consulting Services and Masterplan Consultants.

27. Mansfield, B. and Hutchinson, M. (1992) *Liberality of Opportunity: a History of Macquarie University 1964-1989*, Hale & Iremonger, Sydney, p.24.

28. Lukovich and Colman (1992) *op. cit.*

29. NSW Department of Planning (1991) *Employment Monitoring of Commercial Centres and Industrial Areas*, Department of Planning 91/71, Sydney, p.ii.

30. Australian Institute of Urban Studies (1986) *Private Office Suburbanization in Sydney*, Report prepared by Plant Location International (Australia) Pty Ltd, Canberra, p.10.

31. WSROC (1989) *op. cit.*, pp.8-9.

32. Cardew and Rich (1982) *op. cit.*, p.133.

33. Stilwell (1992) *op. cit.*, p.192.

34. Lukovich and Colman (1992) *op. cit.*

35. Ferguson, R. (1992) 'Sydney business parks recover from rocky start', *Weekend Australian*, 22 March.

36. Lukovich and Colman (1992) *op. cit.*

37. McKittrick, J. (1989) 'A Review of the Draft Centres Policy Relating to the Provision of Business Parks in Sydney', Master Thesis of Environmental Planning, Graduate School of the Environment, Macquarie University.

38. Brotchie, J. et al. (eds) *Cities of the 21st Century: New Technologies and Spatial Systems*, Longman Cheshire, London, p.xiii.

39. O'Connor, K. and Blakely, E. (1989) 'Suburbia makes the central city: A new interpretation of city suburb relationships', *Urban Policy and Research*, 7, pp.99-105.

40. Logan, M. I. (1968) 'Capital city development in Australia', in Dury, G. H. and Logan, M. I. (eds) *Studies in Australian Geography*, Heinemann, Melbourne: pp.245-301.

41. Matthew, M. R. (1993) 'Towards a general theory of suburban office morphology in North America', *Progress in Human Geography*, 17, pp.471-489; Pivo, G. (1990) 'The net of mixed beads: Suburban office development in six metropolitan regions', *Journal of the American Planning Association*, 56, pp.457-468.

42. Murphy, P. A. and Watson, S. (1994) 'Social polarisation and Australian cities', *International Journal of Urban and Regional Research*, 18 (in press).

43. Joseph, R. A. (1989) 'Technology parks and their contribution to the development of technology-oriented complexes in Australia', *Environment and Planning C*, 7, pp.173-192.

44. NSW Department of Planning (1988) *op. cit.*

45. Scott, A. J. (1988) *New Industrial Spaces*, Pion, London.

46. Joseph (1989) *op. cit.*, pp.186-187.

47. *ibid.*

48. Scott (1988) *op. cit.*

49. JLW Property Research (1990) Business Space in Perspective: A Review of 'High Tech' Development in Australia, *Property Research Paper*, Sydney.

50. NSW Department of Planning (1992) *Updating the Metropolitan Strategy*, NSW Department of Planning, Sydney, p.5.

51. McKittrick (1989) *op. cit.*

52. Leinberger, C. B. and Lockwood, C. (1986) 'How business is reshaping America', *Atlantic Monthly*, October, p.49.

53. Zukin (1991) *op. cit.*

54. Nelson, K. (1985) 'Labor demand, labor supply and the suburbanization of low-wage office work', in Scott, A. J. and Storper, M. (eds.) *Production, Work and Territory*, Allen and Unwin, Boston, pp.149-171.

55. Castells, M. (1991) *The Informational City: A New Framework for Social Change*, Research paper No. 184, Centre for Urban and Community Studies, University of Toronto, p.11.

Part 2

Rethinking urban planning and policy in the nineties

Introduction

Sophie Watson and Katherine Gibson

As we race towards the millennium the questions facing planners and urban policy makers are very different from those confronting their counterparts at the end of the last century. It is not that infrastructure provision and the physical planning of cities no longer matter, they do, but many other issues have come onto the agenda. Cities are not just bricks and mortar, streets and sewers, buildings and freeways, subdivisions and industrial parks. As the population of cities diversifies, both in household form and ethnic composition, and new issues such as cultural processes and practices, the surveillance of public spaces, and the environment hit the urban political agenda, different ways of thinking about cities and planning become an urgent concern.

This book, along with other important interventions in the debate,[1] reflects the growing concern with urban issues in Australia. Not since the heady days of the Whitlam government and the Department of Urban and Regional Development (DURD) have we seen such widespread interest in urban policy. At the government level this is reflected in the Building Better Cities Program, the Urban Development Review, various funding initiatives and the extensive public involvement of the Deputy Prime Minister Brian Howe in urban policy arenas. In academic circles, a conference on Postmodern Cities in Sydney in 1993 drew nearly 200 people from 14 disciplines. This interest in cities from those who have traditionally not been involved in planning and urban debates has enriched and widened the debate — introducing new perspectives and frameworks. This influence is reflected in this part of the book where contributions have come from anthropologists, geographers, sociologists and cultural studies theorists as well as urban planners and designers.

Many of the problems now faced in cities derive not only from the sometimes unfettered development that has taken place, but also from the often limited perspectives of planners and politicians. Hopefully, the insights presented here will extend planning and urban policy beyond its established boundaries so that new questions are asked and new solutions found.

Various themes are addressed in this section. Drawing on the work of Michel Foucault, Matthew Allen is interested in examining the place of surveillance, in this case video security systems, in city life. He argues that these systems create localised places of surveillance whose effects are ambiguous in that they provide security for vulnerable groups at the same time as they create others as trouble-makers or vandals. In the context of a growing concern with the decline of democratic public space[2] the issues raised here are important ones.

Margo Huxley's chapter also adopts a Foucauldian perspective. Going to the heart of planning theory and practice Huxley argues that social control is central to the development and control of land through zoning. Zoning she argues has had far more influence on the form of cities and the constitution of citizens than any other aspect of planning. But it is not an uncontested site, resistance to zoning and land use control occurs in all sorts of ways. Rather than getting rid of zoning, since it has many positive benefits, or seeing it simply as an un-problematic set of technical regulations, Huxley argues that zoning schemes should be more openly and extensively debated.

Peter Phibbs and Gary Cox take a rather different tack. In their chapter they address the important question of who should pay for urban services. Given the growing trend across the world to shift from public provision of a whole range of goods to privatisation,[3] this is a key issue for urban policy makers and planners. In this chapter Phibbs and Cox look at the adoption of user pay systems focusing in particular on charges for museums. They conclude that the introduction of these charges has serious ramifications and in particular negative social, environmental and cultural effects. These need to be taken into account and discussed. If a relentless path of privatisation is pursued we are likely to see cities that are more and more socially and spatially divided.

In the next three chapters the focus is on culture, spectacle, the creation of meanings and the place of the imagination in thinking about cities and the built environment. The ideas introduced are influenced by various forms of postmodern theory,[4] and are here applied to concrete issues in the city which have important implications for planning.

In her chapter, Rachel Fensham considers the cultural constructions of the spectacle of recent Olympic Games and their implications. In the context of Sydney's successful Olympic bid, this chapter challenges us to think about different questions than those posed by the International Olympic Committee. Linking the spectacle with different forms of power, in particular those of production and representation, she illustrates the links between pleasure, leisure and amazement and the world of business, banks, politics and media ownership. In a period where public spectacles, and their media representation, are used by cities to enhance their global status, Fensham's analysis is a salutory one.

In her chapter, Jan Larbalastier is particularly concerned to explore how discourses of cities constitute not just subjectivities but also relations of difference. Her argument is important in showing how planners need to continually work with diversity and contradiction in finding creative ways that city users can give shape and substance to ways of experiencing cities. A romantic imagining of places, spaces and subjects, she suggests, is central in shaping discourses about and experiences of cities.

In her chapter on older women and public housing Bette O'Brien is also concerned to introduce the realm of the imagination into the policy arena. In order to address older women's housing needs, which will be increasingly on the policy agenda with growing longevity, we will need to establish more appropriate models of housing provision. O'Brien suggests that an important part of this project will be new forms of enquiry to explore what older women want and need, bearing in mind the diversity of this population. She suggests that ethnographic approaches, which have been well developed within feminist work since the 1970s, could well be incorporated in the policy making process.

The next two chapters shift the focus to specifically cultural questions. In their chapter on the implications of cultural diversity for urban policy and planning Sophie Watson and Alec McGillivray argue that the planning framework in Australia has been governed by Anglo-Australian values which are no longer appropriate given the large numbers of migrants from many different countries living in Australian cities. Examining two local government areas in Sydney, Watson and McGillivray consider what kind of strategies will be necessary in the future if planning is to break out from the more restricted frameworks of the past. Like other authors in this section they emphasise the importance of wider democratic participation in the planning process and more open debate around the sometimes contentious issues that arise.

Gay Hawkins and Katherine Gibson take up related themes in their chapter on cultural planning. They trace the recent emergence of 'culture' onto the local planning agenda to the influences of State arts ministeries, the community arts movement and interest in the international work on cultural industries. Hawkins and Gibson argue that local governments have always been involved in cultural planning, usually by default. To illustrate this point, they explore some of the cultural impacts of mainstream planning procedures and decisions on the town centre of Parramatta in Sydney's near west.

In the final chapter Peter Droege exhorts us to take on board a green perspective. He sees education as crucial for shifting some of the current myths about environmentally sustainable development. But, he argues, this will not be enough. Major barriers need to be surmounted—from aggression and ignorance to denial and fatigue. Facing the green challenge will not be an easy task.

In different ways each of the chapters in this section provide a challenge to planners and policy makers to think more laterally and flexibly than ever before. Drawing on new ideas across a range of disciplines, many of which have been influenced by postmodern concepts and analyses, the authors have attempted to shift the boundaries of planning theories and practices. We hope that these ideas will find their way into the arenas of planning education and professional and policy practices.

NOTES

1. Freestone, R. (ed.) (1993) *Spirited Cities*, Federation Press, Sydney; Watson, S. and Gibson, K. (eds.) (1994) *Postmodern Cities and Spaces*, Blackwell, Oxford.
2. Sennett, R. (1974) *The Fall of Public Man New York*, Alfred A. Knopf; and Watson, S. (1994) 'Recreating Democratic Public Space', Working Paper, available from the author, Department of Urban and Regional Planning, University of Sydney, NSW 2006.
3. See Rees, S., Rodley, G. and Stilwell, F., (1993) *Beyond the Market: Alternatives to Economic Rationalism*, Pluto Press, Sydney.
4. See Watson and Gibson (1994), *op. cit.*

9

'See you in the city!': Perth's citiplace and the space of surveillance

Matthew Allen

In the past few years, the consumer residents of Perth, Australia have been subjected to a widespread advertising campaign by Perth City Council (PCC) which is designed to attract them out of the suburbs and into the urban centre of Perth, the area directly controlled by the PCC. The campaign was a response to declining city retail returns in the face of competition from major suburban shopping malls, including the vast Garden City complex (the largest in the southern hemisphere). The slogan, which can be found on billboards and in newspapers, as well as radio and television, is 'See You in the city!'. And in Citiplace, the main shopping precinct in Perth's urban centre, the PCC will quite literally see you in the city. With the aid of nearly 50 video surveillance cameras, council security staff ceaselessly monitor the people and events within Citiplace.

Any potential for subversion in this ironic coherence between advertising and monitoring is all but eliminated by the 'spectacularity' of postmodern culture. Big Idea Productions, a 'guerrilla theatre group', put a small kink in the seamless flow of the city's discourse when, as part of a street performance, players and audience gathered together to wave at the cameras and re/cite 'See You in the City!'.[1] But, by and large, my own observations in Citiplace reveal no apparent awareness by the shoppers, window gazers and the rest who temporarily inhabit this part of the city, that they are playing a part in the actualisation of the advertising agency's fantasy. They rarely seem to see the cameras seeing them. They hardly even notice that I am videoing them myself. Instead they have that indifference to the camera that is part of the extreme televisualisation of contemporary society.

Now the camera—the technologically remote, disembodied eye— serves not merely as a tool of surveillance but also as its sign. Despite the much broader array of meanings which can attach to 'surveillance',[2] it is the metaphoric power of the visual which lies at the heart of such analysis. And, more popularly, Orwell's classic and unavoidable text of surveillance, *Nineteen Eighty Four*, has ensured that whatever else 'Big Brother' is doing to monitor society, 'he' is always and first 'watching you'.[3] The video camera system has taken over from the 19th century Panopticon, Bentham's revolutionary prison in which all the inmates lived in a circle of cells with the constant possibility of being observed from a central watch tower, as the most representative sign of a surveillance society. Thus, in *Blake's Seven*, a British science-fiction television program, it is a lingering close-up of a video surveillance camera that initiates the opening title sequence and which, in the first shot, precedes and frames the introduction of the chief character.[4]

I do not intend to use my investigation of the PCC security cameras to generate some totalising picture of a surveillance society of an Orwellian character. Yet I wish to cast aside at least some of the indifference which Perth's shoppers and consumers seem to have to this new development in Australia's urban landscape.

A CITY SPACE BECOMES CITIPLACE

First let me lay out the geography of Citiplace. Its area consists of a city block-sized section in which the parallel Hay and Murray Streets have been turned into pedestrian malls. A central attraction in Murray St is a major shopping complex (Forrest Chase) and a public forum (Forrest Place). Many small, lateral arcades link the two malls. Citiplace is next to a major railway and bus terminal, plus plentiful parking, all of which give access to the malls through overhead walkways. Citiplace also connects to the galleries, museum and library of Perth's Cultural Area. Bounded on east and west by major traffic corridors, on the north by another road and rail-line and on the south by the business district's main street, 'the Terrace', Citiplace is a discrete component of the urban centre of Perth.

While Citiplace is adjacent to Northbridge, the major entertainment district in central Perth, and contains a few cinema complexes, restaurants and hotels, the principal activity is retail and associated services. There are few people to be found in both the city and Citiplace especially after the shops have closed. Only on Friday nights, when trading hours extend to 9.00 pm does Citiplace remain active after dark. It is the dominant urban location for retail businesses of all types: while numerous shops lie empty in other parts of the city's central business district, there are no vacancies in Citiplace itself.

It was in this area that, in mid-1991, the council began to install what is the first major public shopping mall video surveillance system in Australia. Forty-eight cameras, mostly mounted in perspex domes about three metres above the street, observe the activities of the thousands of people in Citiplace. They are arranged so as to ensure that very little (if any) of the area escapes observation; they come complete with 360 degrees traverse and pan, tilt and zoom features. At least according to media reports, these cameras have extremely good resolution of detail.[5] The cameras are monitored from a central control room, collocated with the police station which services this part of the city. There are a number of monitor screens which automatically switch from scene to scene, though of course the operator can override to focus on any particular camera. Moreover, at any time the operator can activate a video recording from one or more of the cameras, as well as produce still photographs of impressive clarity.[6]

The cameras are operated by council employees who, on seeing some activity which they wish to halt or investigate, summon by radio either PCC security guards or the police who are dispatched to the location under observation. Both by the proximity of the control room and the police station, there is a strong connection with the police. There is an administrative system that prevents direct operational control passing to the police. However, this system was only introduced after it was found that police had been regularly giving directions to the camera operators about what photographs and video tapes they wanted.

The PCC is notably sensitive to criticisms that the surveillance operation is an infringement of civil liberties. Yet adverse public reaction to the video security system, despite its obviousness, has been limited. The council received some complaints about the threat to privacy which the cameras posed, but it claims that positive responses outweigh these criticisms. After paying it some initial attention, the media has lost interest. The cameras seem to have blended into the cityscape as easily as Citiplace streetlights to which they bear an uncanny resemblance — despite the fact that the PCC wishes them to be as visible as possible so as to increase the deterrent effect!

Given that the system cost some $750 000 to install and over $200 000 per year to maintain and operate, what might have led PCC to spend these funds in the midst of a recession? In one reading of the council's 1992 briefing paper, the decision appears to have been made in light of 'continual media hype' about crime in the Citiplace area, especially at night when the city's workers and shoppers returned home to the suburbs. It was thought that the hype, which overemphasised the threat to personal safety, had contributed to the decline in retail sales in Citiplace. Occasional glowing media reports about the value of the cameras in apprehending gangs of loutish youths, paedophiles and other persons deemed dangerous to the general population tend to support this reading.[7] However, this concern with personal safety is at odds with the stated views of the two senior PCC officers whom I interviewed in 1993, who emphasised that the cameras were primarily installed to protect the built environment of the shopping precinct and the stock and fittings of the retailers. Nor should this motivation really be surprising given the strong links between the retailers and the council and the relatively weak links between the council and the general public which utilises those places under its authority.

Yet, the cameras serve a third significant surveillance function. While at night they deter or detect the stealing of goods, vandalism and graffiti, during the day when Citiplace is usually crowded with people (and such crimes unlikely), they assist in maintaining an orderly shopping environment. For example, people littering can be seen and security guards can arrive within minutes to issue stern warnings about keeping the city clean. Interestingly, the PCC briefing paper on the camera system is indiscriminate about the use of surveillance: it has assisted in dealing with 'assault, arson, drug dealing, heart attack and collapse, epileptic fit, breaking and entering, vandalism and graffiti'— as if all were equally offensive to the sensibilities of consumer and retailer.

The PCC planners seem to identify two distinct groups whom the cameras might observe. First there are visitors to Citiplace, who are seen as legitimate users of the place because their intention, evident in the very fact that they are coming into the city, is to consume the merchandise on offer. Second, there are, in the eyes of the council, the undesirable semi-residents ('welfare recipients', the 'homeless', 'drug addicted' and we can add landless urban Aborigines) whose legitimacy is questionable because they fundamentally challenge the council's attempts to define Citiplace as a shopping precinct. Their permanence and general disregard for shopping in a part of the city defined precisely as a place for consuming visitors makes them a special target of surveillance.

Yet the 'unruly groups' that the PCC is most keen to monitor belong to a third, unrecognised category: those who are visitors but who do not wish to buy much and merely seek out Citiplace as a potential site for self-entertainment. They are usually teenaged, sometimes poor and as suburban as the 'legitimate' visitors. This 'anti-social element', as the official discourse labels them, challenges the established meanings of Citiplace by turning it into a potential playground — for example, by running up the down-moving escalator. While these groups are usually not committing a crime, they do — in the eyes of the council — threaten to disrupt the shopping activities of others in Citiplace, either at the time or by dissuading shoppers from returning.

Whether or not the 'trouble-makers' the cameras are designed to police have changed their behaviour is less obvious: teenaged gangs continue to 'loiter', and appear quite happy to defy or play up to the authority represented by the cameras. Although the council proudly points to its statistics on crime to prove the effectiveness of the cameras, arrest rates are not the same as crime rates and changes in either are caused by a complex mix of factors. Thus these figures are of little help in determining the effectiveness of the cameras. The only evidence for changed behaviour under the gaze of the camera comes from two anecdotes about graffiti artists. First, while the level of graffiti in Citiplace appears to have declined, it has increased in adjacent, unmonitored areas (leading to some pressure on the council to extend the area under surveillance). Second, the camera operators have, on occasion, reported seeing 'gangs of youths' gathering around one of the many public seats in the mall. The operator cannot see what is happening at the centre of the crowd but, when the camera next observes the scene, the crowd has disappeared leaving behind a seat freshly covered in graffiti. Generally, however, it appears that the retailers feel safer about the security of their merchandise and the PCC believes its built environment is less at risk. Like TV ratings, it hardly matters what is actually happening, so long as everyone believes the cameras are effective.

RECONFIGURING CITIPLACE

Let me now re-draw this partial map of surveillance in Citiplace so that I can make some more general conclusions about surveillance. Firstly, although people figure prominently in the images produced by the cameras in Citiplace, it is at heart a system for creating a surveillance place, not a surveillance society. The need for the cameras was prompted in part by changes in the built environment flowing from the Forrest Chase development, with its numerous covered walkways and secluded corners. Moreover, the cameras are located in such a way that they cover Citiplace and no more; indeed they help to delimit this area of Perth in much the same way as do the major traffic roads on its four sides. At least in terms of retail properties, the cameras define what are safe and less safe areas of the city. As a result we might, in the future, see different property values based in part on the desirability of a location within the safety of Citiplace, especially if vandalism and theft become more common outside the boundaries of surveillance. Already, in another part of Perth, the marketing of leases on office space in a new skyscraper emphasises the integrated, fully functional security system (including a network of surveillance cameras).

It is irrelevant to ask whether there is any real threat to be combated by this system (i.e. whether or not the system is actually useful to its 'purchasers', the building's tenants), for the marketing is designed simply to differentiate this building from the many others in a city where, due to the recession, office accommodation is extraordinarily plentiful. Again, whether or not the security system has any use-value is irrelevant when the system is used simply to justify the higher cost of accommodation in this new building. Surveillance here is part of the commodity aesthetic of the place, teasing the customer with its 'novelty and distinctiveness'.[8]

Visual surveillance in Citiplace is further concerned with place rather than people in that it defines the categories of good and bad subjects of surveillance not by reference to a mental category but by their occupation of an urban space. In fact it helps to turn this city location into Citiplace by preventing alternative, non-consumer oriented practices, antithetical to the urban planners who determined that Citiplace would be a shopping precinct, and which are the way in which space emerges from place.[9] The 'good' subjects must neither steal nor damage the goods for sale; nor must they interfere with the built infrastructure of Citiplace. They must not disrupt the 'good' shopping behaviour of other subjects within the mall area, whether by assaulting them directly or by distracting and unnerving them by having an accident, fit or heart attack. The 'bad' subjects are, in the minds of the risk assessors and managers, no different from hazards such as fire which physically threaten the places they are seeking to protect.[10] Thus although the system of surveillance disciplines people, it does so in the context of the important goal of constituting an effective consumer environment and within a dominant discourse that has already established the shopping precinct as place.

Obviously it is not only about place, for the cameras help enforce the dominant ideology of consumer society—but they do so via the mechanism of a place which people may or may not enter, and which they inhabit with far more agency than, for example, the inhabitants of the futuristic city in *Blake's Seven*, in which the urban architecture serves the surveillance system, delimiting the total viewing space and holding its inhabitants within range of the cameras. Although people who wish to participate as consumers have little choice in whether or not they become subjects of a surveillance network generated by that consumer society,[11] the difference is that this society seduces rather than coerces people into joining the surveillance regime. The security cameras in Citiplace do not constitute people as good consuming subjects independent of the sites of consumption, rather they are part of the way that a site for consumption is created which then, in its entirety, disciplines people to consume.

Second, my reading of the video security system in Citiplace suggests that surveillance does not simply erase private life altogether, as Orwell suggests in *Nineteen Eighty Four*.[12] Rather it resets the boundaries between public and private, without ever eliminating either. The power of surveillance is based on the unequal relation between the observer and the observed. Any decrease in privacy for one means an increase in privacy for the other. Citiplace's surveillance system shows how the public/private dichotomy fundamentally concerns the operation of the power relations by which 'human beings are made subjects'.[13] Shopping plazas like Citiplace (which are not privately owned, though they are the location of private shops and businesses) are commonly regarded as public space, into which people project their own, private subject-selves. These subjects might fit in with accepted patterns of behaviour in such consumer environments or, as with the graffiti artists, might be in fact constituted in direct opposition to normative behaviour. These subjectivities are, in effect, created by the play between public and private and by the relationship between the two.

When under surveillance Citiplace remains public, but there is then established another private location—the control room—which is not at all within the agency of the subjects of surveillance, but which still relates to the public space through the bodies of those subjects. The individuals being monitored, who do not know for certain that they are being watched, also do not know who exactly, in the hidden control room, is watching them. Thus they cannot enter into the usual dialogue of self-creation which mediates between our inner selves and our public projections. For example, on one occasion a female operator observed a certain male person walking through Citiplace late at night. She took a number of video still photographs of that person and displayed them prominently in the control room — completely without his knowledge of course. In this way, Craig Turley, resident of Perth, sometime inhabitant of Citiplace, became (once more) Craig Turley, much admired West Coast Eagles footballer and sex symbol. The operator was herself working at the interface between public and private, constructing herself as the admiring fan. While the operator was caught in the web of surveillance because of the opportunity that it offered to her to become the admiring fan, she had more agency in this matter than did Turley.

Third, the Citiplace camera system demonstrates how power and knowledge coalesce in the form of surveillance. It was revealing that the interviews with the bureaucrats responsible for Citiplace were conducted in an office some eight stories above the city (a considerable height, given that Perth does not have many skyscrapers). From the window, we could see Citiplace almost in its entirety. But rather than producing power through knowledge, this view produced pleasure: to paraphrase Michel de Certeau, our elevation transformed us into voyeurs, 'looking down on, totalizing the most immoderate of human texts'— the city. If there was knowledge, it was fictional and produced not from the view itself but only from 'this lust to be a viewpoint'. [14] What cannot be seen or experienced from this viewpoint, as de Certeau argued, are the practices of the space of the city, the operations which create a 'migrational, or metaphoric city'. [15]

The video surveillance cameras, down amongst the hurly-burly of Citiplace and the movements and practices of its inhabitants, do of course provide such knowledge. Not only are they located within (rather than above) the city, these movements and practices are reproduced in the control room, when the operators 'move' through Citiplace as the screens switch from camera to camera and as they focus in on particular activities and events. However it is not an unmediated knowledge. Though surveillance is advertised as 'Truth-seeking technologies [which] claim to be capable of going beneath the surface reality to deeper subterranean truths', [16] surveillance does not find knowledge, but creates it. Knowledge resides in the relationship between the investigator and the subject under investigation: a subject actually constituted by the act of investigation. [17] Thus surveillance extends the expression of power relations between the observer and the observed because the subject can only tell a truth 'through a mode of domination'.[18]

CONCLUSION

The Citiplace surveillance system is not the only such camera installation in Perth. There are, indeed, thousands of security cameras in the city, all monitoring particular sites (courts, bus terminals, trains and railway stations, shopping complexes — the list is almost endless). Like all these surveillance systems, the one in Citiplace is strictly limited in its geography and is not connected with any other systems. The fragmentation of surveillance, which is quite different from the all-encompassing observation depicted in *Nineteen Eighty Four* and similar texts, is generated by the specific placement of video cameras in a contemporary city landscape which is already divided and fragmented; broken up by capitalism's dependence on private ownership and by the strictly delimited lines of authority for certain places of government departments.

But does the development of so extensive a system in Citiplace suggest some move towards some totality of surveillance? Some critics would certainly argue in this manner. Yet their interpretations tend to depend on a crude reading of the metaphor of the Panopticon.[19] However, as Foucault argued, it is more frightening to conceive of networks of decentralised surveillance systems which provide little possibility of resistance: at least in a unified panopticon, a dialectic of resistance might emerge from the confrontation between periphery and centre. In a dispersed society, surveillance spreads so far and wide that everyone is implicated in its operation. Not only would its inhabitants be both the watchers and the watched, but the power which surveillance generates would become completely dissociated from the social relations between these groups.[20]

But it is possible to be too pessimistic about the operation of decentralised networks of surveillance in which 'Those watched become (willingly and knowingly or not) active participants in their own monitoring, which is often self-activated and [thus] automatic'.[21] In this reading the Panopticon turns into a 'polyopticon'. This term, as Haraway pointed out, still retains much of the mystic paranoia directed towards the singular eye[22] while concealing this fact with inappropriately pluralised postmodern language. Indeed the reconstruction of the Cyclopean surveillance eye of modernity into a postmodern multi-faceted insect eye reveals a critical tension in the concept that power becomes autonomous both through the visibility of the system of surveillance and through its decentralisation into everyday routines. For, as we can see from the operation of the many discrete, discreet camera systems in Perth, the more that surveillance spreads out, the less visible it becomes.

Perhaps, then, the threatening Foucauldian model is not so assured as it is impossible to have the dispersion of surveillance necessary for a totally disciplined society, while still retaining the visibility of the surveillance apparatus crucial to Foucault's theorisation of how society becomes self-disciplining. For much of the time, the Citiplace surveillance system is not sufficiently visible to its subjects for all of them to become self-policing. It only produces self-policing in those people who, having formed a certain subjectivity away from the public domain of Citiplace, then must modify it once inside Citiplace so as to conform to the norms of good consumer behaviour which were outlined above.

Instead of dispersion, then, we find fragmentation and just as there is no totality to the surveillance system, there are no absolute arguments either for or against camera installations as found in Citiplace The modernist assumptions of free, autonomous individuals which underpin the extreme judgements of the civil libertarians who opposed the installation of the Citiplace cameras no longer seem satisfactory as we consider the ethical problems raised by a system which at one moment improves the capacity of women to move about more safely in public places and at another further subjects Aborigines to type-casting as vandals and trouble-makers; which might assist in preventing child abuse but which labels young people criminals for trying to have fun in the city. American artist Julia Scher, who is also a leading security system consultant (especially on issues concerning women's safety), confronts such problems in her work. Her installations are created from high technology security equipment, often including video cameras and monitors only available through her membership of the security profession. Such work, in both its origin and its expression, 'is highly ambivalent in the way it juxtaposes the need for protection with the possibility of ultimately becoming the victim of the protective apparatus'.[23] These dilemmas shatter the discursive regularity of responses to surveillance just as surely as the patchwork geography of the city breaks up the networks of security cameras into discrete sites of monitoring. The specificity of place undercuts the possibility of a generalised society of surveillance.

NOTES

1. Bucknell, M. (Performance Artist) (1993) Interview.
2. As suggested by Michel Foucault's use of the word 'discipline' (Foucault, M. (1976) *Discipline and Punish: The Birth of the Prison*, Penguin, Harmondsworth).
3. Is it possible to find any popular or even academic writing (my own included, of course) which does not mention Orwell's book? Orwell, G. (1984) *Nineteen Eighty Four*, Basil Blackwell, Oxford.
4. I explore *Blake's Seven*, *Nineteen Eighty Four* and Foucault's *Discipline and Punish* and various theoretical issues concerning surveillance in more detail in the conference paper on which this chapter is based. See Allen, M. (1993) 'Maps and Explorations of Citiplace: Perth's micro-society of surveillance', in *Postmodern Cities Conference Proceedings*, University of Sydney, Sydney, pp.1-16.
5. Treweek, A. (1992) 'Cameras click as city crime dwindles', *Sunday Times*, 22 March, p.8.
6. The following three sources, plus personal observation, provide the information contained in the succeeding paragraphs: Perth City Council (1992) *Closed Circuit TV System*, PCC, Perth; Perth City Council, Acting Citiplace Manager (1993) Interview, February; and Perth City Council, Citiplace Manager (1993) Interview, July.
7. Treweek (1992) *op. cit.*
8. Haug, W. (1986) *Critique of Commodity Aesthetics*, Polity, Cambridge, p.18.
9. de Certeau, M. (1984) *The Practice of Everday Life*, University of California Press, Berkeley, p.117.
10. CCD Consulting Engineers (1993) Interview.
11. Marx, G. (1985) 'I'll Be Watching You', *Dissent*, Winter, p.32.
12. Orwell (1984) *op. cit.*, p.335.
13. Foucault, M. (1982) 'The subject and power', in H. L.Dreyfus and P. Rabinow, *Michel Foucault: Beyond Structuralism and Hermeneutics*, Harvester, Brighton, p.208.
14. de Certeau (1984) *op. cit.* p.92.
15. *ibid.*, p.93.
16. Marx (1985) *op. cit.*, p.30.
17. Bourdieu, P. (1992) 'Thinking about Limits', *Theory, Culture and Society*, 9, p.44.
18. Foucault, M. (1988) 'Critical Theory/Intellectual History' in Kritzman, L. D. (ed) *Michel Foucault: Politics, Philosohpy, Culture*, Routledge, New York, p.40.
19. Marx (1985) *op. cit.*, p.27.
20. Cohen, S. (1979) 'The Punitive City: notes on the dispersal of social control', *Contemporary Crises*, 3, pp.358-359.
21. Marx (1985) *op. cit.*, p.30.
22. Penley, C. and Ross, A. (1991) 'Cyborgs at large: An interview with Donna Haraway', in Penley, C. and Ross, A. (eds) *Technoculture*, University of Minnesota Press, Minneapolis, p.18.
23. Pomeroy, J. (1991) 'Black Box S-Thetix: Labor, Research and Survival in the [He]art of the Beast' in Penley and Ross (eds) *op. cit.*, p.290.

10

Panoptica: utilitarianism and land-use control

Margo Huxley

In much traditional, or even 'radical' work on urban planning, there is a reluctance to see its basis in land-use control as having much theoretical signficance beyond the obvious — an activity of the state mediating between private property rights and the 'public interest', and/or operating to preserve the interest of property owners.[1] Most previous analyses have little to say about the social control implicit in the details of land-use regulation.

However, other writers have suggested subtler approaches to understanding planning as a crucial aspect of wider projects of domination, and as a pivotal point of 'the spatialisation of modernity and the strategic "planning" of everyday life that has allowed capitalism to survive, to reproduce successfully its essential relations of production'.[2] This form of power over everyday life resides in the performance of land-use regulation and it is the history of this pervasive aspect of planning that needs excavating and interpreting.[3]

The reformist double-edged sword of improvement and social control, so intricately described by Foucault — in prisons, in asylums, in sexuality, in medicine, in public health and in poor laws — is evident in planning regulations.[4] Like the forms of surveillance and control that Foucault traces to Bentham's Panopticon, planning discourse too, derives from Utilitarian origins.

Utilitarianism was extremely influential in government strategies in 19th century England in a variety of fields of reform including medicine, education, penal institutions, poor laws and the urban environment. Utilitarianism, as propounded by Jeremy Bentham, James Mill and John Stuart Mill, was based on the notion of 'utility'— the greatest good for the greatest number. Since an individual's maximum utility (or happiness) might not always accord with the general happiness of society, government must set constraints on personal freedom.

However, the ways government could intervene were likely to be costly and therefore contribute to a diminuition of the general good if the costs outweighed the benefits. Since Utilitarianism stressed 'reason' and 'economy' in calculating maximum utility, any measure that could produce self-limiting behaviours in citizens was to be encouraged. Thus, Bentham conceived of the Panopticon as the most efficient, humane and reasonable way of producing, in recalcitrant criminals, behaviour that would accord with the principles of general utility.

The Panopticon isolated prisoners housed in separate cells, so designed that the interiors were continously visible from a central watch tower. The inmates could not see into the watch tower and could not tell whether or not they were under surveillance. This was the crucial point: under conditions of uncertainty, the prisoners would automatically come to behave as if they were being watched; the invisibilty of surveillance and the uncertainty of its presence was the guarantee of order.[5]

Bentham's whole project was to envision a citizenry in whom duty and self-interest coincided: 'a code of laws — and more generally, a social system — which would automatically make men [sic] virtuous'.[6] The Panopticon was one method of creating such individuals when all other methods had failed.[7] Eventually, individuals would become 'socialised' into doing good by doing right and there would be no need for repressive measures.

In England, Canada, the US and Australia, planning has specifically used Utilitarian arguments to justify its control of urban development, and in the process has become part of the state's involvement in the creation and control of gendered and productive citizens/subjects.

In proposing a connection between Utilitarian reform and the practice of zoning, I am specifically breaking with the usual historiography of urban planning that either sees an unimpeded, Whig-like progression from urban reform to metropolitan modelling and/or advocacy planning, or seeks to maintain the professional and academic legitimacy of theory and practice. Rather than papering over the cracks by seeking a 'metalanguage for [planning] discourse',[8] the gaps, discontinuities and contradictions in the origins of urban planning discourses need to be uncovered and examined for their effects on contemporary conditions. If we can uncover a history of zoning, we might be in a better position to see how zoning itself can be transformed. Rather than being an unproblematic set of technical regulations or the means to utopian reforms that traditional planning literature indicates, a zoning scheme which is openly debated could be part of a planning system that helps reconstitute actively participatory, gendered and differentiated, radical subjects.

SPACE, POWER AND THE BIRTH OF THE UTILITARIAN CITY

'Space is fundamental in any form of communal life; space is fundamental in any exercise of power',[9] and planning can be seen as part of this. Normalisation is a process achieved through disciplinary institutions and the objectification and control of bodies. 'The perpetual penalty that traverses all points and supervises every instant in the disciplinary institutions compares, differentiates, hierarchises, homogenises, excludes. In short, it normalises.'[10]

The same impulse to produce self-regulating behaviours can be seen at the base of land-use planning and these spatial-control strategies have direct links to the origins of public health, the creation of categories of poverty, crime and disease, the incarceration of the indigent, the insane, the sick and the criminal. The separation of land uses can be seen as a form of preventive medicine: 'Doctors were, along with the military, the first managers of collective space',[11] and many 19th century reforming doctors were influenced by Utilitarian philosophies. Edwin Chadwick's reforms of 19th century London were a conscious attempt to put Bentham's ideas into practice.[12]

Utilitarianism proved to be an enduring, if not always conscious, strand in subsequent manifestations of urban planning thought and practice. The 'felicific calculus' of pleasure and pain could justify encroachments on individual property rights that would bring about greater common good than the sum of the individuals' pain.[13]

Town planning added eugenics and environmental determinism to the basic Utilitarian equation; the reform of the city would bring about the reform — morally and physically — of the individual, especially the working-class individual. Zoning separating residential areas from industry would ensure that the working classes could see and be seen. The reform of the city and the individual went hand in hand; garden cities, improved housing and social insurance undermined the mode of life based on itinerant and casual work and the informal systems of mutual support that the working class created in the outcast slums. Disciplinary and scientific policies would reform the 'dangerous classes' by creating necessary dependence on the state, by examples of respectable workers in salubrious garden suburbs and by strategies of normalisation that could not be applied while the outcasts had inhabited the 'rookeries'.[14]

THE DIFFUSION OF UTILITARIAN URBANISMS

The Utililtarian underpinnings of urban reform, planning and zoning did not take identical forms in subsequent colonial and ex-colonial adaptations. It is possible to identify variations on the Utilitarian theme which accord with dominant ideas about land and citizenship in the UK, US, Canada and Australia at the turn of the century, when the idea of town planning was being spread around the ex-colonial world.

ZONED BRITISH

In Britain, attempts to introduce town planning and housing reform had a long history which gathered momentum towards the end of the last century and resulted in the passage of the Town and Country Planning Act in 1909. Even so, the early advocate of town planning, Henry Aldridge, felt it necessary to explicitly set out the advantages of town planning to local governments in improving the lot of the poor by taking up the measures allowed for in the Act. He claimed that zoning ensured that 'under a well-prepared scheme the owner of a house need not fear that the value of his [sic] property will be diminished or destroyed by the erection in close proximity to it of a factory, for it is possible under the Act to reserve certain areas entirely for residential purposes'.[15]

But the very visibility and openness of the new housing areas would create conditions under which surveillance and self-discipline could take place: the municipal building inspector must make sure that yards were not built over, and kept in good order with appropriate plantings of flowers and vegetables.[16] Planning and zoning would increase the visibilty of poor housing and create the conditions for its automatic eradication:

> . . . bad housing and bad planning are the two sides of the one shield. The two problems are so interwoven that they cannot be separated. If the wretched little back to back stood in a main

street in which the passerby could see it, then it would disappear before long, but as a result of bad planning it is placed in a small squalid street or in a closely-packed court, and the great mass of citizens are not aware that it exists.[17]

This reverses the argument from Engels' description of Manchester in the 1840s where, on the main streets, rows of 'shops . . . suffice to conceal from the eyes of the wealthy men and women of strong stomach and weak nerves the misery and grime which form the complement of their wealth'.[18] The horrors of unbridled industrialism had been somewhat ameliorated by 50 years of sanitary reforms, and attention now turned to the creation of model workers in model environments.[19] It was a strategy which could be applied to the reformulation of identities in other situations, and the diffusion of town planning spread rapidly even in those situations where urban reform might, at first glance, appear to have been a less urgent priority.

ZONED CANADIAN

Thomas Adams, a contemporary of Aldridge, helped to spread the gospel of town planning in Britain and North America. In Canada, he reported to the government on the need for proper rural and town planning, even though Canadian cities were, by and large, untouched by the horrors of rapid manufacturing development. The Canadian population was dispersed in more-or-less self-sufficient rural communities, and Adams' conscious Utilitarianism accorded with the Canadian motto of 'peace, order and good government'. It stressed mutual self-help and the importance of community values, was concerned about the iniquities of land speculation and the problems of uncurbed urban expansion.[20]

Adams recommended town planning as a solution to these ills, and advocated the application of zoning to new urban areas, where the expectations of landowners would not be upset as they would be if zoning were to be imposed on existing urban development. Industrial and agricultural cooperative settlements could be set up to employ and house the returning (World War I) soldiers. Land-use planning as proposed by Adams was part of a strategy to reconstruct a national economy and social relations in the aftermath of a cataclysmic European war:

> To make co-operative settlements permanently successful care
> has to be taken to keep them free, on the one hand, from coercive

or paternalistic control and, on the other hand, from unbridled speculation . . . In a co-operative scheme artifical control should be limited to the prevention of wrongdoing, including the prevention of such forms of land development as are economically unsound and socially injurious. [21]

In Canada then, the project of urban and rural planning was not so much the reform of the individual as the encouragement of natural abilites which had been wasted by lack of government guidance. However, the cooperative strand of Canadian planning discourse soon joined with the more pragmatic zoning for the regulation of exisiting urban areas to produce residential 'amenity'— or 'quality of life'.

The planning concept of amenity therefore fitted the principle of utility and Bentham's vision of a virtuous society. High amenity environments were in the public good because they enlarged the happiness and well-being of their residents. And ultimately, if all the population could be housed in such environments the public good would be maximised, and the most efficient form of city would have been created. [22]

ZONED AMERICAN

Thomas Adams then turned his attentions to the United States and became consultant to the Regional Plan of New York and its Environs Committee (1921) which drew up the first comprehensive plan for the New York metropolitan region to treat the city as an interrelated whole. Despite this new kind of aspiration (to plan regions rather than merely to regulate localised development), Adams retained his Utilitarian faith in the efficacy of zoning to attain efficient and equitable outcomes.

The purpose of zoning, according to Adams, 'is the promotion of health, safety, morals and the general welfare, in connection with which the police power can be invoked'[23] — an 18th century concept of government with a long history preceding Bentham's use of it — is essentially to ensure the orderly conduct of local affairs and hence, was not an intrusion on individual property rights.

Writing on *Recent Advances in Town Planning* (1932) for all three of his audiences, but with particular missionary zeal for the Americans, he defended zoning thus:

Those who think of zoning as an interference with the liberty of individuals have a narrow conception of its purpose. It is true of course that it involves applying restraint against one owner from doing things that will injure his neighbours or the community. But as there is a harmony of interest between all owners in a neighbourhood and those who represent the community, reasonable and proper restriction of abuses in land development should result in enlarging and not lessening the liberties of owners as a whole. [24]

Here the restrictions are discussed not in terms relating to use rights nor economic returns, but in relation to restrictions on liberty—the right given in the American Constitution to 'life, liberty and the pursuit of happiness'. In order to sell the benefits of town planning in the US context, the Utilitarian emphasis on economy and efficiency had to be made compatible with American concepts of liberty and happiness. Elsewhere Adams in a specifically US work admonishes his readers for their distorted conception of liberty:

Great benefits have accrued from the expansion of public freedom, but it has had the defect of its excesses — among other defects, improprieties in the use of land and in tolerating haphazard growth of cities. These have been an expression of a spirit of license rather than of true liberty.

True liberty is as consistent with the reasonable discipline of disorderly conditions in civic growth as it is with the discipline of disorderly actions of indviduals. [25]

Here again, planning is connected to a wider project of creating effective 'citizens' who understand and accept that controls are required on their behaviour in order to bring about the greater good. However, this project was not an unqualified success, and the rationale for zoning became separated from these purposes of urban reform and instead remained firmly attached to the myth of the Jeffersonian property-owning, agrarian democracy, which implied maximum individual liberty of movement and settlement and the right to the appropriation of land. Thus, zoning came to serve the interests of property owners and reinforced the middle-class exclusionary homogenisation of residential space. [26]

ZONED AUSTRALIAN

In Australia by the early 1900s, planning and zoning had been the objects of civic concern for some time, especially since the depression of the 1890s had exposed the unsanitary conditions of the working classes in this supposedly vigorous, egalitarian and healthy country.[27] Many town planning advocates were imported on 'study tours' (missionary ventures) of Australia in the years before 1914, including the leading lights of the British Garden City movement, and much correspondence was entered into with the likes of Thomas Adams.[28] These early Australian concerns echoed the British, in connecting slum reclamation and housing to town planning in order to reform the city and the citizen.

The Melbourne Metropolitan Town Planning Commission Act of 1922 set up a Commission of Inquiry into the need for town planning in Melbourne, which published its report in 1929. The report recommended land-use zoning, road planning and the creation of systems of open space and was much closer to the spirit of the New York Regional Plan.[29] The discourse of social reform was much subdued and implicitly, the task of reconstructing the non-property-owning classes was left to the Slum Abolition Board.

'A city must be planned with two objects in view — that of conducting its business in the most efficient manner, and that of conferring the greatest benefits on the greater number. City planning aims to bring about order in urban physical development . . .'[30] In this view, zoning is justified for its ability to stabilise property values and perpetuate the low-density residential areas which were already seen as 'characteristically Australian and unquestionably desirable'.[31] Even by the time the Panopticon of Sydney Cove had been transformed into a reforming social environment for freed convicts by the granting of land, the strategy of the creation of Australian colonial subjects in whom duty and self-interest coincided with the ownership of land had already been accepted.[32]

The advent of the town planning movement in Australia then, was already preceded by nearly a century of belief in the social efficacy of owner-occupancy of land. However, the Depression, political instability and World War II intervened to prevent the passage of the recommendations of the 1929 Report into legislation. In Victoria at least, planning did not become a matter of concern until 1944, when federal and State governments began to turn their thoughts to postwar reconstruction.

Mr. Oldham, the Honorable Minister for Town and Country

Planning, introducing the Bill in September, 1944, used explicitly Utilitarian rhetoric to persuade the Victorian Parliament that town planning was of the utmost importance to the future of the State and the metropolis: 'Town planning endeavours so to order the development of our towns that the use of land shall be regulated for the benefit of the greatest number of people . . . A properly considered town plan when carried into effect will make impossible the creation of slums.'[33] Planning would prevent/control in advance the conditions that gave rise to slums, but housing was the responsibility of either the private housing market or the Housing Commission. This enabled politicians to portray town planning as virtually costless, because the costs would be far outweighed by the returns to the health and wealth of the whole community.

The 1954 Melbourne Metropolitan Planning Scheme was a product of a particularly Australian/Victorian understanding of the role of town planning, housing and land-ownership in the construction of the self-regulating citizen. Zoning played a fundamental part in reinforcing the already-accepted desirability of the low-density suburb. The zoning scheme, installed to keep 'incompatible' land uses separate, was based on the old assumptions about the reforming effects of light, fresh air and clean water, but also now employed the latest technical information, statistics and surveys to increase urban efficiency and residential amenity.[34]

> Human effort, expressed as work, provides the wherewithal of living, and within the limits of the resources of the region, the standard of living depends on the efficiency of working. To obtain the maximum results from his labours man [sic] must have not only the facilities for avoiding unproductive effort, but the means of happy and healthful living, and the opportunity for recuperative leisure.
> . . . The purpose and aim of town planning is to show how all these inter-dependent functions of a city can operate, without interference with one another . . . The happiness, well-being, and contentment of the citizens of the city will, in a large measure, depend on how this is done.[35]

Bentham and Chadwick could not have put it better themselves.

CONCLUSION

. . . we need not take established meanings, values and power relations for granted. It is possible to demonstrate where they come from, whose interests they support, how they maintain sovereignty and where they are susceptible to specific pressures for change. [36]

The examples I have given here from different cultural and historical contexts are intended to show that urban planning and particularly, land-use control and zoning, are part of wider projects of subject-formation, processes that, by various routes and byways, some success-ful, others not, with active resistance or passive acceptance, lead to the emergence of new types of workers and new types of urban individuals. [37]

The mundane practice of zoning has had far more influence on the form of cities and the constitution of citizens than most other attempts to carry out either the reformist or the scientific programs of urban planning. 'That, in fact, was the whole point of the [zoning] exercise — to supplant the traditional working-class districts by 'neighbourhood units' from which the workplace would be banished altogether and in which every aspect of day-to-day living would be assigned to a place especially designed for the purpose.'[38]

Land-use control has been highly successful, to the point where we no longer have to be inspected in order to keep our gardens correctly planted, our streets quietly out-of-bounds for human activity, our neighbourhoods homogenously designed for a particular style of living; in the Panoptica of suburbia, we watch ourselves watching each other. But as George Morgan points out in his chapter, this has had consequences of feeding into other forms of moral panic and fears of the stranger in our midst.

Zoning sets the frameworks within which conflicts are fought out — very rarely is the whole legal structure of control itself questioned. Such questioning that does take place is usually precipitated by the search for new forms of control on the part of dominant interests, such as the Thatcherite incursions into the British planning system in the 1980s,[39] or the proposals for sweeping changes to the planning system of the State of Victoria by the Liberal (ultra-conservative) government.[40] In both cases these changes aim to create more certainty in the system for property interests by modifying and making more efficient systems of zoning. Thus, zoning, like the poor, is likely to be with us for some time: it is not just a modernist discourse applicable only to the creation of urban subjects in the industrial/'Fordist' city. Zoning is a disciplin-ary project adaptable to discourses of social control under varying historical and cultural conditions.

Nevertheless, no form of social control is total or hegemonically complete. Zoning and social homogeneity are consciously and unconsciously contested and resisted by multiple intersecting practices. For example, changes to household composition (gay, lesbian, single-parent households, etc); the increasing visibility of women in the paid workforce; attempts to prevent the intrusion of exclusionary, non-traditional developments into community locales, and legal appeals through the planning system, all pose challenges to the taken-for-grantedness of dominant modes of division and regulation of space.

A history of zoning that examines zoning's connections to strategies of social control and which questions the conventional acceptance of zoning as unproblematic can contribute to strategies to create responsive systems of co-regulation of participatory, productive, gendered, culturally-specific, alternative uses and development of social space.

ACKNOWLEDGEMENTS

Much of the work for this chapter was done while I was a Visiting Professor at the Centre for Research and Teaching on Women at McGill University, Montreal, in 1992. My heartfelt thanks to everyone there for providing such a warm and supportive atmosphere for research, and especially to Peta Tancred of the Centre, Jeanne Wolfe of the Planning Department and Annemarie Adams of Architecture. Many thanks too, to Brian McLoughlin for savage editing and for innumerable lively breakfast seminars on the perverse nature of urban planning.

NOTES

1. For example, Harvey, D. (1985) 'On planning the ideology of planning', in *The Urbanization of Capital*, Basil Blackwell, Oxford; and Scott, A. and Roweis, S. (1977) 'Urban Planning in Theory and Practice: a re-appraisal', *Environment and Planning A*, 9, pp.1097-1119.
2. Soja, E. (1989) *Postmodern Geographies: the reassertion of space in critical social theory*, Verso, London, p.50.
3. Huxley, M. (1989) 'Massey, Foucault and the Melbourne Metropolitan Planning Scheme', *Environment and Planning A*, 21, pp.659-661.
4. Topalov, C. (1990) 'From the 'social question' to 'urban problems': reformers and the working classes at the turn of the twentieth century', *International Social Science Journal*, 125, pp.319-336.

5. Foucault, M. (1977) *Discipline and Punish: the birth of the prison*, Penguin, Harmondsworth, pp.200-201.

6. Smith, P. J. (1979) 'The principle of utility and the origins of planning legislation in Alberta, 1912-1975', in Artibise, A. and Stelter, G. (eds.) *The Usable Urban Past: planning and politics in the modern Canadian city*, Macmillan, Toronto, p.200.

7. Campos Boralevi, L. (1984) *Bentham and the Oppressed*, Walter de Gruyter, New York; and Hume, L. (1981) *Bentham and Bureaucracy*, Cambridge University Press, Cambridge.

8. Dear, M. (1986) 'Postmodernism and planning', *Environment and Planning D: Society and Space*, 7, pp.367-384.

9. Foucault, M. (1984) *The Foucault Reader*, (ed. P. Rabinow), Penguin, Harmondsworth, p.252.

10. *ibid.*, p195.

11. Foucault, M. (1980) *Power/Knowledge: selected interviews and other writings*, (ed. C. Gordon), Harvester Press, Brighton, UK, p.150. See also Foucault (1984) *op. cit.*, p.282; and Foucault (1977) *op. cit.*

12. Finer, S. (1952) *The Life and Times of Sir Edwin Chadwick*, Methuen, London; and Flinn, M. (1965) Introduction to *The Sanitary Condition of the Labouring Population of Great Britain*, by Edwin Chadwick (1842), University Press, Edinburgh.

13. Smith (1979) *op. cit.*

14. Stallybrass, P. and White, A. (1986) *The Politics and Poetics of Transgression*, Cornell University Press, Ithaca, N. Y; and Topalov (1990) *op. cit.*

15. Aldridge, H. R. (1915) *The Case for Town Planning: a practical manual for the use of Councillors, Officers and others engaged in the preparation of town planning schemes*, National Housing and Planning Council, London, p.201.

16. *ibid.*, p.99.

17. *ibid.*, p.126.

18. Engels, F. (1969) *The Condition of the Working Class in England*, Panther Books, London, p.80.

19. Topalov (1990) *op. cit.*, p.333.

20. Smith (1979) *op. cit.*

21. Adams, T. (1917) *Rural Planning and Development: a study of rural conditions and problems in Canada*, Commission of Conservation, Ottawa, p.247.

22. Smith (1979) *op. cit.*, p.211.

23. Adams, T. (1932) *Recent Advances in Town Planning*, J. and A. Churchill, London, p.300.

24. *ibid.*, pp.202-203.

25. Adams, T. (1935) *Outline of Town and City Planning: a review of past efforts and modern aims*, Russell Sage Foundation, New York, p.145.

26. See, for example, Boyer, M. C. (1986) *lDreaming the Rational City: the myth of American city planning*, MIT Press, Cambridge, Massachusetts; Johnston, R. J. (1984) *Residential Segregation, The State and Constitutional Conflict in American*

Urban Areas, Academic Press, London; Perin, C. (1977) *Everything in its Place: social order and land use in America*, Princeton University Press, Princeton, N.J.

27. Davison, G. (1983) 'The city-bred child and urban reform in Melbourne 1900-1940', in P. Williams ed. *Social Process and the City*, George Allen and Unwin, Sydney; Fitzgerald, S. (1987) *Rising Damp: Sydney 1870-1891*, Oxford University Press, Melbourne; Sandercock, L. (1990) *Property, Politics and Planning: a history of Australian city planning 1890-1990*, (second edition of *Cities for Sale*, 1975), Transaction Publishers, New Brunswick, N.J.

28. Freestone, R. (1989) *Model Communities: the Garden City Movement in Australia*, Thomas Nelson, Melbourne.

29. Commissioner Stapley toured America and plans were collected from many US sources. See McLoughlin, J. B. (1992) *Shaping Melbourne's Future? town planning, the state and civil society*, Cambridge University Press, Melbourne, pp.32-35.

30. Metropolitan Town Planning Commission (1929), quoted in Sandercock (1990) *op. cit.*, p.110.

31. Sandercock (1990) *op. cit.*, p.110.

32. Davidson, A. (1991) *The Invisible State: the formation of the Australian state 1788-1901*, Cambridge University Press, Melbourne.

33. Hansard (1944) *Legislative Assembly*, 12 September, p.840.

34. McLoughlin (1992) *op. cit.*

35. MMBW (Melbourne and Metropolitan Board Works) (1954) *Melbourne Metropolitan Planning Scheme: Vol. 1. Report; Vol. 2. Survey and Analysis*, MMBW, Melbourne, p.19.

36. Weedon, C. (1987) *Feminist Practice and Post-structuralist Theory*, Basil Blackwell, Oxford, p.174.

37. See, Gramsci, A. (1971) *Selections from the Prison Notebooks*, Lawrence and Wishart, London; and Topalov (1990) *op. cit.*

38. Topalov (1990) *op. cit.*, p.332.

39. Thornley, A. (1991) *Urban Planning under Thatcherism: the challenge of the market*, Routledge, London.

40. Maclellan, R. (1993) 'Future Directions for Planning in Victoria: a message to Victorian planners from the Minister for Planning and Development', *Planning News*, Vol.19, No.1, pp.1-2.

11

User pays cities

Peter Phibbs and Gary Cox

In the past five years, the user pays edict has become increasingly common in Australian cities. The broad implications of such an approach, however, appear to have been neglected — to the detriment of residents of those cities. This chapter outlines some of the problems inherent in user pays policies and argues for a more critical analysis of their impact.

The introduction of user pays has occurred through two main mechanisms. The first is the adoption by governments around Australia of user pays systems to fund their urban services; the second is private sector provision of infrastructure (traditionally the domain of the public sector) and the consequent introduction of user charges to fund such investment. This chapter looks at the implications of the first of these mechanisms.

Examples cover a wide variety of urban 'goods'. One council in Sydney charges non-residents $5 to visit one of its parks. Another council has considered charging residents for the exclusive right to park in their own street. Beaches are hired out for exclusive use for private functions. Libraries have had to campaign hard to prevent charges being introduced for general services.[1] Museums are starting to charge for entry. Our contention is that often user pays systems of finance have been instituted with scant regard for their likely impacts. This is demonstrated by reviewing the impact of admission fees recently introduced into two Sydney museums.

THE BACKGROUND

In Australia, public services provided by all levels of government have come under increasing financial pressure during the past 10 years. During the 1980s, the federal government has achieved fiscal restraint by curtailing its own expenditure and also reducing the real level of payments to State governments. Hand in hand with this has been a political reluctance to increase taxes, whether these be on income or property. Corporatisation and privatisation have been suggested as alternatives to the traditional structure of public services.

At the service delivery end of government enterprise, the consequence of this fiscal restraint has been a reduction in services or the introduction of new ways of financing them. The doctrine of 'user pays', once the preserve of a few 'small government' economists,[2] has become a recurring theme amongst the economic rationalists. Treasury officials, other bureaucrats, politicians, business groups, and conservative think tanks have promoted the concept.[3] User pays has some immediate attractions, especially for hard-pressed managers of public services and facilities. It is relatively easy to implement. It devolves financial control from government to the managers of services. On face value, there appears certainty in cash flow.

However, there are some fundamental flaws with the policy. The issue is reasonably straightforward. There are some goods which provide a wider benefit than those merely accruing to the individual. These are sometimes called social goods.[4] The need for such goods is experienced collectively not individually. Thus, the market, relying as it does on private individual preferences, is an inappropriate way of providing social goods or services. In the market system, social goods will always be underproduced since effective demand from individuals will be less than the amount of the good or service required or desired by society. The recent Industry Commission report on Taxation and Financial Policy Impacts on Urban Settlement refers to this issue when it states: 'The fact that social infrastructure facilities and services are publicly provided and frequently subsidised means that private demands for such infrastructure should not be the only determinant of its provision.'[5]

It is normal, therefore, for these social infrastructure goods (libraries, schools, community centres etc) to be subsidised by the public sector. It is also considered that most of these goods and services should be paid for according to the individual's *ability to pay*. It is generally assumed that income is the best measure of this, therefore the most appropriate source of finance is an income tax.[6]

These social or merit goods are contrasted with goods where there is mainly a private benefit. Lang calls this the distinction between beneficiary and redistributional services.[7] She considers the mistake policy makers have made is that the principles developed for the big expenditure items such as roads, water and sewerage have been simply translated as being appropriate for social infrastructure as well. Spiller addresses the same issue, and labels items which are deliberately subsidised as *social* infrastructure, which he contrasts with *private benefit* infrastructure.[8] Spiller suggests that infrastructure does not fall into two discrete social and private benefit groups, but rather there is a continuum of infrastructure items from those that involve almost 100% user subsidy (e.g. schools, police) to those where full cost recovery from users may be seen to be appropriate. Spiller provides a notional continuum which is reproduced in Table 11.1.

The main problem with the adoption of user charges for social or merit goods is that if you charge you will reduce demand. But this is counterproductive since you want people to consume the good to generate benefits for society. Or, in other words, user pays is not appropriate when the consumption of the good or service generates external benefits to society or when equity standards require that lower income groups be assured of obtaining the services.[9]

Another issue often overlooked is that user charges may be inappropriate when collection costs are relatively high. Whilst user charges are appropriate for goods like water they make much less sense when social and cultural facilities are being considered.

THE CASE OF MUSEUMS

Museums and art galleries are a good illustration of social goods that have traditionally been provided by governments. While there have always existed private collections and galleries, the large city museums have been the product of 19th century government endeavour to educate the population. In particular, the museums established by local city councils in provincial England were provided to cater for the educational and recreational needs of the working classes.[10] By an act of parliament they were required to be open free of charge three days a week.

Public museums both in the UK and Australia were funded by the state and often supplemented by private donations (often in kind), bequests and more recently sponsorship from industry. Perhaps because exhibiting for public education was often a subsidiary goal to amassing collections, charging the public for entrance was not

Table 11.1
The infrastructure continuum

Items with a high warranted user subsidy component	• Primary schools • Secondary schools • Metropolitan open space • Emergency services • Community services • Police • Community health care • Pre-schools • Neighbourhood centres • Library services • Hospitals • District open space • Childcare centres • Universities & TAFE • Sporting, recreation & cultural facilities • Public transport • Arterial roads • Local parks
Items with a high 'user pays' component	• Dams • Water treatment plants • Trunk water mains • Water supply pump stations, service reservoirs, feeder mains & lead-in mains • Estate reticulation • (Sewerage) water treatment & outfall • Trunk sewer • Pump stations, intermediate carriers & lead-in mains • Estate sewer reticulation • District stormwater management • Sub-arterial roads • Trunk energy • Estate road • Energy reticulation • Telecommunications

Source: Spiller, M. (1993) 'Urban Infrastructure Funding Strategies: Responding to the Industry Commission Agenda'– Background Paper in Gibbins R. (ed) *Infrastructure Funding Techniques*, Paper 7, Occasional Paper Series 1, Better Cities Program, Commonwealth Department of Health, Housing, Local Government and Community Services.

seriously considered. Added to this, industry sponsorship occurred early on in Britain making charging less of an issue. The environment in which museums now operate has changed markedly from these times. In the last 10 to 15 years governments have sought to reduce their expenditures; consequently, museums and galleries around the world have introduced user charges—admission fees—in an attempt to bolster diminishing funds from government. Such charges have tended to be introduced with little consideration for the likely impacts, especially on attendance numbers. Museums have grappled with whether charges can be introduced without contravening their charters, but in the Australian case there appears to have been little public debate about the role of cultural facilities in society and how charging alters that role. Often nowadays museums appear to be regarded as solely tourist attractions. [11]

In the last year or so, a number of Sydney museums have introduced entrance fees. Both the Powerhouse Museum and the Australian Museum have started charging admission. By contrast, the Art Gallery of NSW has publicly stated it will not charge the public to view the permanent collection. [12] The Powerhouse instituted admission charges in September 1991 ($5 adult, $2 concession, $12 family group). The decision to charge admission followed a $3m cut in State funding for 1991-92, representing around 12 per cent of budget for the Museum of Applied Arts and Sciences (which incorporates the Powerhouse Museum, the Sydney Observatory and The Mint). A further cut of $2m was anticipated for 1992-93. [13] A fall-off of 40 per cent in patronage was anticipated, however, after the first 6 weeks attendance was down 52 per cent. For a full year, revenue from charges is estimated to be around $924,000. [14] This revenue intake is clearly insufficient to redress the kind of revenue shortfalls experienced by the Powerhouse. Details of an internal Powerhouse report were later revealed in Parliament indicating a drop of 71 per cent: 47,000 visitors in October 1991, 120,000 down on the same period in 1990. [15] In its first year of full operation 1988-89, the Powerhouse had attracted 2.5 million visitors and was the envy of the museum world. [16]

The Australian Museum faced cuts in funding too and consequently announced admission charges to be introduced on 1 February 1992. The charges of $4 adults, $1.50 concession, and $8 family were considered 'modest' by the Museum deputy director Hal Cogger. [17] Press reports indicated that they experienced a decline in their patronage, although not as drastic as the Powerhouse Museum's.

IMPLICATIONS OF USER CHARGES FOR MUSEUMS

One of the main questions raised is the impact of user charges on public facilities, especially their effect in changing the nature of the service or facility. Another area of debate relates to when it may be appropriate or justified to charge and when not. As stated earlier, user charges have caused dramatic declines in attendance levels at all the institutions which have introduced admission fees. There is some debate as to whether this decline will be sustained in the long run. There are indications that attendance levels are slowly increasing in the UK museums that introduced charges in the late 1980s. However, these increases may be mostly due to consumer adjustment to the free days that most of these museums have now instituted. At the Powerhouse, for instance, attendance levels are 'spectacularly up' on the free days, the first Saturday of the month, while all other days 'you could drive a steam locomotive through the place and not run anyone over'.[18] Local visitors will tend to revisit after a longer period compared to when admission was free. This can amount to a significant proportion of total visits, particularly at times of the year when tourism is low.

This decline in patronage raises equity as a central issue. Since user charges are bound to deny access to certain groups in the community, they are difficult to justify on access and equity grounds. In the context of public facilities, user charges are regressive; lower income groups pay a proportionately higher percentage of their income to avail themselves of the same service than higher income groups. In introducing charges, the poor are relatively disadvantaged. Furthermore, the user pays philosophy ignores the issue that people may stop using a service or facility simply because they cannot afford it, not because they do not want it or do not need it.[19] The issue of the inadequate purchasing power of low income groups in a market economy is often ignored by user pays systems.

In the case of museums, admission charges reduce access, particularly to low income groups and large families. Two major facilities, constructed with public funds, have been changed, for some sections of the community, from public to private spaces. This situation echoes Watson's comments: 'Economic rationalism is producing cities where the public spaces of display are superficially cheerful, relaxed and places of pleasure — but only for those who can afford to be there'.[20]

The introduction of admission fees and the general withdrawal of state support may also change the nature of museums themselves. One effect might be a pursuit of sensationalism at the expense of content. The withdrawal of state funding has led institutions to more vigorously seek corporate sponsorship. Phillips gives a particularly poignant example from the Science Museum in the UK: '. . . in another part of the museum, the visitor stumbles across Food For Thought, an exhibition sponsored by Sainsbury's and the food industry, featuring a

Sainsbury's check-out, a mock McDonald's and a 1920s Sainsbury shop'.[21]

Hamilton lays the blame for the 'tragic realignment' of museums, from encyclopaedic displays to themed exhibitions trying to beat TV and theme parks at their own game, squarely on admission charges: '. . . the policy of museum admission charges, an uncivilised practice that tends to turn every museum visit from one of discovery and enjoyment at the visitor's own pace into one in which money's-worth is demanded, and entertainment part of the deal'.[22]

CONCLUSION

Whilst user pays cities seem part of the current planning paradigm, the blanket application of such a policy has a number of serious ramifications for Australian cities. Such policies do not generate efficient outcomes in the provision of social infrastructure, and they act against the provision of fair outcomes.

From an economic perspective, the main rationale for user charges is where there is a need to *restrict* demand,[23] i.e. when a scarce resource is costly to extract or is being frivolously depleted. However, many public facilities, like museums, do not require price rationing. Congestion rarely occurs, except at special exhibitions. Furthermore, museums are unique resources and there seems no good reason to restrict access to them.

A user pays approach to financing is frequently supported on the grounds of economic efficiency. In the absence of a user charge or price, it is argued that consumers will undervalue the good and consequently consume more of the good than would be the case were charges applied. Howard suggests that the 'fatal flaw' in this philosophy is that it fails to address the issue of inadequate purchasing power in the community.[24] People may stop purchasing or consuming a good simply because they cannot afford it. Hence, expensive capital assets may be underutilised when there are many people who wish or need to use them. The question then arises: why spend large sums of taxpayers' money to construct a facility which will be rationed? For instance, the Powerhouse building budget was $54m.[25] Should an asset that has been financed by the public through general taxation then be rationed to that same public through a user charge? As Edmund Capon, the Director of the Art Gallery of NSW, says: 'There is the philosophical proposition that this building and everything in it belongs to everybody in NSW'.[26] Public policy is clearly contradictory in this area.

User pays also fails to take into account the significant externalities arising from public facilities like museums. Some American and UK cities, for example Glasgow and Liverpool, are basing inner-city regeneration on cultural and arts facilities.[27] The fact that some of these externalities may be awkward to place an exact dollar value on does not make them any the less real. Museums have often been regarded as having a national importance, especially in imparting a sense of shared culture and history.

The user charges debate has wide implications for public facilities and services generally. Managers of *public* facilities often act, or are encouraged to act, as if they were operating *private* profit maximising firms. There are many aspects, such as the social benefits, that can be conveniently ignored in the imperative to balance the books.

Consequently, there is a need for more informed public debate on the implications and appropriateness of user charges. An encouraging sign emerges from a recent seminar organised by the Building Better Cities Program, which reviewed the Industry Commission Report on Taxation and Financial Policy Impacts on Urban Settlement which strongly advocated a User Pays Framework. The record of the seminar contained the following observation:

> Against the background of support for rational pricing mechanisms there are concerns that they may be misapplied. Non-financial costs and benefits relating to, for example, the environment, social cohesion, aesthetics and cultural heritage are likely to be uncosted and hence under-valued. There is a need to better articulate these values. To the extent that they cannot be directly factored into infrastructure prices, there is a clear case for negotiation and planning.[28]

Negotiations and planning indeed. Those advocating user pays facilities, mostly middle and upper-income professionals, have not shown an appreciation of the budget constraints of a significant part of the population. A city dominated by user pays facilities will be a more socially divided city, where a group of residents is excluded from facilities that were once open to all. At the least, issues should be examined on a case by case basis, not lumped together under the banner of an economic ideology which ignores the real impacts of user charges.

NOTES

1. Armitage, C. (1992) 'Charge! Who gains when users pay?', *Sydney Morning Herald*, 15 April, p.13.
2. For example, Friedman, M. (1962) *Capitalism and Freedom*, Chicago University Press, Chicago.
3. Armitage (1992) *op. cit.*
4. Musgrave, R. A. and Musgrave, P. B. (1984) *Public Finance in Theory and Practice*, 4th edn, McGraw-Hill Book Company, New York.
5. Industry Commission (1993) *Taxation and Financial Policy Impacts on Urban Settlement*, Report No 30, Canberra, p.359.
6. Snyder, T. P. and Stegman, M. A. (1987) *Paying for Growth. Using development fees to finance infrastructure*, Urban Land Institute, Washington D.C.
7. Lang, J. (1992) *Developing Cities: Who Pays? Financing Social Infrastructure*, NSW Council of Social Service, Sydney.
8. Spiller, M. (1993) 'Urban Infrastructure Funding Strategies: Responding to the Industry Commission Agenda'– Background Paper in Gibbins R. (ed) *Infrastructure Funding Techniques*, Paper 7, Occasional Paper Series 1, Better Cities Program, Commonwealth Department of Health, Housing, Local Government and Community Services.
9. Due, J. and Friedlaender, A. (1973) *Government Finance: Economics of the Public Sector*, 5th edn, Homewood, Richard D. Irwin Inc., Illinois.
10. Clarke, R. (1991) 'Government Policy and Art Museums in the United Kingdom', in Feldstein, M. (ed.) *The Economics of Art Museums*, The University of Chicago Press, Chicago.
11. Greene, M. (1989) 'Powering ahead', *Museums Journal*, Vol.89, October: pp.23-26.
12. O'Brien, G. (1991) 'Museum to charge "modest" entry fee', *Sydney Morning Herald*, 18 October.
13. Cochrane, P. (1992) 'When is a museum a museum piece?', *Sydney Morning Herald*, 21 March, p.49.
14. *ibid.*
15. *ibid.*
16. Greene (1989) *op. cit.*
17. O'Brien (1991) *op. cit.*
18. Cochrane (1992) *op. cit.*
19. Armitage (1992) *op. cit.*
20. Watson, S. (1993) 'Work and Leisure in Tomorrow's Cities', in Rees, S., Rodley, G. and Stilwell, F. (eds.) *Beyond the Market*, Pluto Press, Sydney, p.117.
21. Phillips, M. (1990) 'The real cost of paying at the door', *Guardian*, 12 January, p.23.
22. Hamilton, J. (1991) 'Pay and display', *Spectator*, 11 May, pp.43-44.
23. Due and Friedlaender (1973) *op. cit.*
24. Howard, M. (1992) quoted in Armitage (1992) *op. cit.*, p.13.
25. Greene (1989) *op. cit.*
26. O'Brien (1991) *op. cit.*

27. Francis, R. (1989) 'A future for museums: funding the arts in inner cities', *Museums Journal*, Vol.88, Mar., p.181.
28. Gibbins, R. (ed.) (1993) *Infrastructure Funding Techniques*, Paper 7, Occasional Paper Series 1, Better Cities Program, Commonwealth Department of Health, Housing, Local Government and Community Services, p.4.

12

Prime time hyperspace: the Olympic city as spectacle

Rachel Fensham

In *Invisible Cities*, perhaps the quintessential novel on the postmodern city, Calvino writes:

> Sophronia is made up of two half cities. In one there is the great roller-coaster with its steel humps, the carousel . . . the Ferris wheel . . . the other half-city is of stone and marble and cement, with the bank, the factories, the palaces, the slaughterhouse, the school and all the rest.[1]

In this passage, Calvino evokes two exemplary sites for the production of cultural meanings in the city: its playgrounds and its official institutions. The first could be held to generate the cultural signs and symbols of the city whereas the second could be thought of as producing social and political effects. Frequently one is considered more important than the other and yet when we consider the city as spectacle these two cities converge and their potential meanings must be considered together. The spectacular city is literally 'the stage in which all prosceniums are unfolding and disappearing'[2] and in which the creativity and capital of the marketplace produce what it is we can see and know.

What cultural symbols are available and vanishing, seen and un-seen, in the spectacular city has implications for how spaces are organised, for whom and to what effect. It is this sense of the city as a mobile landscape which I wish to foreground in relation to public events such as the Olympic games. I propose to examine the 1992 Barcelona Olympics as a global spectacle and investigate the ways in which the representation of the city is manipulated and theatricalised by television in the late 20th century. The recent win by Sydney for the 2000 Olympics was itself a prime-time event and the Games will increasingly focus Australian attention on what the city as spectacle has to offer. It is opportune to reconsider the power of spectacle in relation to public involvement and investment in the future of cities.

When the fireworks burst for a full seven minutes over the Montjuic stadium in Barcelona in 'a display which certainly thrilled the entire world'[3] during the closing ceremony of the XXIVth Olympiad, the moment was all spectacle. Spectacle, defined most simply, produces an immediate experience of awe, euphoria or wonder and is intended for a mass audience. But it is as an orchestrated event of cultural significance that we must make sense of its impact. There are however, different theories of the spectacle and it is somewhere between the optimistic evaluation of anthropologist John MacAloon and the pessimistic Marxist Guy Debord that a contemporary response must be developed.

THEORIES OF THE SPECTACLE

According to MacAloon, 'spectacle', along with festival, ritual and game, is a genre of cultural performance, and is one of those occasions through which 'as a culture or society we reflect upon and define ourselves, dramatise our collective myths and history, present ourselves with alternatives, and eventually change in some ways while remaining the same in others'.[4] Spectacles such as the Olympic Games are therefore powerful, public and reflexive events because through them communities of participants or viewers can make connections between the past, present and future.

But the structure of the spectacle — with its complex interaction of media such as lighting, film, television, staging, music, public address — allows the spectator the choice of distanced observation. And MacAloon argues that it is this very 'distance and optionality' which provides the contemporary audience with a mode of reflecting on the 'problematic of image and reality'[5] in an era of global political awareness. Therefore, the various configurations of spectacular representation, including public events and international broadcasts, *positively* enable the spectator to 'heed moral and social boundaries that have become blurred or banal in daily life'.[6] In his view, the Olympic spectacle can promote greater international awareness and even stimulate public reaction to examples of injustice. On the other hand, televised images are also capable of desensitising viewers to the differences between local, national and global interests.[7]

MacAloon cites the modern Olympics as a type case of spectacle for its form is dynamic, its actors (the sportspeople) are engaged in lively movement, its structured encounters are 'irreducibly visual', and the spectators are excited. As a cultural performance involving most nations in the world, the Games also incorporate wider political and social narratives e.g. the long-term banning of South Africa, the boycotting of the Moscow Olympics, the debate about human rights in relation to Beijing's bid for the year 2000 and the mobilisation of environmental perspectives in the case of Sydney. They also project a sloganistic idealism about the Olympics as a 'festival of human unity'.

The Olympic charter is a reworking of the history of ancient Greek sporting festivals which was articulated by Pierre de Coubertin at the end of the 19th century. He believed these earlier Olympics had celebrated a spirit of amateur physical well-being and endeavour and that their reinvention could be the vehicle for unifying nations in friendly and healthy contest. In fact, the ancient Olympics had also been driven by city-state rivalries, financial competition and various corrupt and violent practices.[8] However, today's Olympics maintain the external appearance of equanimity and order, upholding universalist ideals and yet masking ongoing imperialist and competitive relations between nations. With no note of irony, the closing song of the Barcelona Olympics was *Always Friends* sung by Spaniard, Jose Carreras and American, Sarah Brightman. In a symphonic surge of vocal chords the stadium was rocked by optimistic sentiments about world friendship.

But spectacle does not only seduce, for it consists of contradictory relationships, what MacAloon calls the meta-messages, which are both sceptical: 'admire but do not be deceived' and liberating 'all you *have* to do is watch'.[9] Because the spectacle does not and cannot coerce individuals into fixed positions in relation to what they are seeing, it must offer them a choice. He then argues that it can also liberate individuals 'to *want*, to be free, to do more than watch'[10] therefore functioning as a symbolic medium through which people can become engaged and take up positions in relation to whatever is really at stake. His sympathy for the spectacle is idealistic, emphasising the 'freedom' of spectators to choose what it is they are seeing and to respond accordingly.

On the other hand, there is much critical commentary about the coercive effects of spectacle upon patterns of consumption, which fill spaces with crowds rather than inhabiting them with communities.[11] This persuasive power of the spectacle, and its integration with the popular media, has led to definition of spectacle as 'an explanation of the contemporary operation of power'.[12] Guy Debord, writing in 1967, coined the now-familiar phrase 'society of the spectacle'. He argued that the 'spectacle' was simultaneously the mechanism and the base of a society which produced endless images of images, signs with no meanings, realities with no substances, texts with no narratives. Therefore, the spectacle dominates contemporary society because the manufacture of representations is essential to capitalist production. The outcome of this argument is to think of social relations as constituted not by being, or having, but through appearing. 'The spectacle is not a collection of images, but a social relation among people, mediated by images'.[13]

In Debord's analysis the late 20th century commodification of culture is a totalising phenomenon: 'The spectacle is the moment when the commodity has attained the total occupation of social life . . . the relation to the commodity is all one sees'.[14] For example, the mediated appearances of 'Sydney 2000' (the current slogan) and its marketable products will dominate the event. Spectators will be alienated from other potential sources of meaning, for 'the pseudo-events which rush by in spectacular dramatisations have not been lived by those informed of them'.[15] To Debord the meta-message of the spectacle is 'that which appears is good, that which is good appears'.[16] The spectacle with its power to become social life and to produce the illusion of abundant commodities is, therefore, the hegemonising tool of late-capitalist society, but it is also the domain of politics. Since the reproduction of representations has replaced other forms of reality, the public can be designated a passive consumer of spectacles but is nonetheless addressed as an active constituent.

The bleak analysis of the spectacle within society, with its function of rewriting the past and eroding human memory, has been further developed by the theorists of postmodernism. To Baudrillard 'the age of simulation thus begins with a liquidation of all referentials',[17] producing a 'hyper-reality'; and for Barthes we live in 'a world without contradictions because it is without depth, a world wide-open and wallowing in the evident'.[18] In a society of surfaces, the spectacle is proposed as 'a new heraldic insignia for the emerging postindustrial, postmodern age of electronic communications'.[19] According to this argument, the Olympic city produced through global telecommunications networks is an illusory space, which can be played out with no actual referentials to the space/time of location. In its multiple transmissions through prime-time television the spectacular city circulates as a hyperspace detached from other historical and social meanings.

These two approaches to the theory of the spectacle differ in their emphasis on the politics of representation. MacAloon believes the genre of spectacle can provide sufficient distance for the audience to understand, with some scepticism, the playing out of global and large-scale narratives and ambiguities. Whereas Debord maintains there is little critical distance for the audience, because the production of meanings is determined by the embracing organisation of the means of representation and the collapsing of historical references. Both, however, insist upon the necessity of engagement with representation and therefore I would argue that in assuming an active relation to urban spectacle the public can contribute to the interplay between those media (persons, institutions and technologies) which will shape the city in any particular historical context.

As diverse spectators, we may be 'fascinated by the pomp, the "ostentatious signs" of power'[20] and their distortion or magnification of a city we know or inhabit, but beyond the immediacy of an orchestrated display, other social narratives and structures can be located. In the manipulation of symbols, economic and social changes are taking place and it is this power of the urban spectacle to produce effects which I propose to examine.

URBAN SPECTACLE

The association between public ceremonies and social and political struggles is familiar to many urban historians. Roy Strong, for instance, has described the Renaissance city festivals as an alliance of art and power, 'Allegories de l'Estat des temps'.[21] They were designed to glorify the monarch, whose secular power was replacing religious authority during the period which led to the establishment of the modern state. These elaborate royal spectacles included 'tournaments, ballets, state entries, firework displays, water spectacles, alfresco fetes, intermezzi, masques and masquerades',[22] and the redecorating of the city with arches and porticoes for the entry and procession of the monarch. Citizens were hired to hold flags and wave banners as the monarch was carried past. This public staging of royal magnificence was designed to signify new relations of economic importance for the city, and ushered in a mercantile class whose allegiances were to the throne.

Strong's descriptions of the lavish entertainments, the deployment of artists at the service of new political realities and the co-option of the citizens are not dissimilar to the visual presentations of the Olympic spectacle with its fireworks, its mass displays, its colourful banners, its theatrical entertainments and its broadcast music designed to impress. This historical example of urban spectacle, although informed by different economic and political institutions, foregrounds the political negotiations and promotion of public and private interests which is behind the public rhetoric and managed appearances of cultural events. The global networks of commercial, media and political entrepreneurialism which produce the modern Olympics make them however relatively difficult to analyse.

In Simson and Jennings' expose of 'power, money and drugs in the modern Olympics', they claim that access to the figures and facts of decisions made by the governing International Olympic Committee (IOC) was the hardest journalistic assignment they have undertaken.[23] And yet they do investigate some of the social and political relations being mediated by the pleasures of the sporting spectacle. When the march of the athletes begins or the medals are tallied, I sense that what I am seeing might be far from the professed ideal of the 'equality of nations' and it is on the basis of a similar hunch that they research alternative points of view. It is, nonetheless, possible to enjoy the event (even without being a sporting fan) and recognise its use of cultural symbols in the cause of global unity, as well as to analyse the politics of its creation or the politics of this enjoyment.

What concerns me here is the emphasis which is placed on the Olympic host cities and the intensive and expensive rivalry they engage in for the 'privilege' of being a 'winning city'. Millions of dollars are spent on wooing the votes of the 90 member IOC committee, but the evidence on whether a city gains or loses from the experience is contradictory. Most cities which have hosted the Olympics during the last 15 years have been left with a net deficit, except Los Angeles which made a somewhat controversial profit because it benefited the City but not the IOC.[24] And much is made of the broader economic benefits that will accrue to host cities in the belief that the Games will enhance their growth and development far beyond the immediate sporting benefits. In Barcelona, for instance, it is argued that it facilitated economic restructuring which led to greater political autonomy for the city.[25] Frequently money is spent on developing competitive sporting and cultural facilities which could have been better spent on necessary urban infrastructure. On the other hand, the dominating aspects of these programmed public events are not always experienced negatively by the inhabitants of host cities and the influx of visitors can provide the opportunity for popular and positive social transactions.[26]

Once a city has been chosen it must provide not only the venue but the dressing which will magnify and accommodate the spirit of the Games. Every city must agree to sponsor a cultural festival which will 'symbolise the universality and diversity of human culture'.[27] In Montreal (1976) before Juan Samaranch, the current President of the IOC, came to power, the non-sporting spectacle of the Olympics was officially down-played. In Moscow (1980), apparently due to Samaranch's emerging influence upon the organising committee, the mass of human bodies in the opening ceremony amazed the world. Since then the Olympic opening and closing ceremonies have been given greater attention, not only by the IOC which insists that athletes attend, but by host nations whose lavish musical and theatrical productions are designed to inspire supra-patriotic sentiment. Television networks have increasingly paid for and influenced the schedule and presentation of major events broadcast from the Olympics in order to maximise their potential audience of millions.[28]

THE BARCELONA SPECTACLE

In the Barcelona Olympics the two ceremonies were elaborately staged events performed against the backdrop of the city and lasting three hours each.[29] I want to look at these ceremonies as a set of performance genres, including the categories of game, ritual and festival[30] as well as the theatrical, allegorical and televisual. I am proposing that these genres, or modes of symbolic action, produce spaces which are metaphoric within the spectacle but which also involve reorganisation of the physical environment of the city and the redistribution of social positions. My text is a recording of the Barcelona ceremonies in which the viewing experience is interpolated by the enthusiastic Australian commentator.[31] I have supplemented these 'pictures' with information which has appeared intermittently in the printed media.

Game implies that anyone can win in fair and free contest and includes the contest of athletes and the contest of countries but is also a contest for gold, whether it be medals or money. The game space is enshrined by the construction of physical infrastructure, bought and sold before and after the games. Barcelona's investment in the reconstruction of facilities has not yet been recuperated. Its Olympic Village of 2000 apartments is still virtually uninhabited and its stadiums are struggling to find tenants.[32] In fact, the choice of sports in the Games, and the provision of particular kinds of sporting facilites to poorer nations by the IOC, is in fact determined by those interests which have most buying power.[33] The city's public debt is $2.06 billion dollars[34] whereas the financial well-being of the IOC and television corporations from the Games continues.

Ritual designates the audience as participants. At Barcelona gold masks were distributed to spectators upon entry, unifying them as viewers and viewed: 'Just imagine to be a spectator, an athlete, *a participant*. There are 650 million people who want to go and only 65 000 privileged people who are able to attend the opening ceremonies.' Despite the exclusive ticket prices ($1000 for the ceremony), the visible endorsement of the crowd was critical to its effectiveness as a ritual confirming belief in the Olympic spirit.[35]

The *theatrical* genre utilised a mythical narrative of the Greek warrior Hercules as the city's founding figure returning to Barcelona in order to induce a cosmological blessing for the event. The performance enacted a binary struggle between heaven and hell with demonic figures grovelling on the ground and airborne wonders floating above: 'It is a piece of great theatre!' An Australian event director and Barcelona's artists were the creative forces behind the opening and closing ceremonies, which nonetheless required the involvement of hundreds of volunteer actors subject to an overriding artistic vision.

The *festival* included the 'street life', the harbourside playground of the rich and famous, the artistic monuments and the frenzy of shops and traffic. Together they were transformed into the fantasy of a seasonal and libidinous space: 'It is party-time, people are dancing in the streets'. The 'freedom' of these locations was dependent upon a 'cleaning up', both physical and social, of the inner city. In fact, the elderly were moved out of apartments to make temporary residences for tourists, the prostitution industry flourished but was moved into a licensed zone of the city, and the citizens of Barcelona still pay a much resented Olympic tax.[36]

The *allegorical* carefully differentiated leaders including kings, mayors, business sponsors, and IOC delegates and assigned them to the appropriate privileged positions. The mayor of Barcelona, representing Catalonia, was officially more important than the king of Spain but the highly visible presence of the king in the stadium as the city's guest enhanced the status of Catalonia as an autonomous region. The meeting between the mayor (representing Socialist resistance), the king (monarchical power) and the President of the IOC (an ex-Franco minister) on the platform of honour was a deceptively simple gesture which masked long-term political differences. These figures of public patronage are ostensive of national interests whereas the influence of capital exchange as another form of power is less visible. This theme underpins Simson and Jennings' discussion of the fascist past of President Samaranch and some of the corrupt business dealings of his associates.[37]

The *televisual* is created by the mediating voice of the reporter and the eye of the camera which has ordered and designated the preceding spaces as transparent, neutral and available for our consumption. The reporter's role is to take the viewers on a symbolic journey—'All roads are leading to the stadium'—and up an ascending escalator to the highest realm of an aesthetic space in which the extraordinary becomes possible—'a spectacle unparalleled in the Games' long history! in the history of this planet! Of course we are overwhelmed, awestruck!'

Ultimately, it is in this prime-time hyperspace produced through television that the city of Barcelona circulates in the popular imaginary, persuading faraway individuals to watch until three in the morning. It works as a spectacle because it reveals only part of the potential realities of an Olympic city and because it demonstrates symbolic and spatial relationships which are reproducible by all 'winning cities'. The spectacle becomes integrated with the city as sign, for 'Barcelona' is naming rights and a sponsorship contract. They were the 'Barcelona Olympics' and each TV segment was marked with a trailer captioned 'Barcelona' and showing some aspect of street or city life, for example, a moped, pretty young women, or men playing bowls. Vox populi endorsements provided the viewer with a complicitous place in the willing crowd (we are them) and the enthusiastic commentator offered the disturbing rejoinder: 'Barcelona will never be the same!'

The emergence of city spectacles, not all as grand as the Olympics, but including events such as the Americas Cup, International Festivals, and World Sporting Events, can be linked to the erosion of the city's power over its economic fortune at the national level and its reassertion at the global level. In *The Condition of Postmodernity*, David Harvey argues that: 'Imaging a city through the organisation of spectacular urban spaces is a means to attract capital and people (of the right sort) in a period (since 1973) of intensified inter-urban competition and urban entrepeneurialism'.[38] In the face of the diminished power of the city as a centre for local commercial activity, the nexus of state/nation is increasingly promoting and utilising the city as a centre for cultural consumption in order to more effectively compete in the global economy. Despite the excitement of the Olympic Games spectacle something was really, and symbolically, at stake and this returns us to the city. Barcelona was both stage, player, audience and script for the Olympic prize: gold medal, golden handshake, gold-toothed smile of victory. Tourism pays and clean, hard businesses are attracted to a city which is imaged through the organisation of spectacular spaces. Harvey goes on to argue that the spectacle is used to 'build the idea of the city as a community, a city which could believe in itself sufficiently'[39] to show itself to the world. Contemporary city spectacles overcome ethnic divisions in order to add colour to the image of an harmonious community, and revitalise urban public spaces and promote artists as cultural commodities in order to project an image of safety and cleanliness combined with local vitality.

I developed a personal interest in the mythification and spectacularisation of the Olympic Games living in Melbourne whilst they were trying to win the bid for the 1996 Olympics. The city and in particular its inhabitants were coerced through the media, through slogans, through advertising, through schools and through various preliminary public events into symbolic participation in the bid. Yet many I knew were concerned about the social implications for the city and others actively tried to question the desirability of hosting the Olympics. When it was all over, billboards around the town carried the message: 'Thank You For Carrying the Torch for Melbourne'. The reinvention of Melbourne as Olympic spectacle had occurred despite a period of local economic and social crisis and, in part, as a response to the symbolic necessity of reaffirming the city's future. I wondered whether people were persuaded by the propaganda? The global illusion of participation in the Olympic spectacle seemed to permeate reality and became a principal focus for the city through its integration with policy and planning agendas. Debord argues that as a result of the integrated spectacle, 'spectacular government possesses all the means necessary to falsify the whole of production and perception'.[40]

But Melbourne did not win and the next day's headlines said 'Atlanta spoils the party: Festivities fade as Melbourne finishes fourth.'[41] The message then became that the city/state and nation's desire to compete in the world arena through global spectacle had been displaced for the 'almighty dollar had won'.[42] It is commonly accepted that the decision to send the Olympics to North America for the fourth time in 14 years was not unrelated to the television rights worth one billion dollars in direct telecasting to the Northern Hemisphere and the fact that Atlanta is the home of Coke, the Olympics' most long-standing sponsor, and of CNN, the US cable television network. The playing field was not after all flat and the production and perception of Melbourne as cultural commodity could not be falsified as inevitable winner. The ruptures in the representation made it possible for spectators to see what was behind the 'visible', and to address the competing interests of other nations and other economic forces.

Therefore it is particularly interesting to watch the process of Sydney's winning bid being transformed from euphoria, complete with its own burst of fireworks and celebratory partying, into a dialectic between material progress and 'secret' revelations. Much acclaim has been given in Australian papers to the integrity of the Sydney bid — a win for the 'true spirit' of the Olympics — emphasising healthy Australian policies on drug-testing, an environmentally progressive planning approach, a focus on sport and the athletes over everything else. But many things were not being said and were not being discussed until after the bid was over. These include the representation of women on the organising committee, the hidden costs of the Olympic construction program, false promises about the ParaOlympics, toxic wastes on the Homebush construction site,[43] little or no assessment of social displacement, weak and co-opted journalism, strains upon federal/State relations, etcetera.[44] In just three months, these questions have begun to negotiate the competing realities of the spectacle and the task for independent commentators will be to maintain a critical will and insight into these struggles as the excitement of the event comes closer.

The city will acquire new relationships to the nation, the international economy, and diverse political interests in the final staging of the spectacle. Whether the voices, which I can only describe as 'from below', of local residents, multicultural differences and Aboriginal rights are ultimately given much space or time remains to be seen. Even more problematic is the likely relationship of the Sydney Olympics to a burgeoning nationalism which will be harnessed to this event: will it reinforce old stereotypes about the sporting robustness of the 'real' Australian or allow for more pluralistic images of Australia to emerge? When the juggernaut of international capital in terms of investment, sponsorship and viewing rights has halted, will Sydney appear as a complex urban formation or simply a seaside playground? The proposed spectacle of 'The Harbour of Life' (to cost a relatively modest $14 million over four years and culminate in the year 2000) intends to represent diversity of cultural expression but is disappointingly unimaginative in its present choice of imagery and limited base of involvement.[45] Whether we like it or not, the Olympics will have made its mark on the urban landscape, on the political character of nationhood and in the pockets of Australian taxpayers.

Having suggested some of the consequences of spectacle perhaps I should reiterate that it is the power of spectacle to produce collective pleasure which makes the city both desirable and knowable.[46] In the popularity of the spectacle, we glimpse its social structures and can produce counter-representations where necessary. Since major cultural and sporting events are increasingly key components in the image of a city for its international competitiveness, the city as a spectacle will be undoubtedly influenced by those systems of power with the money and means to transform the city. But it will also be dependent on the collective participation of the public. These powers with their local effects may be peripheral to the greater power of mass-media spectacle, particularly television, which desires and dominates global networks.

Spectacle is not, therefore, the product of a hegemonic power but it is powerful. Spectacle, or hoped-for spectacle, can transform the city for a brief period and entertain members of its population, even as it diverts public attention from more disturbing or incomplete pictures of the city's past and future. Local knowledges and practices will often escape the design of the spectacle because the powers of the spectacle seek to administer and display only those social spaces which are 'good' and 'light'. Postmodern spectacle does not occupy all of social life because no illusion of instant glory can replace the fractured and uncertain social and economic operations of a contemporary city. However the power of urban spectacle to reproduce particular hierarchies of involvement must be questioned and the space for audience 'distance', if not dissent, to say 'we can't pay we won't pay' (the title of a Dario Fo play) or to point out 'the power of the crowd to make or break an event',[47] must be acknowledged.

Whether we are more bemused than seduced by the city as spectacle, the presentation of the ideas of spectacle — pleasure, leisure, wonder, amazement — as if distinct from the world of business, banks, politics and media ownership is a false one. The spaces of market and stage meet, unfold and disappear. The Olympics or any other cultural performance of a city is complicitous with both the powers of production and the powers of representation. In Calvino's city of Sophronia half the city is taken away on trailers for six months at a time; the permanent half-city is that of the carousels and the roller coaster. What disappears on its annual itinerary and reappears elsewhere is the half-city of markets and monuments which has no constant location and can attach itself to the settings of the desireable city. But the sights of the spectacle are not inducements to amnesia for they do, and will, impact upon the physical and social structures of the city in complex and pervasive ways. Therefore, it is important to attend to prime-time hyperspace for what it performs of the roving economic and political circumstances of any known city, whether Barcelona or Sydney, on the global stage.

NOTES

1. Calvino, I. (1979) *Invisible Cities*, Pan, London, p.52.
2. Molesworth, C. (1991) 'The City: Some Classical Moments', in Caws, M. (ed.) *City Images: Perspectives from Literature, Philosophy and Film*, Gordon and Breach, New York, p.14.
3. McAvaney, B. (1992) 'XXVth Olympiad Broadcast', Channel 7 Sport.
4. MacAloon, J. (ed.) (1984) *Rite, Drama Festival, Spectacle: Rehearsals Towards a Theory of Cultural Performance*, Institute for the Study of Human Issues, Philadelphia, p.8.
5. *ibid.*, p.272.
6. *ibid.*, p.273.
7. Larson, J. & Rivenburgh, N. (1991) 'A Comparative Analysis of the Australian, US, and British Telecasts of the Seoul Olympic Opening Ceremony', *Journal of Broadcasting and Electronic Media*, Vol.35, No.1, Winter, pp.75-94.
8. Takacs, F. (1992) 'Ethos and Olympism: The Ethic Principles of Olympism', *International Review for the Sociology of Sport*, Vol.27, No.3, pp.223-234.
9. *ibid.*
10. MacAloon (1984) *op. cit.*, p.269.
11. Morris, M. (1988) 'Panorama: The Live, the Death and the Living', in Foss, P. (ed.) *Island in the Stream: Myths of Place in Australian Culture*, Pluto Press, Leichhardt, p.182.
12. Crary, J. (1989) 'Spectacle, Attention, Counter-Memory', *October*, 50, Fall, p.97.
13. Debord, G. (1970) *The Society of the Spectacle*, Black and Red, Michigan, p.4.
14. *ibid.*, p.42.
15. *ibid.*, p.157.
16. *ibid.*, p.13.
17. Baudrillard, J. (1983) *Simulations*, Semiotext (3), New York, p.4.
18. Barthes, R. (1983) 'Myth Today', in Sontag, S. (ed.) *A Barthes Reader*, Hill and Wang, New York, p.132.
19. Banes, S. (1990) 'Will the Real . . . Please Stand Up? An Introduction to the Issue', *The Drama Review*, 1128, Winter, p.21.

20. Rajchman, J. (1988) 'Foucault's Art of Seeing', *October*, 44, Spring, p.195.

21. Strong, R. (1984) *Art and Power: Renaissance Festivals 1450-1650*, The Boydell Press, Woodbridge, p.173.

22. *ibid.*, p.21.

23. Simson, V. and Jennings, A. (1992) *The Lords of the Rings: Power, Money and Drugs in the Modern Olympics*, Simon & Schuster, London.

24. Lawson, C. (1985) 'Intergovernmental Challenges of the 1984 Olympic Games', *Publius*, Vol.15, No.3, Summer, pp.127-141.

25. Garcia, S. and Eyraud, D. (1991) 'Urban Economic Policies and Local Autonomy: The Case of Barcelona', *Sociologie-du-Travail*, Vol.33, No.4, pp.485-502.

26. Hiller, H. (1990) 'The Urban Transformation of a Landmark Event: The 1988 Calgary Olympics', *Urban Affairs Quarterly*, Vol.26, No.1, Sept. pp.118-137; and Ley, D. and Olds, K. (1988) 'Landscape as Spectacle: world fairs and the culture of heroic consumption', Environment and Planning D, 6, pp.191-212.

27. Simson and Jennings (1992) *op. cit.*, p.81.

28. Min, G. (1987) 'Over-Commercialization of the Olympics 1988: The Role of US Television Networks', *International Review for the Sociology of Sport*, 22, 2, pp.137-142.

29. For different methods of socio-cultural analysis of Olympic events, see Bouet, M. (1977) 'The Significance of the Olympic Phenomenon. A Preliminary Attempt at Systematic and Semiotic Analysis', *International Review of Sport Sociology*, Vol.12, No.3, pp.5-21; MacAloon, J. (1992) 'The Ethnographic Imperative in Comparative Olympic Research', *Sociology of Sport Journal*, Vol.9, No.2, June, pp.104-130; Serini, S. (1988) 'Towards an Understanding of the Social/Cultural Aspects of Special Events', *Central States Speech Journal* Vol.39, No.2, Summer, pp.146-157.

30. MacAloon (1984) *op. cit.*

31. McAvaney, B. (1992) *op. cit.*

32. *Sydney Morning Herald*, 25/9/93.

33. Eichburg, H. (1984) 'Olympic Sport — Neocolonization and Alternatives', *International Review for the Sociology of Sport*, Vol.19, No.1, pp.97-106.

34. *Sydney Morning Herald*, 25/9/93.

35. Peacock, J. (1985) 'An Anthropologist Goes to the Olympics', *Social Science Newsletter*, Vol.70, No.2, Summer, pp.77-81.

36. *Sydney Morning Herald*, 25/9/93.

37. Simson and Jennings (1992) *op. cit.*

38. Harvey, D. (1989) *The Condition of Postmodernity: Selected Interviews and Other Writings* (ed.) Gordon, C., Basil Blackwell, Oxford, p.92.

39. *ibid.*, p.89.

40. Debord, G. (1990) *Comments on the Society of the Spectacle*, Verso, London, p.19.

41. *The Age*, 19/9/1990.

42. *ibid.*

43. Beder, S. (1993) 'Sydney's Toxic Green Olympics', *Current Affairs Bulletin*, Nov., pp.12-18.

44. *Sydney Morning Herald*, September-November 1993.
45. Sydney Olympic 2000 Bid Limited (1993) *Sydney 2000: Harbour of Life*, Cultural Program Promotional Document.
46. Foucault, M. (1984) *Power/Knowledge*, Pantheon, New York.
47. Morris (1988) *op. cit.*, p.184.

13

Imagining the city: contradictory tales of space and place

Jan Larbalestier

In this chapter I explore some of the ways in which discourses about cities constitute subjectivities and relations of difference.[1] Locating ourselves and others in cities is an engagement with processes of social differentiation. Such processes are embedded in various social relations of inequality: social relations of power and privilege, of age, class, ethnicity, sex, sexuality and race. In the planning, design and development of urban environments we need to consider the diversity of human needs and the culturally diverse, contested and complex ways of locating ourselves and others in 'place'.

Discourses about cities reaffirm boundaries and places as fixed points of reference in terms of a logic of binary opposition. At the same time such discourses highlight the fluidity and indeterminacy of boundaries. Cities are firmly fixed within a rural/urban process of differentiation. This contrasting of 'town and country' has often been noted: we have Jane Austen's Darcy claiming that in 'a country neighbourhood you move in a very confined and unvarying society',[2] and Carol Clover, writing on contemporary film, observing that in horror films, people 'from the country (. . . people construed as the threatening rural Other) are people not like us'.[3] A pervasive and continuing thread in shaping such discourses is an aesthetic sensibility: a romanticism of difference. This is to say that 'the city', as experience, as location, as concept is mediated by and through various romantic images.[4]

Elizabeth Wilson argues that the idea of the 'sublime' in the tradition of romanticism — ranging from Edmond Burke's suggestion that the 'sublime' was 'productive of the strongest emotion' to vaguer intimations of terror and beauty, to contemporary understandings of the sublime as the representation of the unrepresentable — has 'seeped into our collective consciousness to become one of the ways in which [experiences of urbanisation are] understood, re-evaluated and transformed'.[5] Jukes presents a similar view, suggesting that modern metropolitan markets provide not only physical necessities 'but the imaginative requirements of existence: fantasy, escapism, glamour, magic, romance'.[6] Romantic sensibilities then have important implications for ways in which people locate themselves and are located by others in spaces and places.

Belonging and relating are bound up with space and place. In distinguishing places and spaces I follow de Certeau.[7] Place has a distinct location which it defines, place is fixed. Two things can not be in the same location. The city of Sydney is located on the east coast of Australia beside a harbour, it cannot at the same time be located in the centre of Australia next to Alice Springs. Space in contrast is composed of intersections of mobile elements with shifting often indeterminate borders (see below).

As Barthes suggests '[we] speak our city . . . inhabit it, walk through it, look at it'.[8] City places and spaces are continually 'read' (interpreted) in various ways, by a variety of people pursuing a variety of endeavours, in walking, in working, in reading, in speaking, in all or any of our everyday practices. The point I want to stress is that who we are, or might be, is constantly negotiated. We (our places and spaces) are in a sense continually coming into being. We are continually acting on and reacting to our environments. At the same time, attachments to specific locations and being located in place and space provide possibilities for a sense of continuity in our experiences of individuality and self-awareness.

CITY TALES

'Cities' are places where contemporary cultural offerings provide fetishised blurring of boundaries, marvellous, fantastic and absurd contradictions. Consumers are presented with such objects of desire as Country Road's 'Wilderness' clothing for city life and freshly squeezed orange juice from bottles (admittedly with a limited shelf life). Elvis is alive and well in Franklin's 'BIG FRESH' supermarket, strolling aisles, loving us tenderly while we make choices, interpreting, consuming sounds, sights and spaces. Amid increasing poverty for many there are ever increasing possibilities for consumption: cities for pleasure on Golden Sunshine coasts with Australia's highest rate of unemployment.[9] I find street scenes with women marching to 'take back the night'; street scenes with increasing violence toward homosexual strangers while Gay and Lesbian Mardi Gras festivals celebrate gay cultures. Streets I walk reveal private practices in public spaces, plenty of room, home for the homeless. Resident aliens?

Writing thus about cities from 'my place', situates that place in various ways: academic, geographic, political, yet indeterminant. In imagining 'the city' we also imaginatively constitute subjectivities, both our own and others, we tell stories of place which valorise, maintain and reproduce differences: different places and spaces, different people, different subjects.

I will explore these issues of differentiation and subjectivity by recounting some tales of the city. I aim to show the interweaving of both imaginative understandings and processes of romanticism in constituting and situating ourselves and others in city sites: to illustrate various 'spatialising practices' which are engendered and embedded in particular social relations.[10] Unlike de Certeau's sexless subjects, however, the subjects of these tales have relationships which are embedded in relations of age, class, gender, and race. These stories attest to effects of 'micro-technologies of power', as well as to resistance, collusion and contradiction.

The first narrative, a feminist tale, is taken from a short story by Barbara Wilson.[11] The opening pages describe attempts by persons unknown to reappropriate certain city places (in this case London). In the process new spaces were created while the ambiguity and indeterminacy of sites were highlighted. An enamel plaque at 22 Hyde Park Gate stating that Leslie Stephen had lived there was joined by a new plate informing the passerby that this was where writer Virginia Woolf and painter Vanessa Bell had spent their childhoods. In the following weeks other blue plaques were attached to buildings. Joining a plaque in Primrose Hill which read that Yeats had lived in the house was another informing readers that Sylvia Plath wrote *Ariel* poems here before committing suicide in 1963. At 20 Marsfield Gardens a plaque stating that Sigmund Freud spent the last year of his life there was joined by another recording that Anna Freud had lived for 42 years at the address. The new plaques not only destabilised notions of places as male, they also served to represent the past in the present as part of contemporary struggles about women's place in, and use of, urban spaces.

My second city tale is an amalgam of many stories. A mother and daughter come to Sydney for a holiday. The women are not complete strangers to the big city, but it is not home. They view their home town as friendlier, safer and, although not without glamour, less multi-cultural, less sophisticated, far less exciting. Being in Sydney reinforces their sense of themselves, as belonging to and coming from another place. Both women continually constitute 'the city' as experience, as location, as concept. Such imaginings of space shape contexts in which mother/daughter relations are constituted, negotiated, reinforced and possibly transformed.

For the mother and daughter Sydney is romanticised and 'othered' as a place of fascination, of danger, of pleasure, of increased possibilities for consumption and most importantly increased opportunities for sociability. They stay with friends in an inner-city suburb, close to transport and the city centre. Both women enjoy the visit, shopping, visiting museums, art galleries and Darling Harbour — sometimes together, sometimes singularly, sometimes with friends. The daughter goes to nightclubs noted for their great dance music and sexual harassment free environments. Sydney is experienced as pleasurable, exciting and liberating for women, liberating for mothers and daughters. They feel 'good' there. [12]

Another view of the city, however, is generated by the daughter's intended visit to friends living in a distant suburb. The ground of the women's interaction shifts, in relation to each other and in relation to 'the city'. The proposed visit generates tension between mother and daughter. The mother becomes afraid for her daughter, fearful of this city. To reach her friends the daughter must walk to the railway station — an inner-city station, a site sensationalised/sexualised/exoticised by sections of the media as a place of deviancy, of violence, a place frequented by would-be rapists, bag snatchers, muggers, misfits in general — people not like us. More alien residents?

Integral to media representations of this inner-city station is its proximity to Koori residents living in what one magazine writer sensationalises as Australia's 'most notorious street'. [13] As de Certeau suggests 'rumours propagated by the media' totalise, 'wipe out' diversity, rumours 'wipe out' other ways of knowing. [14] In the process of such 'spatialising practices' a 'notorious' place is thus construed as encompassing the station which then becomes part of a marginalised space: a black urban ghetto. A Koori presence, as nearby residents and users of Redfern Station, becomes an imaginary association with an imagined space and thus a basis for explaining any and all delinquent behaviours at the station.

The mother's fears, though vaguely expressed, are clearly indicated. Big cities are dangerous for women. Young women should not 'walk unattended upon city streets',[15] or at least these city streets, or travel alone on this city's trains. Sydney train stations are dangerous places and some more dangerous than others. The daughter, although not sharing her mother's fears, needs to negotiate permitted conditions of travel. Agreement is reached following assurances on the daughter's part of careful, appropriate and motherly acceptable behaviour during the journey. The daughter is then able and enabled to make her journey across the city. She is given a lift to the station and attended by a friend while waiting on the platform for her train. The waiters/watchers see all sorts and manner of people alighting from and catching trains, numerous possibilities for labelling, categorising, stigmatising, and thereby constituting other subjectivities: Kooris, Greek, Irish, Italian, Lebanese, parents, grandparents, mothers, fathers, residents, non-residents, would-be-attackers, bag-snatchers? Who and what are they? All or any of these?

Urban/rural distinctions in Australian contexts take on particular complexities, particular contradictions. As a colonised place, struggles over land reflect, among other things, powerful political and symbolic struggles in the realm of what de Certeau refers to as 'spatialising practices'. Britain's cultural appropriation of another's place and space acts to reduce its spatial dimensions to a civilisation/ wilderness, city/outback divide. Indigenous landscapes, sites of symbolic, textual and political meanings are written over, appropriated, demolished, reconstructed — different stories were told. Stories of taming the land, overcoming the barbarians: a conquest by the 'brave-hearted' who then lay their victories 'at the feet of great cities', an heroic mythologising of a made-over world — a necropolis.[16]

My final city tale was headlined in the Australian media recently as: 'City v Country in Video Battle'.[17] The city location was Marrickville, about eight kilometres from Sydney's city centre marked as the General Post Office (GPO). Moss Vale was the country location about 121 kilometres south-west of Sydney. Local government councils in both locations had rejected applications for fun parlours. The appellate body, the Land and Environment Court, heard appeals against the decisions of each council. Similar evidence was presented in each case as 'respected citizens from both municipalities' expressed their fears to the court.[18] Fun parlours, it was claimed, were venues for 'children already under-motivated and low in self-esteem. [Such children] need to share their disillusion, to engage in activities of a mindless and fantastical nature and generally to become susceptible to behaviour that borders on or transgresses the legal.'[19] In brief fun parlours served to increase crime rates, encourage 'drugs and delinquency', 'truancy and disorder'.[20]

The court decided to allow a fun parlour to be established in Moss Vale but decided against such an establishment for Marrickville. Shaping decisions in both cases were the ways in which the areas were represented to the court. Urban Marrickville was said to have a juvenile problem that was 'almost a situation of anarchy', its population was ethnically diverse, there was 'very high unemployment and a youth crime rate that ran about double the Sydney average'.[21] In contrast Moss Vale was seen as more law abiding, more ethnically homogeneous, with more employed (employable?) people. A fun parlour for this untroubled, orderly rural area the court decided, 'may well be beneficial' and 'might help reduce juvenile *misbehaviour* [as opposed to crime?] by giving children a leisure activity other than organised sport'.[22] Evidence from a planning consultant attempted to counter doubts expressed by some of Moss Vale's concerned citizens. The consultant suggested that 'amusement centres caused trouble only where there was a background of crime, which meant that there was a lower risk in Moss Vale than in Sydney'.[23] In presenting his case the consultant invented a new and stigmatised space as Marrickville was made to encompass all Sydney.

Pin-ball machines, in twos or threes, do exist in some Marrickville retail establishments, apparently without generating disorder in the form of increased juvenile crime. The court, however, concluded that the allocation of whole establishments to pinball machines with its accompanying cacophony of 'blazing electronics' and 'blaring music' would, in the light of views presented to the court, 'be equivalent to dousing a smouldering bushfire with a liberal quantity of petrol'.[24]

Cultural perceptions about difference inform the court's decisions. Evidence given to the Land and Environment Court fitted into already existing cultural understandings about rural/urban distinctions. The boundaries can (and do) shift (Moss Vale was represented in the same newspaper the next day as an 'outer urban area')[25] but a city/country, urban/rural distinction remains. In the present text Marrickville and Moss Vale were viewed as inherently different places and spaces. The text is framed by the 'City v Country' heading, while the substance of the text itself reinforces those divisions. Marrickville-Sydney-the City has juvenile *crime*, Moss Vale-the Town-the Country has juvenile *misbehaviour*. The country town Moss Vale is ordered, relatively harmonious but restricted ('a very confined and unvarying society'?) in terms of its leisure offerings for 'kids'. Marrickville's diversity, however, is only negatively assessed — kids there presumably do not have opportunities to play organised sport and without a fun parlour they have 'nothing to do' except apparently contribute to disorder and anarchy.

Fun parlours, the newspaper article suggests in regard to the court's decisions, are 'good for country kids' but 'bad for city kids'.[26] Despite views to the contrary that fun parlours are inherently 'bad' the qualities of 'badness' or 'goodness' attached to them are considered by the court to be determined by particular environments. Environments shaped by unstated assumptions of class and ethnicity and inhabited by similarly classified individuals.

The young in both areas inhabit the text as sexless bodies. Two accompanying photographs in the newspaper report tell a story of their own. The bodies in the visual images are male. One photograph is much larger than the other. The larger photograph shows three 'European' looking male Moss Vale youths playing 'Lethal Enforcers' while the smaller visual shows seven 'Asian' looking males, mostly seated, and not playing a sex-specific fun parlour game.[27] The 'City v Country' battle in this context has clear racist and sexist implications — drugs, disorder, delinquency are attributes of young Asian males, corrupting yet corrupted by city life. Paradoxically, the chief assessor's use of metaphor 'dousing a smouldering bushfire with . . . petrol', conjures a brief glimpse of the unpredictable dangers of country life as he allows the country to inhabit the city in his text.

CONCLUSION

Cities, like totems, are good 'to think'.[28] What is problematic and needs to be resisted is the impulse to allow particular understandings and individual experiences to serve as representative of all possible experience and knowledge of places and spaces. The city tales described above indicate ways in which our romantic imaginings of spaces and places take on specific romanticised, sexed, racialised and classed forms. They are replete with contradictory and contested meanings.

Linking people with places, constituting spaces, stigmatising people and spaces in certain contexts have potential contradictory effects. On the one hand diverse experiences are elided and counter-discourses silenced, processes serving to maintain and reinforce relations of power and inequality. On the other hand, they serve to illuminate struggles over meaning.

In the case of Redfern Station such struggles over meaning are a legacy of Australia's colonial heritage: the ongoing attempts to control and reproduce the conditions of being subject for indigenous Australians; conditions of being subject which are constituted in relation to 'other' undifferentiated Australians. Such struggles over meaning may act as 'micro technologies of power', but may also serve to generate counter-discourses in academic papers, in everyday practices and most significantly by indigenous people themselves.[29]

Cities, like bodies, are sites of symbolic, textual and political interpretation and struggle.[30] Our location in them in relation to our sense of self and others is constantly being transformed. Spaces and places are continually created and recreated in stories, fiction of all kinds, in the media, in appellate courts, in everyday talk, in everyday practices. Cities (sui generis) are beyond our universalising gaze: 'Totalising visions . . . can never capture all the meanings and significations of the urban . . .'.[31] Despite the materiality of everyday experiences, cities like Benedict Anderson's nations[32] are constituted (inter alia) as imagined places for imagined communities.

Representing cities, their sites and subjects, in academic discourses, in Land and Environment Courts, in urban planning, is a difficult, partial and political process. We need to continually explore the limits and possibilities of such analyses; to be critically aware of ways in which discourses work towards closure and so work to negate diversity, contradiction and contestation.

Much has been said and written about making cities better places for their inhabitants. Writers stress the need to integrate physical and social planning and to consider the variety of people and cultures in cites; the need to enable the relatively disadvantaged to participate in planning.[33] Unless we acknowledge and continually work with diversity and contradiction the majority of city users, along with aspects of their 'sublime' and 'imaginative' requirements of existence, will be caught between 'a rock and a very hard place' indeed.

NOTES

1. Shaping my interest in discourses about cities is a concern with politics of cultural representation and constitutions of difference in western discourses; an interest which grew out of my work on western representations of indigenous peoples in Australia. See, for example, Fabian, J. (1983) *Time and the Other: How Anthropology Makes its Object*, Columbia University Press, New York; Larbalestier, J. (1990) ' "Amity and Kindness" in the Never Never: Ideology and Aboriginal-European Relations in the Northern Territory', in Marcus, J. (ed.) *Writing Australian Culture*, Special Issue Series (Social Analysis), No.27; Larbalestier, J. (1991) 'Through Their Own Eyes: An Interpretation of Aboriginal women's Writing', in Bottomley, G. de Lepervanche, M. & Martin, J. (eds.) *Intersexions*, Allen & Unwin, Sydney; McGrane, B. (1989) *Beyond Anthropology*, Columbia University Press, New York; Said, E. (1985) 'Orientalism Reconsidered', *Cultural Critique*, 1. Fall, pp.89-107. Western representations of its 'others' is constituted (inter alia) by classed, racialised and sexed shaping of differences. It is these interests (strongly informed by feminist theory) that have helped to shape my reading on cities and processes of urbanisation.

2. Austin, J. (1813) *Pride and Prejudice*, Gordon Classic Library, p.36.

3. Clover, C. (1992) *Men, Women and Chainsaws*, Princeton University Press, New Jersey, p.124.

4. Wilson, E. (1991) *The Sphinx in the City: Urban Life, the Control of Disorder, and Women*, University of California Press, Berkeley.

5. *ibid.*, pp.21-23.

6. Jukes, P. (1990) *A Shout in the Streets*, Faber & Faber, London, p.99. See also Ewen, S & E. (1982) *Channels of Desire: Mass Images and the Shaping of American Consciousness*, McGraw Hill, New York.

7. de Certeau (1988) *ibid.*

8. Cited in de Certeau, (1988) *op. cit.*, p.219.

9. Mullins, P. (1993) 'Decline of the Old, Rise of the New: Late Twentieth Century Australian Urbanisation', in Najman, J. M. and Western, J. S. (eds.) *A Sociology of Australian Society*, Macmillan, Melbourne.

10. de Certeau (1988) *op. cit.*, p.116; Dickens, P. (1990) *Urban Sociology: Society, Locality and Human Nature*, Harvester Wheatsheaf, Hertfordshire; Modjeska, D. (ed.) (1989) *Inner Cities*, Penguin, Victoria.

11. Wilson, B. (1992) 'Theft of the Poet', in Paretsky, S. (ed.) *A Woman's Eye*, Virago.

12. de Certeau (1988) *op. cit.*, p.108.

13. Leser, D. (1990) 'Our Place', *G.H.*, June, p.51.

14. de Certeau (1988) *op. cit.*, pp.107-108.

15. Wilson (1992) *op. cit.*, p.74.

16. The story of European cultural appropriations is of course more complex than I indicate here. See Gunn, A. (1908) *We of the Never-Never*, Hutchinson of Australia, Melbourne, p.57, p.237.

17. *Sydney Morning Herald*, 6/4/93.

18. *ibid.*
19. *ibid.*
20. *ibid.*
21. *ibid.*
22. *ibid.*
23. *ibid.*
24. *ibid.*
25. *Sydney Morning Herald*, 7/4/93.
26. *ibid.*
27. Fun-parlours are represented in the text as masculine spaces with masculine technologies for male players: toys for the boys!
28. cf. Levi-Strauss, C. (1964) *Totemism*, Merlin Press, London.
29. For example, Gilbert, K. (1978) *People Are Legends*, University of Queensland Press; and Davis, J. & B. Hodge (eds) (1985) *Aboriginal Writing Today*, AIAS, Canberra.
30. Corrigan, C. (1992) 'Fashion, Beauty and Feminism', *Meanjin*, 1, pp.107-122; Gatens, M. (1988) 'Towards a Feminist Philosophy of the Body', *Crossing Boundaries: Feminisms and the Critique of Knowledges*, Allen & Unwin; Grosz, E. (1987) 'Notes Towards a Corporeal Feminism', *Australian Feminist Studies*, 5, pp.1-16.
31. Soja, E. (1989) *Postmodern Geographies: The Reassertion of Space in Critical Social Theory*, Verso, London, p.247.
32. Anderson, B. (1983) *Imagined Communities*, Verso, NLB, London.
33. Cass, B. (1991) *The Housing Needs of Women and Children*, AGPS, Canberra; Minnery, J. R. (1991) *Urban Form and Development Strategies: Equity, Environmental and Economic Implication*, The National Housing Strategy, AGPS, Canberra; Stretton, H. (1989) *Ideas for Australian Cities*, Transit, Australian Publishing; Watson, S. (1993) 'Cities of Dreams and Fantasy: Social planning in a postmodern era', in Freestone, R. (ed.) *Spirited Cities*, The Federation Press, Sydney.

14

The place of imagination: public housing for older women

Bette O'Brien

'changes in the way we imagine, think, plan and rationalise are bound to have material consequences'[1]

A massive national demand is looming in Australia for public housing for women aged 55 and over. The nature of this demand, and the inadequacy of existing government policies to meet it indicates that there is a need to rethink the current approach to housing older women in the public sector. This rethinking needs, I believe, to move outside the bounds of present perceptions of public housing to a more inventive, innovative, creative and insightful realm; into what I call the place of imagination. The place I have in mind is an arena where we can seek alternate possibilities to the universal housing models which have appeared during the modernist historical period. Our entrance into this place can only occur however if we also recognise the corollary, that imagination has a place in our approach to public housing. Imagination has a place in our thinking, our planning, our rationalising and in the material consequences of this process.

The place of imagination is a thinking space suggested by feminists who have recognised the connection between the experiental and perceptual, and who have given emphasis to the postmodern appreciation of difference. The modernist canon stresses the need for objectivity and rationality in the quest for knowledge. This striving after objective detachment has, however, constrained our imagination. Imagination relies on a style of thinking whereby the objective and the subjective merge and participate in the creation of meaning. Reasoning is enhanced when subjective aspects such as intuition and empathy, the body and senses, and emotions and feelings are called forth as contributing elements of the imaginative thought process. A more fluid, flexible and contingent mode of analysis is sponsored, and solutions of greater richness and complexity are made possible.

Once the subjective aspects of knowledge are incorporated into our thinking, submerged understandings emerge. It becomes impossible to deny the existence of multiple realities, meanings and perspectives, and the significance of alternative subjectivities and experience. Imaginative thinking opens up a place in which suppressed thoughts and experience can reappear. In this place it is possible to become more aware of one's biases, prejudices and ignorance, and to stretch the borders of understanding.

Creativity becomes a vital component when it is recognised that knowledge arises from a creative synthesis of the imagination, involving a mediation between understanding and sense perception.[2] Our imaginative realm provides for engaging the whole human vital repertoire of thinking, willing, desiring and feeling. We can divest ourselves of the previous habits of thought, feeling and action, and enter into the subjunctive mood of what can be imagined. In doing so, we can engage in an activity I refer to as strategies of invention.[3]

Imaginative thoughts about public housing for older women will be reflected in what older women may see as the most important aspect of public housing, the dwelling that is provided. The hammer of the carpenter will continue to be guided by the creativity of the policy maker.

CURRENT NEEDS, FUTURE TRENDS

Public housing policy has failed to take into account the diversity of older women's needs and experiences, and the requirement for a corresponding diversity of housing provision. Feminist perspectives on housing[4] have concentrated on issues such as the location of this housing, size of the accommodation provided, safety and security offered by the residence and surroundings, and the isolation experienced by some older women accommodated in public housing. This literature has also touched upon the importance of design in the ability of housing to provide appropriate living conditions for older women, the need to look at shared public housing as an option, and the absence of female values in housing provision. It is the last three issues to which I will return in my discussion of the place of imagination.

Public housing for older women in Australia has reached crisis point. The large increase currently occuring in national demand for public housing for older women can be expected to continue throughout the next 30 years and beyond. This increase in demand will be dramatic given the fact that Australia's population of persons aged 65 and over is growing at a rate of 2.5% per annum, nearly twice as fast as the population as a whole, and will continue to grow at a considerably faster rate than the total population for several decades. This rapid ageing of the population is being generated by a number of factors, including the international post-World War I 'baby boom' of 1918, the ageing of the massive influx of immigrants in the early post-World War II years,[5] and the mortality reductions which are leading to an increased life expectancy for older people and a corresponding lengthening of the period of ageing.[6] Given the predominance of women in the aged population, there will be an an increased requirement for services and facilities used by older women, including public housing.

A large percentage of the public housing required by older women in the years to come will fall into the 'lone person' category. Over the last two decades there has been a large increase in the number of female single person households and this trend is continuing. Nearly twice as many women as men currently require lone person public housing in NSW in the later years of their life.[7] Reasons for this widening differential include, as the principal cause, the greater longevity of women relative to men (currently five to six years); a longevity which continues to increase. Other reasons include an increase in the number of divorces and separations, and a lower incidence of marriage.[8] These factors will significantly increase the number of older women requiring single person public housing in the future.

One commentator has estimated that there could be an increase of as much as 30% in the number of older single person households between 1986 and 2001.[9] In the case of single person households occupied by older women we could expect this figure to be proportionately higher. Many of the older women requiring lone person accommodation in the future will be in receipt of a government pension, will never have had the opportunity to purchase a house, and will therefore need public housing. Additional demand for public housing will also result from a limitation on the growth rate of nursing home places, and the private sector's reduced capacity to supply low cost rental accommodation, due to, among other factors, a sharp decline in boarding houses in NSW since 1986.[10]

The NSW Department of Housing appears fully aware of the growing demand for public housing for older women, and has stated that this demand 'has serious implications for the directions of housing policies in Australia in general and New South Wales in particular'.[11] The department has recognised the need to 'increase the stock of accommodation, to explore different procurement options and make better use of existing stock' to ease this demand.[12] This is a very important recognition, especially when it is noted that the department's average waiting times for allocation of lone pensioner housing in NSW have varied between 21 months and four years since 1985.[13] Waiting times have been significantly larger for housing requested in particular housing zones, and for certain types of pensioner housing.

In attempting to define the future direction of public housing policies related to older women, demand presents itself as the crucial issue, however this issue does not stand alone. Another issue of particular importance is the nature of the housing models which will be employed by public housing authorities throughout Australia. Older women's housing satisfaction will be dependent on these models.

THE TRADITIONAL APPROACH

The current approach to housing older women in the public sector neglects vital considerations such as the effects of gender, cultural background and age on housing satisfaction. The requirement for a diversity of housing options has been overlooked in favour of universalistic and monocultural solutions. This absence of alternate models to provide for particular needs works to the detriment of older women. For example, many such women from non-English speaking backgrounds experience alienation and isolation because existing allocation policies do not provide for these women being housed in locations where cultural and linguistic support is available. Older women may also be allocated accommodation remote from community facilities and services they have been using for many years, such as churches, community art spaces, social clubs, or even a trusted personal physician. This of course presents numerous problems, including access factors such as transport, time and the cost of fares.[14] Lower

levels of car ownership among older women and their greater reluctance to venture out alone, and at night, contribute to such
problems.

The exclusion of an adequate consideration of gender and cultural
specificity in public housing policy formulation has resulted in
inappropriate forms of public housing for many older women, which
fail to adequately cater for a continuance of the particular and different
lifestyles established by these women during their lifetime. In many
cases the housing provided leads to a severance of this lifestyle. For
example, the provision of a bedsitter or one bedroom flat to a woman
who has been used to overnight visits by family members or friends will
adversely affect her quality of life. Loneliness and other negative
consequences of public housing for older women could be alleviated if
such women were given an adequate opportunity to define their
particular public housing needs and possible solutions.

THE PLACE OF IMAGINATION

An imaginative approach towards public housing solutions for older
women would be far more flexible, inventive and innovative,
democratic and open ended, and aware of its own contingency
and limitations, than has been the case until now. Housing authorities
including the NSW Department of Housing and the Victorian
Ministry of Housing, and a number of local councils in NSW,
have recently added shared housing to the range of accommodation
offered. This is a step in the right direction, but the two types of
housing are still seen as polar opposites, and imaginative options
which rather see them as part of a continuum continue to elude
planning departments.

Design is a vital element in the ability of housing to provide
appropriate living conditions for older women. Speakers at the 1985
and 1987 National Women's Housing Conferences mentioned the
requirement for flexibility and innovation in design. This requirement
calls for both architects and users to participate in an imaginative
dialectic. Design has traditionally commenced with the viewpoint of
the architect and emphasised the importance of form over function. In
contrast, an approach is required which embraces a concern with
environmental meaning and is suspicious of standardised solutions.
Design according to this approach starts with the viewpoint of users
and allows a definition of meaning which incorporates function and
social activities. Public housing designed according to the perspective
of older women would enable these women to positively value their

homes, and would provide spaces that were as adaptable as possible to individual women's needs and wants.[15]

By entering the place of imagination to rethink public housing, policy makers could take account of subjective experiences, be receptive to the incorporation of disparate ideas, and incorporate multiple meanings and perspectives into their policies. Policy makers engaging in this process would also recognise the need to give voice to the 'other', and to make a more concerted effort to bring human values back into the analytical realm. In adopting this approach, an emphasis would be placed on ethnographic discourse to reveal public housing solutions that cater to a diversity of cultural backgrounds.

Exploration would be a prime goal, as would the aim of being creative, insightful, and entertaining alternate possibilities. Investigation would be tentative and exploratory, would incorporate paradox, and would replace the modernist either/or distinction with an and/also approach. This approach to housing older women would not privilege one truth, correct interpretation or right method. Instead knowledges, methods, interpretations would 'be judged and used according to their appropriateness to a given context, a specific strategy and particular effects'.[16] Knowledge would be accessed through communication with older women, emerge holistically and be interpersonal from the start.[17]

This approach to public housing acknowledges that older women from diverse cultural backgrounds will impute different meanings to their living circumstances. A pluralism of values would be represented in public housing to reflect the diverse values of inhabitants. The incorporation of a variety of values, including those related to gender is long overdue, as recognised by a number of feminist scholars who have noted the absence of 'feminine' principles in planning and housing.[18]

The inclusion of such principles can make a significant difference to the built environment. The outcome can be said to be more user oriented than designer oriented, more functional than formal, more flexible than fixed, more organically ordered than abstracted/systematised, and more holistic/complex than specialised/one dimensional.[19]

The place of imagination would be characterised by the interpretation rather than the legislation of values. A departure from the security of modernist moorings and an entrance into the place of imagination would mean we would be able to change the way we think, plan and rationalise. By incorporating the thoughts, values and interets of older women, we would then be in a position to provide more appropriate public housing for older women.

NOTES

1. Harvey, D. (1989) *The Condition of Postmodernity: An Enquiry into the Origins of Cultural Change*, Basil Blackwell, Oxford & Cambridge, p.48.
2. Code, L. (1991) *What Can She Know?: Feminist Theory and the Construction of Knowledge*, Cornell University Press, Ithaca and London, p.56.
3. O'Brien, E. (1993) 'Postmodern Planning: a need for "strategies of invention"', *Postmodern Cities Conference Proceedings*, Department of Urban and Regional Planning, The University of Sydney, April.
4. Coleman, L. and Watson, S. (1987) *Women over Sixty: A Study of the Housing, Economic and Social Circumstances of Older Women*, Australian Institute of Urban Studies, Canberra.
5. Hugo, G. (1989) 'Ageing in Australia: the spatial implications', *Urban Policy and Research*, Vol.5, No.1, pp.24-25.
6. NSW Department of Housing (1990) *Directions on Ageing in NSW: Housing*, Office of the Ageing, NSW Premiers Department, NSW, p.1.
7. *ibid.*, p.2.
8. *ibid.*, p.20.
9. Burnley (1988) cited in NSW Department of Housing (1990) *op. cit.*, p.20.
10. NSW Department of Housing (1990) *op. cit.*, pp.20-25.
11. *ibid.*, p.43.
12. *ibid.*, p.25.
13. NSW Department of Housing (1985/6-1990/1) *Annual Reports*.
14. O'Brien, E. (1992) 'Public Housing for Older Women: developing a postmodern-feminist approach attuned to cultural specificity', (unpublished thesis), Department of Urban and Regional Planning, the University of Sydney, pp.37-39; pp.51-53.
15. Goodchild, B. (1991) 'Postmodernism and Housing: A Guide to Design Theory', *Housing Studies*, Vol.6, No.2, pp.132-133; p.141.
16. Grosz, E. (1986) 'What is Feminist Theory?' in Pateman, C. and Grosz, E. (eds) *Feminist Challenges: Social and Political Theory*, Allen and Unwin, Sydney, p.204.
17. Davidson, D. (1991) 'Epistemology Externalised', *Dialectica*, Vol.45, Nos.2-3, pp.191-202.
18. For example, McDowell, L. (1983) 'Towards an understanding of the gender division of urban space', *Environment & Planning D: Society and Space*, 1, pp.59-72; Watson, S. (1988) *Accommodating Inequality: Gender and Housing*, Allen & Unwin, Sydney.
19. Kennedy, M. I. (1981) 'Toward a Rediscovery of "Feminine" Principles in Architecture and Planning', *Women's Studies International Quarterly*, Vol.4, No.1, pp.75-81.

15

Stirring up the city: housing and planning in a multicultural society

Sophie Watson and Alec McGillivray

The physical picture and, to a large extent, reality of modern urbanism in Australia is of striking skylines, surrounded by still vibrant older areas of terrace housing, three to ten-storey apartments and industry, surrounded by vast expanses of low-density housing and office and industrial parks—this last variant is described as anything from the democratic provision of the 'Australian Dream'[1] to unsustainable, alienating urban sprawl.[2] This chapter fits in to a number of international debates on 'suburbia'—the social pros and cons, ecological considerations, urban consolidation (termed densification in the US, intensification in Canada), the lack of choice in housing form, and others—yet deals with a specific element often overlooked. In recent decades the Australian suburban social landscape has seen a significant influx of migrants from around the world. This represents a growing acceptance of multiculturalism both politically and in terms of the wider population. The question is how has this multiculturalism represented itself in the physical landscape? Outwardly, it seems not to have. As one engineer spoken to in the study researching this question describes housing choice, 'there are standard cluster homes, standard town houses, standard 600 square metre blocks, standard quarter acre blocks'. And these standards are very much based on dominant Anglo-Australian planning and construction models. The focus of this chapter is on housing, but also looks at local government planning to see how it is dealing with issues of multiculturalism, change and difference.

A BRIEF HISTORICAL PICTURE

The history of land subdivision, infrastructure provision and planning is similar to that in the US, England and Canada.[3] It is also based largely on imported ideas from the former two. Early city growth of Sydney, Melbourne and other colonial cities was usually chaotic. In Sydney, harbour and land forms made a simple grid pattern untenable and Robert Freestone notes, 'residential development was largely an uncoordinated staging, by independent actors, of land survey, subdivision, dwelling construction and infrastructure provision'.[4] The single storey cottage/bungalow was the first major housing type, and became the ideal as urban reformers in the late 1800s began campaigning on issues such as sewerage, open space, separation of land use, civic beautification and general slum clearance. Acts like the *New South Wales (NSW) Width of Street and Lanes Act 1881* set up some conventions and early Australian planners such as John Keily, John Sulman, Charles Reade, Saxil Tuxen, Walter Scott Griffith and Walter Burley Griffin started thinking in terms of ordered urban morphology. Most of this early planning was heavily influenced by the British garden city movement, and by Raymond Unwin in particular. The more comprehensive plans were rarely realised, but the ideal housing form that was the cornerstone of much writing was. This was clearly the detached house with prescribed ample yard space and it became the suburban development standard.

In the inter-war period new ideas were incorporated, or added, to some already advocated by Griffin. Most notable was the neigbourhood unit and a hierarchy of automobile transportation roads. This led to a more planned sprawl with a continued similarity in house form. Freestone writes, 'while integrating more diverse and sophisticated influences, and now drawing more directly on American experience, the reform message being pushed in the 1940s and early 1950s was not dissimilar in flavour, or content, to the earlier campaign associated with the garden city movement'.[5] The 'more sophisticated influences' in this more planned expansion of the city were generally technical; a refining of standards. Models were set up that offered rules on how much open space was needed per a set population, how to judge and provide for schools, and how to get people back and forth from the central business district. Suburban public space was thus geared to traffic and generally unused or underused boulevard sidings (providing 'visual amenity' and room to expand road width), school playgrounds, and active recreational facilities such as soccer fields, cricket ovals, and baseball diamonds. Semi-public spaces were set up for churches and clubs for certain groups such as seniors, scouts and veterans. Private spaces were reserved for socialising, in the home or backyard, or shopping and entertainment, in prescribed malls with ample parking. In all, as clear an allocation as the larger land-use planning efforts, and one that, when questioned, is based on one element of a primarily Anglo-Saxon view of separation and need: the privatised suburban house, the privatised nuclear family, and egalitarianism based on homogeneity.

The legacy this history of suburban planning has left is a challenging one. On the large scale, metropolitan areas such as Sydney have grown to such an extent that there are very real problems of city viability, particularly as it relates to transportation. On a much more local scale, there are the issues of isolation and the differences homogeneity subsumes and masks. Poor public transport turns the physical separation of residential and other uses into social isolation for those least likely to have access to a car; women, children, adolescents and the elderly. Far from satisfying women's needs, recent feminist critiques have argued the suburban form traps women into the domestic and consumption spheres and reinforces their exclusion from the masculine worlds of work and influence.[6] In the study presented here, we find that migrants not only face poor public transport, but also confusing timetables in a language they are not yet proficient in, and the difficulty of orientation in the suburban landscape. As one Vietnamese migrant said, 'uniformity is a danger, because you don't know where you are'. Yet the low density form with ample open space has created a firm mind-set that the Australian Dream includes a single detached house on a good sized lot.[7] With housing and planning tied to the desires of the population — or that portion that has the most power — and preference tied to dominant cultural norms,[8] change will be slow.

In this study we consider the specific geography of housing in the large area to the west of central Sydney; an area that makes up over half of the area of greater Sydney and houses over half the population. 'The west'— inhabited by 'westies'— is an often maligned region, characterised by such images as lack of amenity, crime, lack of physical and sometimes even moral character, and high unemployment. This reputation is not fully deserved and is in part a media creation, as explored by Diane Powell in *Out West: Perceptions of Sydney's Western Suburbs*.[9] Yet on a per capita basis, it does tend to be underserviced according to such variables as arts and social services funding. Perhaps most important, it has and continues to provide the bulk of new and/or 'affordable' housing options in an expensive city. Coopers & Lybrand Consultants report that between July 1991 and July 1992, six of the top ten local population growth areas in Sydney were in the west, accounting for much of Sydney's slowing population growth.[10]

The history of suburban growth in West Sydney follows roughly the pattern outlined above, with some variants. The County of Cumberland Planning Scheme of 1948 did hope to guide more comprehensive planning for the growth of Sydney into the area. '[The plan] was an ambitious attempt to contain and rationalise metropolitan development, to establish viable communities rather than dormitory suburbs'.[11] Yet the postwar need for housing and the economics of development for the growing city diminished the lofty plans for a 'green belt'.[12] Further, the subdivision of the medium sized market garden lots that occupied much of this area occurred in a rather haphazard way. Land was relatively inexpensive and building was often done in small groups or through do-it-yourself methods, all with whatever materials were available. More mass-produced and utilitarian were the hostels and housing estates built to house the returning servicemen, a growing flow of migrants, and an inner-city population that was being cleared from 'unsatisfactory slum' housing. Today, new release areas see a much more integrated planning, particularly as it relates to physical infrastructure. 'Sewers before settlement — now taken for granted — is one of the most dramatic changes brought about by planning in the postwar period'.[13] Yet both early and recent developments are striking in their lack of diversity of form.

The flow of migrants into Sydney, often to the western suburbs, is of interest. Sydney's social mix has changed since the mid 1960s. Since the first white invasion and settlement, the city has received immigrants. For much of this time, migrants have primarily been from the UK. In the immediate postwar years northern, southern and eastern European migration increased. Governments were concerned to meet the growing demands by industry for labour. Yet immigration policy was geared not to disrupt the homogeneity of the population. Migrants with fair complexions were favoured as easier to assimilate. Often these groups formed ethnic areas in the inner-city suburbs that were being left in a suburban move by the more established population.

For the past three decades, migration policy has been substantially more open. Large numbers of political refugees, business migrants, and migrants joining family already here through reunion programs have led to a growing population of groups that are more visible as different, and more spread over the metropolitan region. Today nearly half of Sydney's population is of first or second generation non-English speaking background (NESB). Many countries are represented, particularly Asian. In the three months to June 1991, 19 960 out of a total 49 000 permanent and long-term settlers gave their country of birth as one in Asia. Sydney remains the country's largest recipient of immigrants.[14]

THE STUDY

The study focused directly on bringing to light some issues related to how the planning profession is dealing with the needs of migrants in this multicultural urban environment. Forty local government planners, social planners, community workers and migrant resource workers, and a number of developers and migrant representatives were interviewed individually and in small groups. Most interviewees were from two very different western Sydney areas, Fairfield and Penrith, with some interviewees from neighbouring areas as well as several key statewide agencies concerned with migrant issues. Planning documents and the coverage of migrant issues in the local media were also examined. Fairfield was chosen for its reputation as being one of the most multicultural local government areas in Australia, stemming from a history of migrant settlement through a concentration of migrant reception hostels and the propensity for migrants to locate close to family and same-group populations. The proportion of overseas born in this area had risen to 47.9% by 1991.[15] Residents from NESB are from 109 language groups. There is evidence of some change to the physical makeup of the area, at least on commercial streets such as the Vietnamese/Chinese core of Cabramatta. Here almost all shops and businesses display Asian signs and the area has become a well known tourist site for inner-Sydneysiders for dim sim on Sundays. Penrith provides good contrast. It is a country town which has expanded and been integrated into the Sydney metropolis over the last decade. Despite the 13% overseas born population, there is almost no visible change in the forms of housing and landscape.

There were striking differences in the views of the physical planners and the social planners/community workers interviewed. This research supported the conclusions of David Wilmoth's international comparison: 'Unlike urban planners in USA, Asia and even UK, . . . Australian urban planning has clung to its land use planning and development control core, a peculiarly defensive response'.[16] High powered and 'economically significant' issues centre on physical planning: hard service infrastructure, negotiations with developers over financing of some public services through user-pays schemes, the enforcement of building codes, and the allocation of land. Within this often two-dimensional process, certain norms and standards have been developed and legitimised, often with little clarity or questioning of the social objectives reported to being met. Unlike countries like Sweden, where social and physical planning are seen as integrated activities with no clear separation, in Australia social planning exists as an add-on. This was the overwhelming view of the planning structure given by the social planners and service providers. Consultation and the gaining of input on issues of migrant needs 'come in as an afterthought'. 'Social planning input is vital from day one, but other people's jobs are easier if it is not included'. Migrant workers are there to deal with those who are not able to 'fit in'. This view was also backed up by the fact that many of the planners dealing with the physical and land use side of issues concluded that there were no specific migrant problems they could think of.

In *Housing in Australia — Some Stereotypes Examined*, Ross Clare suggests that: 'much of the diversity of Australian housing derives from locational differences and material finishes, rather than from more fundamental differences in housing type. Nearly 80 per cent of housing consists of detached houses, with most of these having three bedrooms.'[17] In light of an emerging multicultural population, this is curious. Barbara Gapps of Fairfield City Council writes: 'Fairfield continues to be one of the most interesting and dynamic Local Government Areas in western Sydney and home to a diverse range of non-English speaking communities. Its human faces, dress and special places of worship and culture reflect its diversity. Its housing, however, is distinctly Australian, despite the fact many people in Fairfield may not be dreaming of the quarter acre block. The challenge, to change housing design, is one that I believe we have not yet faced.'[18] What is the relationship between what is provided and what is desired?

The physical planning departments interviewed acknowledge that there was pressure for both larger and more diverse housing forms. Recognition ranged from such blanket statements as 'Italians like large houses', to specifics on development applications. A planner at a west Sydney office of the New South Wales Department of Planning commented, 'the available built form does not really allow for large or extended families'. This was particularly the case with the existing stock of public housing being made up of one, two and three bedroom housing based on the concept of the nuclear family, 'which was not who we had [making applications]'. Penrith City Council has adopted the philosophy that they 'ought to be able to offer a choice in housing', but it is not clear what this implies in practice. Fairfield City Council planners also expressed the view that non-English speaking groups have different concepts of housing which have not been adequately addressed. It was stressed that zoning was relatively flexible, for instance one planner said, 'I'm not certain that the regulations that are in place would necessarily prevent us responding to [variety] if people brought the product forward'. However planning authorities did tend to identify three problems:

- migrants who move into existing housing have limited opportunities to change the physical layout of the pre-existing structure;
- there is a limited amount that government can do except through that slow process of education and widening the choice of housing that is provided;
- yet, building applications with slightly different layouts or for different usage from the usual often trigger a prejudice born of a particularly 'Australian' social background and history; within the profession as well as the larger public.

The social planners and service providers also identified this lack of choice as an issue. One at the Blacktown Migrant Resources Centre reported that the planning problem migrants always mention is the difficulty of being able to have houses in close proximity.

Most interviewees identified affordability as the driving factor in the homogeneous suburban landscape. One NESB community worker summed it up: 'there is not an outcry because you can't afford anything different, and this is what the market provides'. Still, there is an enduring allure of the single detached home. A 1985 study of housing preferences of Polish, Turkish and Indo-Chinese in Melbourne found the detached house with a large or small garden favoured by 96, 99, and 94% respectively.[19] To what extent known options define demand is difficult to assess without extensive in depth interviewing where other housing forms are properly canvassed. Our interviews revealed that an owned home was seen as a place to be proud of as well as private space to be different in (i.e. grow fresh vegetables and spices not available in the supermarket) (see Susan Thompson's chapter in this volume). Choice is influenced by the larger 'Australian' whole. Ownership of a single family detached home represents success in Australia; talk of *achieving* home ownership is common in government documents.[20] In most cases it also represents success to family and friends in country of origin, as well as being the most secure type of housing choice in terms of an investment and source of capital gain.

This is the area where slow change and education is needed as planning departments work for a greater variety of housing types, and for market acceptance of these. Certain migrant communities with, as one interviewee pointed out, 'experience in living in and creating interesting higher density environments', should be looked on as a resource, while another NESB worker reported that newly arrived Vietnamese liked the higher density dwellings of Cabramatta, liked to be in close proximity to friends and shops. Yet here, as with all research on diverse groups, caution must be excercised. Yes they have experienced higher density living, but with people they were related to and knew well. It is important to remember that 'migrants' are not a generalisable group, nor are ethnic groups within the larger whole. Stereotypes need to be avoided.

DIVERSITY OF HOUSING OR DIVERSITY OF HOUSING DESIGN

The debates on housing and the directions taken by the planning profession are complex. In west Sydney there is a real fear on the part of the community planners and service providers that urban consolidation is looking to better use the hard services infrastructure without giving proper consideration to social services.[22] A *Planning Research Bulletin* report on building approvals from 1987 to 1991 notes the success of consolidation in the outer suburbs and new release areas, as measured by approvals of multiple dwellings, yet states that '[this] needs to be tempered by a recognition that the benefits of urban consolidation — that is improved access by transit systems to employment and to a range of community facilities — are not yet being delivered in outer suburban areas and there is little prospect of the delivery of any significant improvement in services in the foreseeable future'.[23] From a physical planning perspective, the issue of housing choice has tended to mean a variety of housing densities and, to a lesser extent, a variety of housing prices but has not extended to incorporating notions about housing design derived from other than an Anglo-Australian background.

In the planners' defense, they are not developers. Yet they do have a role and function as information providers. As a Health, Hygiene and Welfare Services Supervisor from Penrith said: 'Builders need a bit more encouragement to market their homes in a different way'.

Developers should be made aware that the housing they plan to build may be purchased by people of different ethnic origin, and that flexibility on a number of design fronts could be offered or maintained. It is incumbent on planners to promote a sensitivity to cross-cultural issues and make themselves knowledgeable in these areas. Currently, builders tend to expect purchasers to fit the house, at least those looking to purchase project homes. As stated by a salesperson for a large Australian home construction firm: 'People come in with all kinds of ideas, but you can explain to them what is practical or why it is designed that way. Changes to the standard design usually lead to increases in cost.' To his credit, he does show potential customers how room dividers and screening can work in creating suitable spaces.

What became apparent during the research was that there are many ways in which the standard three bedroom dwelling does not effectively meet the lifestyle needs of the migrant community in general. Specific examples from NESB respondents included such things as the need to accommodate large and extended families, difficulties providing appropriate places of worship within the home, the siting and orientation of the house and/or doors, the desire for kitchen arrangements that facilitated traditional methods of food preparation, the arrangement of rooms to reflect cultural attitudes, even to issues of cleanliness and hygiene. The following comments illustrate these issues: 'For ethnic communities, particularly those recently migrated, their family unit is much bigger, so people want to live in bigger houses that accommodate a larger amount of people, the extended family'. 'Some elderly people in my group [the Vietnamese community] don't have a room or a corner in particular to put their altar. The altar is a very special thing. Ideally there is a special place in the house for the altar'. 'Chinese prefer regular shaped blocks of land rather than being in a cul-de-sac;' while 'some northern Indians dislike a front door facing south'. 'Some Asians and Indians prefer sealed kitchens rather than open plans due to cooking odours. Also better ventilation.' 'Turkish peoples may have need of a foyer where shoes can be left before entering the house. The outdoors and things associated with it are considered "unclean"'. 'For some Middle Eastern nationalities, the standard Australian toilet doesn't meet some cultural needs related to hygiene.' Yet again there is a danger in generalisations. Second generation migrants may well differ from their parents in their desires, needs and views. Without meaningful consultation there is a very real risk of myths developing through misinterpretation. We were told both that Chinese prefer gas stoves because of the utensils used for cooking and that they prefer the safety of electric stoves. What is needed is adaptable design and a consideration of alternative models of housing, not just a review of what already exists.

Once purchased there are often modifications that people want to make to a house and, less often, to apartments. If major, this is the point of contact with planning regulations. Many migrants have come from countries where there are not the same government regulations about what can and cannot be done to a dwelling and land. There were several reports of people making 'unauthorised' alterations to homes due to lack of knowledge of the permit requirements. Regulations are based on minimum acceptable standards, often with quite valid rationale. Shading, privacy, and adequacy of building construction to the Australian climate are fairly value neutral. The problem comes when building applications are judged on 'merit' and more subjective values of the dominant culture are imposed. Some interviewees recognised that it was not always the codes and regulations that were restrictive, but rather the interpretation of what was permissible by those in the position of granting approvals. An illustration was a planner speaking about a recent development application. 'They specifically wanted certain things built into the house that went against our normal strain of where you would put [rooms] . . . not really ordinance 70 problems, just floor plan design that we didn't see as the normal way to do it'. Yet in Fairfield, the Chief Planner indicated an environment where stigmatisation of difference is largely avoided. It is something that had/has to be worked at; recognising that values and codes can change over time. The best evidence of this is the evolution from illegal conversion of garages to provide affordable accommo-dation, to the permissible construction of the so-called 'granny flat', to today when two dwellings on one block of land (dual occupancy) is acceptable regardless of configuration.

A second area where migrants often differ in their perception of home involves the separation of house and work. Home industry includes such things as cooking, clothing manufacture, jewellery making or motor vehicle repair. Unemployment is high in western Sydney and Fairfield is an area where the values and codes are changing. Controlled home industry is looked on as empowering and as an avenue for incubating new businesses. Codes to guide the establishment of home industry are also available in a number of languages. The point where home industry becomes a 'nuisance' and should move to larger quarters is a politically decided question, relating to such things as noise, parking and working conditions, but the opening up of land use is occurring and does represent a response not only to multicultural needs, but also a growth in working from the home by a larger portion of the overall population (Alvin Toffler's 'electronic cottage' forecasts).

PUBLIC SPACE AND SEMI-PUBLIC SPACE

More that the home itself, the housing environment is an area with which many migrants are uncomfortable. The following quotes from a community development worker and a number of migrants sum this up well: 'There is so little happening on the streets; and the cities being quiet, especially after dark, and nobody being out and things like that I think inhibits people. In Italian town and cities, for example, in the evening everybody is out and promenading, chatting and sitting in outdoor cafes. And in Asia there is lots of life on the streets, lots of stalls, but here everybody is in their house.' Where areas exist for this kind of interaction, private transport is usually necessary. 'So you end up with the library being the social place and then there are large complaints from all the sections of the community.' Where congenial public spaces are provided they are well used. 'If you go to Freedom Plaza in Cabramatta you will see that every morning there will be heaps of old people just sitting around on a bench there chatting to each other and getting the sunlight.' 'You know, the piazza where [one can] get together and not necessarily consume as you would have to if you go to a coffee shop or pub.' Malls surrounded by parking lots are alienating to migrants used to street shopping and small social spaces.

During the day, the housing environment is not that much more hospitable. Most of the formal recreation areas in the western suburbs are given over to traditional sporting fields. The predominant users of these spaces are adolescent boys and adult males, with some but less use by girls. Obviously some children of migrants comprise members of these groups and thus make use of these facilities. But these spaces are not conducive to other kinds of uses such as walking, sitting around, bowls, volley ball and other games. The landscape is often barren with few areas that are shaded and pleasant to sit in. Many sporting activities that are played in other countries take place in less formal areas. Yet passive and active, public and semi-public space is being contested. Some migrants 'play on the roads, they occupy the footpaths, they go in the backyard. The boundary of the block doesn't seem to bother them at all. They make full use of the open space that is available to them. Whereas I think the Australians are a bit different, they are very protective of their boundaries.' One park is being redesigned and planted in Fairfield. More importantly, migrants are beginning to push for access to and provision of semi-private areas, often the most important for socialising as well as engaging in specific cultural practices. This has created controversy in the Sydney suburbs, and it is through these that some underlying political and often racist, or at least xenophobic, forces of the social landscape are brought to light. The most contentious has been the siting of religious places of worship. Where religious groups have proposed or established mosques or temples in existing residential areas they tend to encounter resistance by residents and politicians. [24]

Similar resistance is encountered to the establishment of social and sporting clubs for migrant groups. [25] What is important to recognise here is that planners often face a reluctance, by either a majority or a vocal minority, to accommodate change; the NIMBY (not-in-my-backyard) syndrome. Michael Dear, in writing about this reluctance states, 'Opposition arguments, after the initial angry phase, usually express three specific concerns: the perceived threat to property values, personal security, and neighbourhood amenity.'[26] The planner has to take the roles of advocate, facilitator, and educator to help ensure the successful implementation of multiculturalism.

In conclusion, planning and housing policy in Australia can no longer ignore the increasing cultural and social diversity of the population in cities. This will involve new ways of planning which break out of the rational comprehensive framework which has dominated physical planning over the last century. [27] It will mean asking for new forms of participation which are not simply tokenistic, and new ways of thinking about urban and housing form. Just as feminists have illustrated the gendered/sexed nature of planning and housing in Australia, we now also need to examine the ways in which the city is modelled on particular Anglo-Australian notions of how people live.

NOTES

1. Stretton, H. (1975) *Ideas for Australian Cities*, 2nd rev. ed. Georgian House, Melbourne.
2. Greenpeace (1993) *Strategy for Sustainable Sydney*, Greenpeace, Sydney; Kemeny, J. (1983) *The Great Australian Nightmare*, Georgian House, Melbourne.
3. Hall, P. (1988) *Cities of Tomorrow: An Intellectual History of Urban Planning and Design in the Twentieth Century*, Basil Blackwell, Oxford.

4. Freestone, R. (1991) 'An Historical Perspective on the Design of Residential Environments in Australia', *Urban Futures — Special Issue*, No.3, p.1.
5. *ibid.*, p.5.
6. Game, A. and Pringle, R. (1983) *Gender at Work*, Allen & Unwin, Sydney; Watson, S. (1988) *Accommodating Inequality*, Allen & Unwin, Sydney.
7. Brown, J. (1991) 'Attitudes and Values Towards Housing in Australia: Some Preliminary Thoughts and Findings', *Urban Futures — Special Issue*, No.3, p.10; Kemeny (1983) *op. cit.*
8. King, R. (1984) 'Immigration and Urban Inequality', in Birrell, R. et al. (eds.) *Populate and Perish*, Australian Conservation Foundation, Melbourne.
9. Powell, D. (1993) *Out West: Perceptions of Sydney's Western Suburbs*, Allen & Unwin, St. Leonards, NSW.
10. In Salt, B. (1993) 'Population Growth Ranking in Australia: July 1991 and June 1992', Coopers & Lybrand Consultants, Sydney.
11. Powell (1993) *op. cit.*, pp.53-53.
12. Freestone, R. (1992) 'Sydney's Green Belt, 1945-1960', *Australian Planner*, Vol.30, No.2, pp.70-77.
13. Troy, P. (1987) 'Planners and Social Justice', *Australian Planner*, Vol.25, No.1, p.27.
14. Murphy, P. et al. (1990) *Impacts of Immigration on Urban Infrastructure*, Australian Government Publishing Service, Canberra.
15. Australian Bureau of Statistics (1993) *Population Characteristics by LGA 1991 Census*, ABS Service, Sydney.
16. Wilmoth, D. (1987) 'Metropolitan Planning for Sydney', in Hamnet, S. and Bunker, R. (eds.) *Urban Australia: Planning Issues and Policies*, Mansell, London, p.138.
17. Clare, R. (1991) 'Housing in Australia — Some Stereotypes Examined', *Urban Futures*, Vol.1, Nov., p.18.
18. Gapps, B. (1990) 'Consolidation for People: The Impact of Urban Consolidation on the Planning and Provision of Human Services — Proceedings', Western Sydney Regional Organisation of Councils.
19. Social Planning Consortium (1985) 'Housing for all People: A Report on the Housing Preferences of Polish, Turkish and Indo-Chinese People in Melbourne', A Report to the Australian Housing Research Council, Section 4.22.
20. Watson (1988) *op. cit.*
21. Brown (1991) *op. cit.*
22. Gooding, A. (1990) 'Consolidation for People: The Impact of Urban Consolidation on the Planning and Provision of Human Services', Western Sydney Regional Organisation of Councils.
23. Planning Research Centre (1992) 'Building approvals 1987-91 show spatial differentials in impact of the recession', *Planning Research Bulletin*, Vol.1, No.1, pp.10-11.
24. Watson, S. (1992) 'Cross cultural issues in planning', *Cultural Policy*, Vol.4, pp.19-35.

25. *ibid.*
26. Dear, M. (1992) 'Understanding and Overcoming the NIMBY Syndrome', *Journal of the American Planning Association*, Vol.58, No.3, p.298.
27. Watson, S. and Gibson, K. (eds.) (1994) *Postmodern Cities and Spaces*, Blackwell, Oxford.

16

Cultural planning in Australia: policy dreams, economic realities

Gay Hawkins and Katherine Gibson

In Australia 'cultural planning' has become the buzzword of the '90s. It has spread, like a virus, through federal and State arts ministries, community arts associations and some local governments. The growing popularity of this term signals several significant developments. First, the limitations of community arts policy and practice and second, the urgent need for some new ways to think about and intervene in local cultural development.

In the Australian context cultural planning is a term that covers a wide range of activities and approaches. But in general the main push has been to put 'culture' on the urban planning agenda. It's a bit like a forced marriage with those in the field of cultural policy chasing those working in urban policy keen to seduce the urban planner/local government official with the pleasures and profits offered by culture.

In seeking to align the arts with urban development, cultural planning has placed itself right in the midst of major tensions between development versus amenity, public versus private ownership and control, and local versus international culture. But does cultural planning offer useful solutions to some of the problems cities and town centres currently face? Is it just another trendy planning fad coming hot on the heels of social planning, needs based planning and environmental planning? Or is it a genuinely innovative approach to reconciling the pressures on local government to foster economic growth and be sensitive to local needs and identity? This chapter addresses these questions by first exploring where cultural planning in Australia has come from and second analysing some of its current limitations. We then go on to discuss the new economic forces shaping our cities, which have already placed culture on the urban planning agenda. Finally we address how the planning process might mediate the many different forces and interests competing to shape cultural experiences in the city. [1]

CULTURAL PLANNING—AUSTRALIAN STYLE

Understanding the history and context of cultural planning in Australia is useful and necessary for several reasons. First, an awareness of where the push for cultural planning has come from and how it has evolved is crucial to debates about where it should go in the future. Second, it is important to investigate the distinctiveness of the Australian context for cultural planning. After all, cultural planning is an imported idea, taking off in Australia after the Creative Cities conference in the late 1980s and heavily influenced by the approach developed by Partners for Liveable Places in Washington and, to a lesser extent, the work of Bianchini and Worpole in England. Now there is nothing wrong with imported ideas, especially when they are good ideas, but it is important to understand how they have been re-made and adapted in new sites.

Cultural planning means different things in different places according to different political processes, economic conditions and cultural practices and landscapes. The role of local governments in British cultural planning is, for example, something that cannot be replicated in Australia where the economic base and powers of local councils are much more limited and their precinct is more likely to be suburban rather than small city. [2] Cultural planning may be an import but Australian cultural policy makers, artists, planners, local government officials have dramatically re-constituted it in the Autralian context.

In terms of policy development and the promotion of cultural planning in Australia, this process has been largely top down. It is the State arts ministries, particularly in Victoria, and the Community Cultural Development Unit (CCDU) of the Australia Council that have most enthusiastically embraced the cultural planning ethos. Their enthusiasm reflects a certain exhaustion with community arts policy, which has become bogged down in the arts as social integration model. Cultural planning offered new approaches to fostering community development and expanding local culture and local government participation in culture. Lots of reports, projects and models have been produced.[3] The main audience for this work has been local government. In Australia cultural planning has been one of the central forces in trying to develop or foster cultural policies at the local level. This reflects the history of cultural policy, or arts policy, in Australia which largely began with the formation of the Australia Council under former Labor prime Minister, Gough Whitlam. Both State and local governments have borrowed extensively from the ideological models and approaches established in the Australia Council. The evolution of cultural planning in Australia can be seen as a State and federal government push aimed at selling culture to councils.

The arguments these bodies have produced promoting cultural planning are very sound and reflect overseas models. The arts are represented as crucial for local amenity, identity and community development and good for business. These are all important arguments, well developed in numerous reports.[4] The general push is that it is time for councils to move beyond the libraries, Mayor's Art Prize and council colouring-in competition mentality and embrace a wider cultural agenda.

There are serious limitations in the current formulation of cultural planning in Australia because of the dominance of arts funding bodies in its development. Firstly there is an overemphasis on aesthetic definitions of successful cultural planning. While cultural planning policies may point to the value of culture in community development and economic expansion, too many of the examples cited reflect middle-class values and culture. The public sculptures, main streets painted in heritage colours, local festivals etc tend to deny the extraordinary diversity of urban popular culture. In a CCDU funded report on arts development in western Sydney,[5] there was hardly a mention of the extent and variety of commercial culture, from leagues clubs to pub rock. In seeking to foster more art in western Sydney this region was inevitably represented as without culture: the reality of the commercial sector which was market driven and the centre of most people's cultural consumption was not even addressed.

Arts bodies' control over cultural planning discourse has meant that the emphasis is still implicitly on art rather than culture, on galleries and artists' weeks rather than pubs, shopping centres and street life.

There is still an enormous hostility towards commercial culture. Arts bodies still implicitly endorse the subsidised over the profitable, the high over the mass. We have to beware that cultural planning does not become bogged down in the civilising rhetoric of high cultural policies which argue that art is good for you while popular culture is merely soporific pap for the masses. Concepts like 'amenity', 'quality of life' or 'liveable places' are abstract, they are given different meanings by different interest groups. These concepts must not be exclusively defined by middle-class notions of what constitutes a 'nice place to live'.

The second problem with the history of cultural planning in Australia is that it has been built on the assumption that local government knows nothing about culture and that councils need to be educated about the value of culture. There is a certain naivety and arrogance in this assumption. If there is an area of government in Australia that has been most at the vanguard of cultural expansion and development over the last 10 years it is local government.[6] All over Australia councils have been grappling with development applications for large scale shopping malls that have massive implications for main streets, tourist resort developments that transform local economies and local leisure practices. They have also been building massive cultural centres — often reflecting that dangerous combination of money and narcissism; they have been licensing street markets — from Rockdale Markets and Parklea Markets to the Gay and Lesbian Mardi Gras, and supporting Aboriginal museums in order to attract tourists. These are all cultural developments that have phenomenal impacts on local economies, urban form and the ordinary cultural practices of residents — how they shop, what they do in their leisure and so on.

So while State and federal governments may be right in pointing out that local governments need cultural policies i.e. frameworks for cultural provision and regulation, they are wrong to assume that local governments are ignorant of culture. Councils are doing cultural planning all the time unwittingly and by default. They are engaged both in the provision of cultural services and also in facilitating a multitude of developments which have a wide range of cultural impacts.

What is missing in Australian arguments for cultural planning is any sound economic analysis of the forces that are restructuring local economies and the cultural impacts of these changes. Cultural planning in Australia needs to move beyond motherhood statements about how good culture is for local identity and economies. It needs to reflect a more sophisticated understanding of the relationship between political processes and economic forces. The implicit emphasis on the aesthetic benefits of culture (good design, heritage streetscapes, public art) makes cultural planning policy blind to the forces shaping cities. Ultimately, cultural planning is a misnomer. In its current form in Australia it has not really moved beyond arts planning because of the over emphasis on non-technological, 19th century subsidised cultural forms.

While cultural planners argue that the arts and culture have a crucial role to play in urban renewal and development, they have failed to grasp that urban policy is already cultural policy. Urban policy, or the lack of it, has dramatically shaped how we use cities and town centres, who benefits from them, how pleasureable, accessible and commercially viable they are. While it's important to say 'take notice of the value of the arts and cultural industries!', cultural planning also needs to consider the cultural effects of existing urban forms and policies in order to understand how the economic and cultural intersect. Cultural policy makers need to understand the economic organisation of culture and the cultural impacts of various urban developments, from unplanned sprawl to shopping malls.[7]

THE NEW ECONOMIC FORCES SHAPING CITIES

As we see it, the crucial issue facing cultural planning today is that 'culture' has been put on the urban agenda by economic forces, not by planners or bureaucrats. The fact is that the new urban investment companies of late capitalism have taken an extraordinary interest in cultural developments such as tourism, resort construction, leisure shopping complexes, entertainment centres and so on. So the question that arises is not 'how to add culture on to the planning agenda?' but 'whose and what culture is currently shaping our urban experience?'

In contemporary cities, cultural activities are certainly being exploited by urban developers in a different way and on a different scale than ever before. Australian cities have, since the 19th century, been shaped by the excesses of speculative development. During the property boom of the 1960s and early 1970s institutional investors were enticed into the market and 'initiated an era of large-scale investments in office-blocks, shopping centres, industrial estates and giant hotels'.[8] The style of urban development sponsored by these investments clearly had cultural effects. For example, the 'malling' of Sydney created new sorts of shopping spaces and contributed to the death of many inner-suburban high streets. The rise of diversified retail malls changed the nature of many suburbanites' relationship to 'town', the retail, entertainment and services district of the CBD.[9] But while these developments all had cultural effects, many cultural activities were not the focus of economic interest for investors.

By contrast, at the end of the central city office block boom of the 1970s, property investment capital (now less British and more Asian) looking for windfall returns began to move into more risky development ventures.[10] Many of these more speculative projects targeted cultural activities as their primary economic goal — tourism and resort development (Bondi, Manly, Cronulla, the Rocks, Kings Cross); leisure shopping and entertainment (Darling Harbour, Eastgardens, theatre/office complexes e.g. MLC Building, Entertainment Centre, cinema complexes). The cultural effects of most of these developments involves the promotion of internationalised, homogenised, yuppie experiences. Increasingly each harbourside, whether Baltimore or Sydney, looks alike, each five-star hotel has the regulation plant filled atrium and each cinema complex looks like an international transit lounge. The urban commentator David Harvey sees this last round of investment in glitzy CBD redevelopments (especially around outmoded docklands and wholesaling/market areas), and the associated marrying of economic functions with entertainment and leisure functions, as a significant feature of the historical evolution of capitalist economies and the built environment.[11]

Whether we buy all of Harvey's argument or not, there is something to be said for trying to discern how changing patterns of investment are influencing cities and our everyday practices within them. Many of the recent cultural cum economic developments we see in Sydney have been pushed by new style investment/developers, rather than the older urban redevelopers such as Westfields and Lend Lease.[12] And because in some cases established planning practice has been disregarded in favour of fast track planning to get these developments off the ground, the opportunity for conflict and competition over urban space and ultimately cultural experience has increased.

Parramatta offers an interesting recent case study of how the city remains an arena for struggle between different economic interests. In our study of Parramatta's downtown we were able to observe a conflict between the 'old style' developer, Westfields, and a 'new style' developer, Merlin Investments, over an urban development which had major ramifications for the cultural amenity of Parramatta CBD.

Church Street is the old shopping spine of the Parramatta which once was a regional shopping node for residents in the mid-western suburbs of Sydney. At the southern end of Church Street, below the railway overpass and right next to the railway station, Westfields built an integrated shopping mall in 1974. The smaller shops along Church

Street rapidly declined and the whole high street became down at heel, much to the dismay of retailers, especially those larger companies such as David Jones who had previously located within the traditional shopping area, at its northern end. Under pressure from local small businesses Parramatta Council attempted a beautification and revitalisation program for Church Street. The Church Street Mall was constructed by closing off part of the street to traffic, paving, building performance areas and creating a civic space which is used and enjoyed, particularly by the office workers who, during the 1970s, became the main daily migrant market for this retailing area.[13]

At its northern end Church Street crosses the Parramatta River into a run down section of shops and hotels. It is here that a tale of two cultures gets played out on a nightly basis, for, despite its decrepit image, the northern end of town is the site of Parra's two most important cultural edifices. Adjacent to the football stadium we find the Parramatta Leagues Club (a well-attended venue which offers a diverse cultural menu to a variety of people from far and near), and hugging the river bank is the Parramatta Riverside Theatre complex (a publicly funded Bicentennial white elephant, much less well-attended than the Leagues Club).

Just south of the bridge over the Parramatta River and opposite the Riverside complex is David Jones and a number of smaller, rundown retail sites. It was this parcel of land around DJ's that the struggle between Westfields and Merlin was all about.

Westfields is a corporation with a strong and relatively solid base in property, particularly retail, development. Its formula for success has traditionally lain with secure financing and long-term planning of phased developments. The security of financing for large scale retail developments has been based upon the binding long-term agreements Westfields exacts with large department stores to be primary tenants of any one site (and more recently with large cinema chains to be secondary tenants). Development, Westfields style, involves advance acquisition of property for redevelopment and a strategic plan for the whole city which aims to ensure that every Sydneysider will be only 20 minutes drive from a major shopping complex.

Merlin Investments, by contrast, is a relatvely recent arrival on the property development scene. Formed in 1987, based upon a small real estate firm with property interests in Kings Cross, Merlin moved into retail development when the residential development market experienced a downturn in the late 1980s. Merlin entered a joint venture with McNamara Pty Ltd (a Parramatta based construction company) to redevelop Darling Harbour as a leisure/tourist/retailing complex. It also redeveloped Manly Pier. With water as a seeming winner, Merlin embarked on a project to redevelop the Parramatta site into a 24-hour complex with speciality retailing, food outlets, terrace cafes, waterfront restaurants, entertainment and amusement facilities. To be financed by vast borrowings, the plan involved extension of Church Street Mall, redevelopment of David Jones as part of the complex, development of the river frontage opposite Riverside Theatre and closure of Lennox Bridge.

For years Parramatta had been centred on the railway with its back to the river. Merlin proposed to turn the city around, refocusing it on the attractive environmental amenity offered by the Parramatta River. The Rivercentre complex involved partial extension of public space, revitalisation of the dead end of town, economic rescue for David Jones and the development of a 24-hour leisure retailing focus. What's more it offered potential for the emergence of a cultural precinct in Parramatta, providing a commercial context for the public investment in high culture across the river.

But what it also offered was a significant challenge to the established dominance of Westfields over Parramatta retailing. In the very same year (1988) that Merlin lodged its development application with council, Westfields had opened its level three extension adding an extra 27 shops to its Shoppingtown. Clearly, Westfields did not welcome the proposition of major competition in the local area for the retail dollar and secretly launched its own offensive — the acquisition of even more land around its established site to enable further extensions, negotiations with David Jones to lure it away from the Merlin magic, and later a strategic $200 000 donation to the Riverside Theatre, at a time when its subsidies were running out and the complex was in dire financial straits.

In the vicious struggle of competing investment interests that ensued local council planners/authorities were buffeted by corporate powers, large and small, the NSW State government, the Chamber of Commerce and statutory authorities overseeing environmental issues. Merlin's development application was delayed by eight months as various interests bickered over who was to meet the costs of further street closures. Aldermen were in turn doubtful about traffic provisions, bus access, the bridge closure and car parking. While the battle raged, global banking interest rates fluctuated in the background and interest bills on Merlin's significant debts mounted. The planning regulations that Premier Wran had conveniently removed at the Darling Harbour site were adhered to in Parramatta to the last letter, and finally an environmental report declared much of the plan subject to major (1 in 100 year) flood risk. In the end the financial system pulled the rug from Merlin's feet and Westfields became the corporate victor. Soon after, the jubilant Westfields announced its further extensions which included underground tunnels connecting it to Church Street mall and pedestrian walkways to its new sites.

The Parramatta case illustrates the complexity of economic and political forces which shape town centres. It highlights the importance of unpacking different types of investments in the built environment and their cultural consequences. In this case the proposal to develop a commercially viable 'permanent and organised spectacle'[14] failed in the face of yet another victory for formula retailing. It failed partly because of the established and vested interests embedded in the built environment of Parramatta, represented to varying degrees in the structure of the local council.

Further this study shows how, long before cultural planning took off in Australia, Parramatta council was already busy making a whole lot of decisions with cultural effects — investing in a large cultural centre, allowing major office block developments and changes in the daytime economy of the city, facilitating the development of Westfields and then having to deal with the consequences of a depressed high street and downtown. In the face of intense commercial struggles over public amenity such as took place in Parramatta we are tempted to ask how a more enlightened cultural planning practice might emerge?

PLANNING TO HEAR THE DIVERSITY OF VOICES IN THE CITY

Cultural planning in Australia has been promoted with a missionary zeal aimed at expanding the vision of local government beyond roads, rates and rubbish. But what we have argued here is that culture is already on the agenda, placed there by new patterns of investment in so-called service industries and by expansion in the commercial cultural market place (from tourist resorts to suburban multiplex cinemas). In many places cultural development is really an outcome of struggles between different corporate interests and their vision of amenity. The real challenge for cultural planning is to offer an alternative to that type of corporate cultural development. This doesn't mean offering 'art' as some sort of superior cultural form, rather it means planning to hear the diversity of cultural voices and identities that make cities interesting and allowing them to flourish.

From our research into local cultural economies there are three principles we would endorse as central to the development of good cultural planning in Australia. Such planning must be proactive rather than reactive; must move beyond the arts and into the wider cultural community; and must facilitate diversity, both cultural and economic.

Proactive rather than reactive

The great value in cultural planning models is that they offer both a critique of and an alternative to existing practices in urban planning. Despite the vision of planning as a value free, technical process which manages the urban environment, the reality is that planning in many sites is little more than a mediation process. Several important critiques of urban planning argue that planning is largely a process of negotiating between different economic pressures from retailers, residential developers, industrialists, office developers and property speculators.[15] In this view planning is purely reactive and functions to facilitate the expansion of capital accumulation and maintain the spatial status quo.

But the economic forces which shape our cities are not themselves planned, nor coherently organised. In the competitive and contradictory processes of investment in the built environment there are many opportunities for intervention and redirection. Cultural planning can have the potential to intervene in larger economic processes and orient development around specific cultural, social and economic objectives. However, a necessary precondition for proactivity is that cultural planning have a realistic economic analysis of the forces with which it is at play.

Good proactive cultural planning would also involve a truly collaborative process which includes representative groups and interests — from residents to local artists to business interests both large and small — not just in a tokenistic review context, but at every stage of the planning procedure. There are a number of interesting overseas models that could be drawn on such as the Town Centre Management Committees and Worpole's concept of the 'city workshop'.[16]

Beyond the arts' into the wider cultural economy

Cultural planning in Australia has to recognise the diversity of what counts as culture for most people. While the arts are part of culture, they are not its sum. For a large percentage of the population art still has a major image problem. Many people's cultural pleasures are market based, technological (from TV to heavy metal rock) and home based. The challenge for cultural planning is to work out how to embrace the continuum of culture — public and private, high and low, home-based and city-based. The way forward is to develop a more economic and industrial analysis of culture. The cultural industries approach developed in some local government areas in England has been barely explored in Australia. This approach focuses upon public investment in local cultural industries and is geared at improving both cultural production and distribution in order to reach wider local audiences.[17]

Facilitating diversity, both cultural and economic

In the midst of trends towards cultural standardisation in Australia cities we have seen an interesting and unpredicted flowering of culturally diverse spaces within the urban fabric. Some of the most culturally distinctive and vibrant areas of Sydney have been unplanned. Their popularity has been based upon the variety and pleasures of an active street life organised around small businesses with strong links to the local community. In Cabramatta, Vietnamese small businesses clustered along the old shopping strip have transformed this suburban node into an exotic and thriving local cultural economy. While this area has become an important site for the Asian community's identity and development, it has also become a destination for Sydney-based tourism.

Similarly in Paddington, Oxford Steet has now become the spatial and economic centre for the gay community in Sydney. The annual Mardi Gras parade draws a massive local and growing international audience and is both commercially successful and an important vehicle for the positive expression of gay solidarity.[18]

These are two of many possible examples that could be drawn upon to highlight the surprising tendencies to be found in contemporary cities which counter visions of cultural standardisation and economic concentration. These places show how local economies can have an organic relationship with different cultural constituencies. They also show how culture and economics can be aligned to nurture diversity, foster amenity and mobilise urban spectacles of a genuinely local rather than an international order.

NOTES

1. This chapter is based on a paper presented at the Cultural Planning Conference, Bondi, 3-4th December, 1991.
2. Brisbane City Council is one of the few 'local' governments which has jurusdiction over a whole urban area, as do many councils in the United

Kingdom (for example, Sheffield or Glasgow). The Brisbane Cultural Development Strategy is focused, like many of the British examples that Worpole discusses, on the Central Business District and surrounds. But for most local councils in Australia, cultural planning is necessarily geared to the suburban and to nodes within a complex and much larger metropolis. See Mercer, C. (1991) 'Brisbane's Cultural Development Strategy: the process, the politics and the products', *Proceedings of the Cultural Planning Conference*, Engineering Information Transfer Pty Ltd, Sydney.

3.   cf Chesterman, C. and Schwager, J. (1990) *Arts Development in Western Sydney*, Australia Council, Sydney.

4.   cf Local Government and Arts Task Force (1991) *Local Government's Role in Arts and Cultural Development*, Australia Council, Sydney.

5.   Chesterman and Schwager (1990) *op. cit.*

6.   Cameron, J. (1989) *Local Government Cultural Funding*, Discussion draft report for the Australia Council.

7.   The cultural impacts of suburbia and retail restructuring have, of course, been sensitively explored by feminist geographers and urban theorists interested in the ways in which women's lives are shaped by city structures. The lines of analysis persued by feminist urban analysis might well be noted by cultural policy makers. See, for example, Bowlby, S. (1988) 'From corner shop to hypermarket: women and food retailing', in Little, J., Peake, L. and Richardson, P. (eds.), *Women in Cities*, Macmillan, London, pp 61-83; Wilson, E. (1991) *The Sphinx in the City: Urban Life, the Control of Disorder, and Women*, Virago, London.

8.   Daly, M. T. (1982) *Sydney Boom Sydney Bust: The City and its Property Market 1850-1981*, George Allen & Unwin, Sydney, p.71.

9.   Hawkins, G. and Gibson, K. (1991) 'Local Cultures Supplement', *Australian Left Review*, 130, July.

10.   Daly (1982) *op. cit.*, p.69.

11.   Specifically, for Harvey, the transition from Fordist to post-Fordist production systems and modern to post-modern cities. Harvey, D. (1989) *The Condition of Postmodernity: An Enquiry into the Origins of Cultural Change*, Basil Blackwell, London.

12.   Huxley, M. (1991) 'Making cities fun: Darling Harbour and the immobilisation of the spectacle', in Carroll, P., Donohue, K., McGovern, M. and McMillen, J. (eds.) *Tourism in Australia*, Harcourt Brace Jovanovich, Sydney.

13.   During the 1980s many government departments and authorities have relocated from the CBD to offices in Parramatta.

14.   Harvey (1989) *op. cit.*, p.89.

15.   cf Paris, 1984.

16.   Fisher, M. and Owen, U. (1991) *Whose Cities?* Penguin Books, London.

17.   Hawkins and Gibson (1991) *op. cit.*

18.   Hawkins, G. (1993) *From Nimbin to Mardi Gras*, Allen & Unwin, Sydney.

17

Green dreams of planning: is there life after development?

Peter Droege

The 1980s have featured an enormous amount of green rhetoric, and a good deal of wide-eyed optimism about getting a grip on the mounting environmental disaster, whether one thinks of urban development strategies, or pitches for biodegradable soap. An increasing number of countries has adopted environmental regulations for development, and there has been a flurry of 'green city', 'ecotopia', 'ecopolis' and 'eco-city' initiatives, most notably in those countries that are least well-known for sustainable practices. Green talk has had a heyday in urban politics worldwide, and the EC has enjoyed a tough Commissioner, Ripa di Meana, who took destructive development projects and their all-too-obliging host cities to task, and indeed to court.

Extraordinary and far-reaching successes have been achieved, most notably in urban air and water pollution measures, impact assessment procedures and development controls. Yet the overall gain has been extremely disappointing: some largely local improvements aside, it is difficult to detect environmental indicators that suggest real and significant improvements along the lines intended. Forests die, apparently inexorably, in sulphur, carbon dioxide or ammonia clouds, or disappear through mechanical destruction. Species diversity is in rapid decline, and global pollution levels soar with the human population. In the face of all this, the basic development premises remain as an unprecedented urban development and resource destruction wave charges across East Asia. Here and elsewhere, attempts at real change are entangled in many-fold thickets of individual and institutional barriers, including aggression, ignorance, denial, self-interest, inability, expediency, negligence and fatigue.

Up until now, most mainstream environmental activists and theoreticians seem to have concluded that cities don't matter. For the theoreticians they are too small, and for the activists too big, and in any event, they seem too complicated for both. Yet urban agglomerations do contain the policy and action apparatus that in principle could impact crucial areas of the environmental challenge. This perception, after a long hiatus since the public-policy hopes of the 1970s, is slowly re-gaining ground. A renewed wave of attention is focusing on cities. But so far the realisation is that while the best possible measures may be taken, they do not appear to be enough, or good enough. It is now time to leap onto the next level of engagement, departing from the admirable yet still inadequate achievements made.

To any idealist, education lies at the focus of all hope for betterment. The opportunities to improve general education in environmental and resource management issues are enormous, simply because the current level is so utterly basic. Elementary aspects of an educative agenda for change continue to be ecological sensitisation, reconnection to one's emotional life, motivation for self-education and network building; consolidation economics, environmental accounting, webbed policy measures, deeper environment-development correlations, thorough analysis of successful cases, radical transformation of conventional architecture and urban planning curricula etc pose more complex challenges. Even more complex, more fundamental and more challenging yet is the much-needed conversion of the development-ideologically predominant, seemingly pragmatic ethical systems (Judaeo Christian and Confucian) into more intelligent, more wholly encompassing models, akin to the buried animist tradition of Japan.[1] Furthermore, many argue that a more vigorous feminist agenda holds promise if it can lead to more matriarchically guided social change, in a line of thinking that aligns the female interpretation of the meaning in environmental maintenance and change more with the Neolithic, nurturing, agricultural logic, while the currently dominant, more blindly strident, male view of the world is more akin to Palaeolithic hunting and tribal warrior traditions.[2]

Better education, a newly charged activism and appropriate economics continue to be basic prerogatives in the struggle to revolutionise mainstream perceptions of development. Because of their commercial and political nature, design and physical planning have come to sorely lag behind their true challenge: to synthesise the kind of integral solutions that other, more precise and narrowly focused disciplines are not very good at. Given the current crisis in local governance, extraordinary compensating measures are required—in the nurturing of professional ethics; self-policing institutions for planning, design, and construction, but, importantly, also for aid, trade and investment; instruction in zero-option programming and task reassessment tactics; and even the formation of environmental unions.

In this, education towards sounder practices will focus on deconstructing the following five myths of environmentally sustainable development (ESD). These pertain to the attitude about technology, scale, program, symbolic narrative and cost of 'green projects'. The first myth holds that there is a specific set of technologies supporting the move towards more sustainable forms of development, technologies that might be called 'green', 'intermediate' or 'appropriate'. These qualifiers serve their purpose in labelling intentions and applications, but do not describe a particular set. In fact, public, industrial and private sector-derived technologies in urban development are being applied across a wide spectrum of advancement, and with varying degrees of success. The underlying fear of a technological determinism is well-founded, however: the dominant credo still holds that technological innovation in itself is good for societal progress—despite overwhelming evidence to the contrary.[3]

The second myth assumes that 'ecological' projects are of small scale. The reality points to the need to introduce radically different approaches precisely into the large endeavours that litter the global cityscapes and set the tone for the aspirations of the much larger number of smaller and secondary development authors. The third myth says that green developments and planning procedures tend to embrace a certain set of 'environmentally correct' programmatic contents, in the nature, intention or organisation of the projects and programs involved. In reality, however, even global fast-food chains and logging companies sail increasingly under green flags, and occasionally with some justification. Fourthly, there is the very persistent myth that there is a specific form, or a visible symbolic narrative to new development, transparently expressive of the ambitions of the program, with a more natural, organic, perhaps even nostalgic, in short, 'sustainable' look. This sort of exclusive thinking carries great danger to the aim of nurturing more rational attitudes towards ecology and resources on a broader, mainstream basis. Nevertheless, legitimacy lurks in the argument that as part of a general critique on the manufacture and manipulation of desire there must be scope for visibly deconstructing and exposing the ideological content of environmental form. It is difficult to argue, however, that a 'greener', perhaps more village-like and rustic look somehow espouses or can be taken as a guarantee for a more humane, democratic and environmentally sustainable world.

Finally, the most clearly exposed myth is the notion that ESD is more costly. Environmental or 'green' economics and methods of accounting for the long-term and external costs of development have been extraordinarily helpful in pointing out the fallacy of conventional productivity measures. Yet certain taxation policies and other counter-incentive measures aside, they elude broader implementation, in the general climate of ever shortening planning horizons and profit realisation cycles.

For the direction of professional skills and education in architecture and planning fields, five conclusions can be drawn from the current stirrings of hope for achieving tolerable long-term development impacts. For one, much remains to be done to broadly, meaningfully and precisely share an understanding of what constitutes 'ecology', 'ecological design and strategies', 'environmentally sound' or 'sustainable.' Across the disciplines centrally involved, there is not yet such a critically important shared sense. Second, there is enormous scope for expanding the horizon of the architectural, urban development, design and planning professions in pure technical terms. Energy, water management, waste cycles, material and resource use: all these concerns place new and extraordinary demands on both technical capability in project development and upstream programming intelligence. Central to the range of new technical skills is also an understanding of the cultural and social ramifications of more sustainable forms of ecological asset management.

The deluge of development-induced global crises challenges the validity of traditional sectorial and layered organisation of the planning, development and design processes. On the surface, this fundamental questioning of the established administrative order appears to also characterise the pressures exerted by neo-liberalist and quasi-privatising competitive doctrines, but under much different objectives. Whereas the latter seeks institutional destabilisation all too often to decrease social awareness and environmental responsibility for the purpose of particular gain, the former pursues dramatic institutional change precisely to increase social stability. It seeks to reestablish new and meaningful links driven by public concern and scientific inquisitiveness. Ecological strategies will inevitably cut across institutional divisions, and not infrequently reverse the conventional project programming routine, by placing the environment as a leading concern, not merely as collateral damage to be mitigated later.

Fourth, new ecological challenges mandate tangible visions in the search for their resolution: there is an imperative to plan and design in more intensely researched, creative and compelling ways, and present constituents with practical and desirable alternatives to current, deleterious practices. Visions for the future, new solutions: this also involves a search for new visual semantics, a new formal rhetoric, new symbolics for new conditions and aspirations. Form is never free of content.

Finally, there needs to be a newly charged level of personal engagement, innovation, entrepreneurship, in short, a commitment to leadership through motivation and creative delegation. The very nature of our challenge is such that the personal concerns of practitioners, administrators and academics should not only be tolerated, but firmly required to flow into practice. As pointed out by Greenpeace's urban designer Roderick Simpson, an 'un-professionalism' in the best sense of the word is needed, to usefully re-connect private spheres and public commitments through engaged, 'awake' and responsible forms of professionalism.[4]

SCOPE FOR PESSIMISM: HOMO SAPIENS VS THE EARTH

During 1992, numerous celebrations commemorated Columbus' presumed discovery of the New World five hundred years ago. They also recalled the launch of world-wide biological and cultural devastation wreaked by one hemisphere on another. But more frequently this past half millennium is being thought of as the age of global development towards modernity. Both descriptions are accurate.

One special event, while not registered as an official memorial event, ought to have been cheered as a most ingenious and appropriately timed neo-Columbian event: the voyage of the Japanese vessel Akatsuki Maru ('MS Red Moon') and its plutonium tonnage, fabriqué en France. The mission was launched in secrecy, against the expressed wishes of a number of countries and without a plausible case of the peaceful need for the type and quantity of fuel. As a symbol of the general collusion within the triad of Northern domination, the US,

Japan and Western Europe, to carry on the battle for world hegemony the shipment sent a shivering signal around the world: ye who do not consent to our dominant development dogma will be fought with secrecy, manipulation and hired guns.

The Akatsuki Maru incident also highlighted how governing elites continue to envision development. Instead of scrambling for clean and sustainable solutions most leading countries seek to turbo-charge their flagging economies with the magic Faustian formula (Dr Faustus gained fame and fortune by selling his soul to Mephistopheles, i.e. the devil). These nations will not concede that cities and their industries do not run on centrally generated energy, mammoth infrastructure and macroeconomic theory alone. The plutonium dispatch also symbolised the third generation of global colonisation, this time aimed at subjects that are already well-primed with readily internalised values: the newly industrialising and recently industrialised nations of East and Southeast Asia.

Since their very beginning cities have been associated with massive deforestation, resource wastefulness and widespread pollution. To the pessimist, the impact of human development on the natural environment has not changed in fundamental, qualitative terms, except that the process of global environmental annihilation has dramatically accelerated over the past 150 years or so. In this, it was largely marked by phenomena referred to as 'urbanisation': today, a majority of the sources for the combined global and regional forms of environmental degradation reside within the jurisdiction of cities and towns.

Since the most recent awakening of widespread environmental concerns a generation ago, cities, towns and some of their leaders, planners and architects have responded with rising and ebbing waves of often admirable initiatives. There has been a string of successes in the protection of ecologically valuable sites, in savings of energy in materials and construction, and recently even development-associated clean-up measures. In Europe, the German IBA (International Building Exposition) Emscher Park effort is perhaps the most comprehensive and promising of such projects, seeking to clean up a central part of the devastated Ruhr area, and in South America, the Brazilian city of Curitiba has long been hailed as an ingenious source of inspiration and hope to transportation and urban planners throughout the world. The record is impressive, even hopeful to some, and the number of 'green cities' being touted is on the rise. But even if the current pace of progress continues, will it make a vital difference?

To begin with, much of what is billed today as major accomplishments in urban development is little else than environmentally and culturally corrosive. The vast global investment in new waterfronts, shopping complexes, industrial parks and residential areas adds virtually nothing to either the relief of the strained environment or the betterment of the social and cultural condition of the larger community. Most new mainstream plans are unimpeded by common sense or environmental concerns, either on the macro- or on the micro-scale.

Increasingly, green rhetoric and ecological gestures are being deployed to mute popular opposition to new developments. And because 'green projects' usually carry an experimental or demonstration status, and aim at technically sophisticated measures such as water quality improvements and the restoration of wetlands, they are also often conveniently placed on greenfield sites — exactly where much of the new development does not belong from an environmental point of view, but where developers and land owners prefer it. Are development and the environment really incompatible? Perhaps many promising earlier initiatives were not unviable in themselves, but merely pursued with insufficient determination. One may never know. It is hard to remember many optimistic ideas, such as the 'petroleum-free city' of the 1970s. What are the barriers to change? What drives us to perpetuate past follies? There are at least eight factors.

AGGRESSION

War almost always involves environmental degradation as a by-product, such as the marine havoc wreaked during the so-called Gulf War. But frequently, dramatic environmental change is actually the weapon of choice. The poisoning of water and air, the bombing of cities or the defoliation of forests are well-known examples of environmental warfare: today, Vietnam's prospective economic growth is hampered by the fact that it has simply not enough forest left to 'develop first and worry about the environment later'.[5] But even in the 'peaceful' times of national betterment and development, we can find naked aggression involved in environmental deterioration. The overt discomfort or even hatred felt by 'modernised', industrialising nations towards their own poor, or their indigenous population, can represent an incentive for 'development', and not merely a cost thereof. Tragically, examples are legion, such as the sustained hounding by development initiatives of indigenous peoples in Australia, Brazil, Canada, Indonesia, Malaysia or the US.

In other words, while displacement and annihilation are often presented as a necessary by-product of development, development sometimes is actually deployed as genocidal weapon, perhaps unconsciously. Scanning recent development history, we discover a staggering arsenal of golf courses, cattle ranches, uranium mines, shopping centres, agricultural areas, roads, dams, airports and new towns, deployed as common weapons of aggression. At the 1992 International Conference on Urban Development Policies and Projects hosted by the United Nations Centre for Regional Development a senior South American planning official argued that spontaneous settlements along new forest roads result from the 'natural' activity of his country's 'city-building' people. He neglected to mention that the roads were there as result of national and World Bank policy, that the settlements were made possible both because of policy and a well-known absence of enforcement capabilities. His definition of 'people' did not embrace forest Indians, who presumably counted among the lower life forms, to be justly eliminated by the cattle ranchers serving Western beef importers, the heinous acts condoned by a government under pressure to reduce its foreign debt. The seemingly technical testimony displayed a surprising degree of fear and hatred against the forest itself, the habitat, the home of our despised, city-less ancestral neighbours.

IGNORANCE

In the eyes of optimists, environmental ignorance is the root cause of our environmental conundrum today. It is defined as a state of absent data, lack of intelligent insight, or lost memory. Superficially, lack of insight can be claimed by fewer and fewer as a working excuse — since information has become, by and large, more readily available, even in the daily press. However, feigned ignorance disguising wilful concealment or non-disclosure of information, such as in the sale or use of polluted land or contaminated buildings, is still endemic to the problem.

In formal education, exposure to environmental facts and theory is still far from being as popularly available as would be desirable. Broad analytical capacity is lacking: access to information or insight on a particular aspect of the environment is not the same as understanding the links between causes and effects, or the relations between different causes, or different effects. This involves a higher state of environmental and politico-economical education, even less available to most people.

The most daunting challenge is memory loss — such as the evaporation of previously learned lessons. In current urban development conferences one finds very little genuine and sanguine concern for any sort of environmental issue. Airports rule the day, and even the old automobile still inspires planners from Bangkok to Beijing, and from Stockholm to Seoul.

DENIAL

Again, ignorance often is deliberately induced, consciously and unconsciously chosen to attain a tolerable level of comfort, through denial. It is quite human to hide from ourselves painful memories, unpleasant facts, or daunting prospects. Denial is a basic dimension of human psychology, and has long been described in its basic dynamics by Elizabeth Kuebler-Ross and others.[6] It can be lethal. Denial kept large numbers of people from fleeing Nazi Germany, rendering them unable or unwilling to believe the coming of the holocaust, even as their neighbours were carted to the murder camps. Denial allows us to stare into the face of global oceanic and general biological disaster, and react merely by purchasing stock in manufacturers of sun-block lotion. It preserves our carefully composed sanity, but renders us unable to act collectively or individually.

Refusing to take responsibility when it does not lie in our immediate area of accountability is a form of denial as well. It is often aided by role codification, procedural conventions and institutional arrangements, which are especially potent in the world of city planning and administration. And because city planning is a form of political activity, it is not immune to deliberate denial, flights of fancy, or plain lies. Another high-ranking government planner from an aspiring newly industrialising country in Southeast Asia claimed at the above mentioned conference in a deadpan way that his country's major metropolis had 'no' environmental problems and that development in his country, famous for its controversial forestry practices, was 'totally in harmony with nature'. The source of trouble? 'Neighbouring countries' were blamed as the cause, such as forest fires in Indonesia, or the eruption of Mount Pinatubo in the Philippines. This conference delegate may not have deliberately distorted the truth. He may have been a happy victim of that comforting sister of denial, delusion. To be fair, we are all victims. In a growing number of countries, optimistic delusion makes people believe that separating garbage into combustibles and non-combustibles is an important contribution to environmental redemption.

SELF-INTEREST

Self-interest is healthy under singularly life-threatening conditions, such as in situations of acute self-defence. Indeed, the dominant world's acquisitive, squirreling urges are sometimes explained by ancestral struggles for basic survival. Is the axiomatic credo of modernity, to live day-by-day and for short-term gain, really programmed by our Palaeolithic ancestors? Be that as it may, the combined effect of individual self-interest is collective socio-pathic behaviour, undermining the long-term viability of society itself.

Self-interest is packaged as the ultimate human value in the dominant, late-industrial ideologies, resulting in the commercialisation of all and everything, including individuals and their very lifetimes, and the dismantling of whole entities into assets: value-added elements and components. Unfettered self-interest positions communities against their very sources of sustenance, ancestral beliefs and children's future. The very skills that may have ensured survival in the dawn of history now threaten to terminate human life.

INABILITY

Many individuals and institutions desire to overcome their limitations, yet tragically fail in their ambitions. But to be administratively and technically incapable of handling a crisis can be comforting and convenient, too, and is indeed often used as excuse for inaction. Institutional inability and unwillingness to learn and change is a widespread phenomenon, as is the difficulty of shifting financial priorities. There are more basic forms of technical ineptitude, such as lack of legal or professional tools, shortage of staff and resources, often due to political inability in providing these. Lack of vision and inventiveness are fatal forms of weakness in planning and public administration as well.

True dilemmas lie in countries with debilitating problems of deprivation, resulting in spiralling environmental deterioration. It will be hypocritical not to make their improvements a primary focus of world attention, beginning with the managed, conditional cancellation of foreign debts and the strengthening of sustainable segments of their economies.

EXPEDIENCY

There is a long and venerable tradition of utopias, but none has proven as difficult to attain as the zero option. Political fortune, administrative limitations, the pressure to turn an instant profit — all argue against not doing something, even when that is the most sensible option. Expediency is also often quoted when calls are raised to do something sensible, such as conducting a search for comprehensive action. Institutional divisiveness is another way of describing sectoral expediencies.

NEGLIGENCE

Social responsibilities are usually neglected due to inattention, logistical convenience, outside or internal pressures, personal greed, or for financial or political gain. In 1992, a widely reported incident in Japan demonstrated to a national audience the effects of a common chain of negligence in picture-book fashion. A powerful politician pressured an environmental minister to approve a Kyushu river dam project in response to pressure by the all-powerful construction minister. To the Japanese voters, this became a case of triple negligence: negligence on part of the construction minister to see the limits of his responsibility and the legitimacy of his portfolio's interests; on the part of the politician towards his duties and code of conduct; and, had the environmental minister succumbed to the pressure, negligence on his part as well, for failing to sacrifice his career in pursuit of his duty.

FATIGUE

People get tired. People move on. And sometimes people have come to rely on assorted environmental regulations as comforting substitute for real change. While fatigue has not affected the environmental movement as a whole, there is some of that sense of eroding continuity that comes with individual episodes of surrender. Yet although the environmental movement certainly has had its share of growing cynicism, loss of heart, and the kind of distancing pragmatism that can accompany advanced age, the daily mounting and changing visions of disasters yet to come have kept us on our toes, and a constantly renewed population active. Surprisingly low levels of real discouragement and the growing enthusiasm and acceptance that environmental ideas evoke make fatigue somewhat less potent among the eight root causes of the environmental malaise. The arrows of perseverance aim at the Achilles heel of dominant development dogmas: cynicism.

A CASE OF OPPORTUNITY AND COMPROMISE: SYDNEY'S GREEN OLYMPIC GAMES BID FOR 2000

The dilemmas of development pressures and the 'green imperative' are well presented in the Olympic bid for the year 2000. The Olympic gods have bestowed their blessing upon Sydney and Australia, making the nation feel good again. Political and industry leaders insist that the regional and national economy is about to surge, or at least be jolted. Great psychological, political and financial capital is said to be gained. A majority of planners asserts that if the Games are cleverly handled, Sydney's urban efficiency and life quality will receive a permanent boost, as other Olympic cities have demonstrated: Munich, or Barcelona—despite their long-term indebtedness. And what excites people most about Sydney's 2000 plans is that they promise to be environmentally responsible, having been endorsed by Greenpeace International. Their much-touted features include energy efficiency, habitat healing, waste and water recycling, the sealing off of toxic soil.

The way Sydney's 2000 games are being envisioned is green, certainly, in a sense that within the frameworks of the Olympic Games, and within the limitations of the Sydney 2000 planning concept, they aim to do the right thing, using state-of-the-art thinking. The dilemma is that the Games in themselves are not sustainable, if sustainable means that environmental accounts will not seriously balloon on the debit side.

Greenpeace and 'Sydney 2000', the Olympic bid planning team, have stumbled into their marriage of convenience on the heel of a blind date, the anonymous Olympic Village competition for Homebush Bay, yielding the Greenpeace team as one of five winners. The encounter resulted from multiple strokes of luck, seized in spirited savvy: Sydney's Greenpeace constituency is one of the very few in the world with an urban conscience, targeting cities and urban development as key villains in the global eco-mess. Other bids, such as the Manchester and Berlin bids, aimed into right directions as well, but their campaigns suffered from a fatal Greenpeace gap.

To cynics, 'sustainable Olympics', if anyone actually dared to use this expression, would win Gold in the Heavyweight Oxymoron class. To them, the Greenpeace-endorsed Sydney 2000 will go down in history as a Herculean contradiction in terms, late-20th century greenspeak at its best. They say: the idea of a green Olympics is a perfect illustration of what is wrong with current unsustainable notions of sustainability. For one, they argue, the concept, while perfect for the three weeks in 2000, is almost all wrong for the post-Olympic age: an isolated, over-venued site soaks up scarce public funds and tends to reinforce our utterly unsustainable car reliance, while inner-urban lands languish, little used. And while there will be an extraordinarily creative and expensive shuffling around, and clay-capping of the poisoned earth in Homebush Bay, some important nurturing and preservation of mangrove forest patches and animal breeding grounds, and a carefully oriented Olympic Village, sporting the best of eco-technology and common sense in urban design[7] — critics will still point out that the modern Olympics in themselves could not be further from the Green Fleece. Fleets of intercontinental Olympia-bound passenger and cargo aircraft will churn their greenhouse gases and ozone depleting chemicals right into high layers of the atmosphere — at a time when sanity should dictate a stop to all non-essential flights. Cubic kilometres of concrete — the least sustainable of all construction materials, barring steel — is poured into largely luxurious landing strips, highways and venues, venues and more venues, not only in Sydney, but also in the furiously proliferating, identical stadia that have been started in vain, and in defiance of the odds, around the world. A universal boost in an already universal junk food frenzy. Another generation conditioned to the dogmas of unlimited growth and individual competitiveness at all cost, perpetuating the myth of higher, faster, farther, mightier.

Even to supporters of the Games, and others who choose not to resort to this sort of breathless, easy mongering of criticism there are some basic dilemmas in the notion of Green Games. They are as fundamental as another Olympic paradox: the espoused sharing of 'the spirit' and universal harmony in the face of nationalist, subtly supremacist sentiments that surfaced during the bid race, an aspect of the Games since their inception.

It is not easy to reconcile the requirements of a fail-safe, highly exposed international event with those of efficiently and imaginatively meeting regional development needs. 'Good' Games demand a close concentration of venues, perfect surveillance and tight security perimeters. By contrast, good city development demands a distribution of resources across space and over time, adaptive reuse and openness. However, a key driving factor in hosting the Olympics is broadly shared hopes for betterment. How this is achieved ought to be subject to careful public scrutiny.

Both sets of interests need to find a happy marriage. Until we do so, we will stand transfixed, hopefully squinting into the green limelight as we watch another go-go development party coast down another lucky hill, cheering wildly while running on empty, confidently skipping the petrol station, or better the public transit stop.

Today's Games are captive to emerging mass communication technologies, and their economics: photographic reproduction, cinema, radio—and now television, by satellite, cable and soon by the former telephone. But as a vehicle of hope and a mass medium, they are also inherently receptive to social and cultural innovations that may well be informed by mass sentiments—and a global fear of ecological doom is inexorably rising. Granted, the Olympic impact on the environment is minuscule, even insignificant when compared to our massive daily ecological onslaught on the life-sustaining capacity of this earth. However, the symbolic role, the function as a message, development model and cultural paradigm is controversial—and will be more so in the future.

Munich in 1972, and Los Angeles in 1984 were perhaps the first 'green' Games. In Munich, the emphasis was boldly placed on public transit and pedestrianisation of the inner city, resulting in an extremely visionary suppression of the automobile, for late 1960s planning concepts, that is. And Los Angeles minimised new construction, stressing re-use and adaptation of existing structures, and concentrated unabashedly on celebrational, 'virtual' venues. No, the International Olympic Committee (IOC) had not gone soft. This great innovation was a fluke, and only possible in this form because the city was the only Olympic contender at that time—and in a very strong bargaining position indeed: the city and its tax payers did not have to underwrite the costs. This is where the resource conservation aspect ends: the LA Olympics still served as a monumental advertising billboard for business-as-usual.

Olympia 2000 will be held at a crossroads. In one direction lies business as usual—a future string of great international pageants going off in living colours yet inexorably like so many fireworks, leaving behind big puffs of smoke. In the other there is greater daring and inventiveness, a resource-conserving and symbolically sophisticated Olympics-stimulated urban healing process, positively affirming the physical, high-touch sweatiness of the real, the here and now, the permanent transience and exhilarating glory of world cities at their best. The richly mixed lessons taught by the best 'civic' Olympics, such as Munich, Los Angeles and Barcelona, will continue to serve as the basis for great innovation in resource conservation and efficiency in venue provision, both in the short and in the long term, and in city form.

It might well be sensible—yet utterly unreasonable—to expect from the IOC that it issue stringent environmental performance guidelines and enforce them, just like it imperially insisted on an extravagantly spiralling splurge in 1976 Montreal. What we need to come to grips with is that the true Olympic achievements have been the brilliant and renegade innovations in city building, coming from within the competing cities. These few maverick achievements owe their impetus to the Games, but their spirit and intelligence to the savvy of the women and men that negotiated the best, most sustainable deal for the long run. This relatively thin history of Intelligent Games is awaiting another chapter now, at this, our time, when unprecedented environmental and technological issues continue their race seemingly all on their own, raising the spectre of the game to end all games—humankind's environmental and technological endgame. We can no longer simply say: 'it's just sports'; or: 'we share the spirit'. We must try harder to understand what sort of spirit it is that we are sharing, whom we are sharing it with, and how on earth we are going to make headway in the race towards salvaging the earth.

NOTES

1. Tsurumi, K. (1993) 'Animism and Science', Research Papers, Series A-58, Institute of International Relations, Sophia University, Tokyo.
2. For an early articulation of this notion, see Mumford, L. (1961) *The City in History*, Harcourt Brace Jovanovich, Orlando.
3. Marx, L. (1987) 'Does Improved Technology Mean Progress?' *Technology Review*, No.1, p.33.
4. 'How to build the Eco-city', professional development series organised by Urban Design Program, University of Sydney, Spring 1994.
5. Hiebert, M. (1994) 'Travelling Trash', *Far Eastern Economic Review*, February 3, p.21.
6. Ross-Kuebler, E. (1969) *On Death and Dying*, Macmillan, New York.
7. See miscellaneous Sydney 2000 Bid Documents and Greenpeace's Strategy for a Sustainable Sydney, 1993.

Index